IBM® RISC SYSTEM/6000™
A BUSINESS PERSPECTIVE
Second Edition

Related Titles of Interest from Wiley . . .

IBM PS/2: A Business Perspective, Fourth Edition, Hoskins (G325-0400)

IBM AS/400: A Business Perspective, Third Edition, Hoskins (GA21-9990)

Managing Software Development Projects: Formula for Success, Whitten

Developing Applications Using DOS, Christopher, Feigenbaum, Saliga

The New DOS 5.0, Christopher, Feigenbaum, Saliga

DOS 5 Reference, Christopher, Feigenbaum, Saliga

OS/2 Presentation Manager Programming, Cheatham, Reich, Robinson

IBM® RISC SYSTEM/6000™
A BUSINESS PERSPECTIVE
Second Edition

Jim Hoskins

John Wiley & Sons, Inc.
New York • Chichester • Brisbane • Toronto • Singapore

Library of Congress Cataloging-in-Publication Data

Hoskins, Jim.
    IBM RISC System/6000 : a business perspective / Jim Hoskins. — 2nd ed.
      p. cm.
    Includes bibliographical references and index.
    ISBN 0-471-55879-6 (pbk.)
    1. IBM RISC System/6000 computers.   2. Business — Data processing.
    I. Title
    QA76.8.I25975H67   1992
    004.165 — dc20   91-34764

Printed in the United States of America

10 9 8 7 6 5 4 3 2 1

Printed and bound by Malloy Lithographing, Inc.

To my three-year-old —
Nikolas . . .
who brings me untold joy without even trying.

Foreword

The RISC System/6000 provides unprecedented IBM value. It melds innovative hardware and industrial strength software into a system that you can count on today and for the foreseeable future.

IBM R&D sites around the globe rallied in support of a new line of systems that would provide a quantum leap in performance at an affordable price. A second-generation RISC (Reduced Instruction Set Computer) processor was to be coupled with new high-speed memory and I/O subsystems into a computer that could be cost-effectively mass produced. Reliability was to be an integral part of the design. Advanced error detection and correction technology would be exploited to yield a system that could run for extended periods without a disruption in service. The resulting product was named the RISC System/6000.

The Advanced Interactive Executive/6000 (AIX/6000) is an open standards-compliant operating system that takes advantage of all of the power of the RISC System/6000. It builds on capabilities found in UNIX, with new features and facilities specifically designed to meet the needs of business. Foremost among these capabilities is an innovative file system, which improves reliability, increases performance, and can be expanded without disrupting service. Other noteworthy AIX/6000 features include compilers that produce extremely efficient code and a high-level management facility that allows the system to be easily administered. And AIX/6000 does all of this while conforming to a wide variety of formal and industry standards.

AIX and the RISC System/6000 provide a solid base for the future. The hardware and software is designed to be extensible while preserving application investment. Over time, you'll see desktop models at prices typical of business PCs. And the high-end of the line will expand to provide performance and throughput that we commonly associate with today's large mainframes.

Jim Hoskins' book provides an excellent business perspective on AIX and the RISC System/6000. It is readable and informative. I think you'll find it worth a modest investment of your time.

JEFF MASON
Advanced Workstations and AIX Systems Director
IBM United States

Trademarks

AIX is a trademark of International Business Machines Corporation.

AIX Version 3 for RISC System/6000 is a trademark of International Business Machines Corporation.

AIXwindows is a trademark of International Business Machines Corporation.

AIX/370 is a trademark of International Business Machines Corporation.

C + + – macs is a trademark of Unipress Software Inc.

Cray is a trademark of Cray Research Corp.

DATAPRODUCTS L2R 2665 is a registered trademark of Dataproducts Inc.

DEC is a trademark of Digital Equipment Corporation.

DEC VT100 and VT220 are registered trademarks of Digital Equipment Corporation.

DECstation is a trademark of Digital Equipment Corporation.

Ethernet is a trademark of Xerox, Inc.

EXDiff, TCAT, TACT-PATH, TDGEN, S-TCAT, SMARTS, and CAPBAK are trademarks of Software Research, Inc.

Glockenspiel C + + from Oasys is a trademark of Glockenspiel Ltd. of Ireland.

graPHIGS is a trademark of International Business Machines Corporation.

GSS is a trademark of Graphic Software Systems, Inc.

Hayes Smartmodem is a trademark of Hayes Inc.

HP is a registered trademark of Hewlett-Packard Inc.

IBM is a registered trademark of International Business Machines Corporation.

IBM System/370 is a trademark of International Business Machines Corporation.

InfoExplorer is a trademark of International Business Machines Corporation.

InfoTrainer is a trademark of International Business Machines Corporation.

InfoWindow is a registered trademark of International Business Machines Corporation.

INGRES is a registered trademark of INGRES Corporation.

Interface Builder is a trademark of NeXT Inc.

Interleaf is a trademark of Interleaf, Inc.

JSB Multiview is a trademark of JSB Computer Systems Limited.

LaserJet II is a trademark of Hewlett-Packard Inc.

Micro Channel is a trademark of International Business Machines Corporation.

NCR is a trademark of National Cash Register.

NETBIOS is a trademark of International Business Machines Corporation.

NetView is a trademark of International Business Machines Corporation.

Network Computing System (NCS) is a trademark of Apollo Computer, Inc.

Network File System and NFS are trademarks of Sun Microsystems, Inc.

NextStep is a trademark of NeXT Inc.

Objective-C is a trademark of Stepstone Corporation.

Omnilaser is a trademark of Texas Instruments Inc.

OS/2 is a registered trademark of International Business Machines Corporation.

OS/400 is a registered trademark of International Business Machines Corporation.

OSF and OSF/Motif are trademarks of the Open Software Foundation.

OSF/1 is a trademark of the Open Software Foundation.

Personal Computer AT and AT are trademarks of the International Business Machines Corporation.

Personal graPHIGS is a trademark of the International Business Machines Corporation.

Personal System/2 and PS/2 are registered trademarks of the International Business Machines Corporation.

PC-DOS is a trademark of the International Business Machines Corporation.

Polytron Version Control System (PVCS) is a trademark of Sage Software, Inc.

POSIX is a trademark of the Institute of Electrical and Electronic Engineers (IEEE).

PostScript and Display PostScript are trademarks of Adobe Systems, Inc.

PROCASE and SMARTsystem are trademarks of PROCASE Corporation, Inc.

PRINTRONIX P9012 is a trademark of Printronix Inc.

Racal-Vadic is a trademark of the RACALVADIC Corp.

Rational Environment is a trademark of Rational.

RISC System/6000 is a trademark of International Business Machines Corporation.

RT, RT PC, and RT Personal Computer are registered trademarks of International Business Machines Corporation.

Saber-C is a trademark of Saber Software.

Screens + + is a trademark of Novum Organum.

Selectric is a registered trademark of International Business Machines Corporation.

Software through Pictures is a trademark of Interactive Development Environments, Inc.

Software BackPlane, Project Softboard, and Integration Softboard are trademarks of Atherton Technology.

SPARCstation is a trademark of Sun Microsystems.

SUN is a trademark of Sun Microsystems.

System Application Architecture (SAA) is a trademark of International Business Machines Corporation.

Teamwork is a trademark of Cadre Technologies, Inc.

TEX is a trademark of the American Mathematical Society.

ULTRIX, VAX, VMS, PDP, and DECNET are trademarks of Digital Equipment Corporation.

UNIX is a registered trademark of AT&T.

VADS is a trademark of Verdix Corporation.

VISUAL is a trademark of VISUAL Technology.

WYSE is a trademark of WYSE Corporation.

Xenix is a trademark of Microsoft Corporation.

Xerox is a trademark of Xerox Corporation.

X/Open is a trademark of X/Open Group Members.

X Window System is a trademark of Massachusetts Institute of Technology.

X.25 is a recommendation by the International Telegraph and Telephone Consultation Committee (CCITT).

386, 486, 80386, 80486, 80386sx, 80387, 80387sx are trademarks of the Intel Corporation.

AIX is used as a short form for AIX operating system.

AIX/6000 V3 is used as a short form of AIX Version 3 for RISC System/6000.

UNIX is used as a short form for UNIX operating system.

Acknowledgments

Many "IBMers" assisted me in the preparation of this revision of the book. Some provided me with information concerning their product areas. Others read the manuscript and provided very helpful comments or supported the project in some other way. To all those who assisted, I thank you.

I would like to give special thanks to Dave Pinkerton for helping me coordinate this revision. I would also like to thank Theresa Abernathy, Dan Cox, Jessie Kempter, Jeff Mason, Linda Ryan, Don Stotts, and Gene Tempas.

Finally, hats off to the entire RISC System/6000 development team and management.

Reader Comments

Any comments you would like to make are welcomed. Send comments to John Wiley & Sons, 605 3rd Ave, New York, NY 10158, attention Katherine Schowalter, or through IBMLink to HONE84(DEV3338).

Disclaimer

This book is not intended to replace IBM product documentation or personnel in determining the specifications and capabilities of the included products. IBM product documentation should always be consulted as the specifications and capabilities of products are subject to frequent modification. The reader is solely responsible for the choice of all configurations and applications of computer hardware and software. All configurations and applications of computer hardware and software should be reviewed with proper IBM representatives prior to making any commitments or using the configuration.

While the author of this book has made reasonable efforts to ensure the accuracy and timeliness of the information contained herein, the author assumes no liability with respect to loss or damage caused or alleged to be caused by reliance on any information contained herein and disclaims any and all warranties, express or implied, as to the accuracy of said information. This book is not sponsored by IBM, and the author is not acting as an IBM agent.

Other Books in the Series

There are two other books in the "Business Perspective" series: *IBM AS/400 — A Business Perspective* (GA21-9990) and *IBM PS/2 — A Business Perspective* (G325-0400). These books are similar in organization and style to this book.

Subscribing to Revisions

You may subscribe through an IBM branch office to automatically receive future updates of *IBM RISC System/6000: A Business Perspective* (GA23-2674) and the other books in the "Business Perspective" series through IBM's System Library Subscription Service (SLSS).

Contents

CHAPTER 2
Options and Peripherals   58

CHAPTER 3
Using Your RS/6000   138

CHAPTER 4
Application Programs   173

CHAPTER 5
AIX for the RS/6000 183

CHAPTER 6
RS/6000 Communications 205

Introduction

WHAT THIS BOOK IS

This book is dedicated to members of a new family of IBM® computers, namely the IBM RISC System/6000® computers. First, the new RISC System/6000 computer products will be introduced. The features of these new computers will be reviewed in a way understandable to noncomputer experts.

Second, you will be guided through a "hands-on" session with a RISC System/6000 computer and the programs that come with each system. The different kinds of software necessary to do "real work" will also be described to help you with software buying decisions.

Finally, the book discusses some ways to apply RISC System/6000 systems to solve problems, improve productivity, create competitive advantages, and so on. Proper selection and usage of RISC System/6000 products are impossible unless you understand how you can use these components to fill your needs. Specific RISC System/6000 hardware and software configurations for typical environments will be offered. Many important computer automation planning issues will also be discussed, such as financial justification, lease versus purchase, ergonomics, and so on.

WHAT THIS BOOK IS NOT

Many computer books try to be all things to all people. They start by explaining checkbook balancing and then finish up by covering the space shuttle's redundant flight computer complex. This book is not a general overview of computers. It is specific to RISC System/6000 computers (a subject more than broad enough for a single book). This book is not a technical reference manual (IBM will sell you that),

1

nor is it intended to teach computer programming. It will provide a good understanding of RISC System/6000 computers and how to use them in various environments.

Finally, this book will not assume you are a computer professional. While some technical discussions are necessary, I have tried to keep these discussions as light and concise as possible while still conveying necessary and useful information.

HOW TO USE THIS BOOK

Chapter 1 first introduces the entire RISC System/6000 family and provides an overview of each RISC System/6000 model. The latter part of the chapter examines the elements (architecture, graphics, auxiliary storage, etc.) that make up RISC System/6000 computers.

Chapter 2 surveys the many hardware options available for RISC System/6000 computers — including displays, ASCII terminals, printers, disk expansion, CD-ROM drives, and communications. It is provided primarily as a reference to help you select the proper options for your RISC System/6000 computer.

Chapter 3 guides you through a "hands-on" session with a RISC System/6000 computer system. You will learn how to use the computer-based education provided with every RISC System/6000 computer. The latter part of the chapter describes the role of the three types of programs that work together to do productive work in a RISC System/6000 computer (application programs, operating systems, and device drivers).

Chapter 4 continues the discussion on application programs. The basic types of application programs useful to almost any organization are described. Further, industry-specific application programs are introduced. Finally, the question of "prewritten" versus "custom" application programs is addressed.

Chapter 5 continues the discussion on operating systems. First, basic operating system concepts such as "multiuser" and "interactive processing" are defined in non-technical terms. Then the AIX® operating system and its optional extension products are described to help you determine what you need.

Chapter 6 shows how specific RISC System/6000 options and software products are used to participate in common computer communications environments.

Chapter 7 discusses issues related to the selection of RISC System/6000 hardware and software to meet the needs of both commercial and technical users. Hypothetical organizations are described and outfitted with the appropriate RISC System/6000 computer systems. Then, important topics such as user training, ergonomics, security, maintenance, and so on, are discussed.

Appendixes are included to provide additional information. Appendix A provides a list of peripheral equipment supported by RISC/6000 computers. Appendix

B provides additional performance information. Appendix C lists IBM publications associated with the RISC/6000 family.

To help you better understand the topics covered in this book, key terms and phrases are defined and given in **boldface** type when they are first introduced. These key terms are also listed in the index at the back of this book. If while reading you forget the definition of a key term or phrase defined elsewhere, the index will quickly point you to the page(s) where the term is discussed.

A GLANCE BACKWARD

To understand the full intent of the RISC System/6000 family and its AIX operating system, one must be familiar with some basic history. The AIX operating system is IBM's version of the UNIX® operating system, which was originally developed by AT&T Bell Labs in 1969. The original UNIX was not intended to be a commercial product but rather a tool for use by computer programmers internal to AT&T. In fact, at that time, AT&T was not in the business of selling computers or operating systems. However, in 1975 AT&T began to license universities to use the UNIX operating system at no charge. This practice caused the UNIX operating system to become widely used in the academic community. Students quickly took advantage of the freedom in the academic world to make their own improvements to the UNIX operating system, often resulting in new commands that while obvious to the creator sometimes seemed cryptic to other users. For example, the "BIFF" command used to pick up electronic mail stored in the computer system was added to the UNIX operating system. Why "BIFF"? Because the student who made the enhancement owned a dog named Biff that was trained to go out and get the newspaper every morning. While this freedom to make unstructured improvements to the UNIX operating system at will helped the UNIX operating system become more powerful, it also left holes in areas such as data security and reliability.

In 1981, the University of California at Berkeley offered its own version of the UNIX operating system with many enhancements of its own. Berkeley's version of the UNIX operating system, known as Berkeley Software Distribution 4 (BSD 4), became a very popular operating system in its own right. So much so that most of the enhancements contained in the Berkeley version were incorporated by AT&T's later versions of the UNIX operating system.

Meanwhile, IBM was busy working on the "801 project," which was started in 1975. Named after the building in which it was resident, the 801 project was an experiment to develop a minicomputer that bucked the existing trend toward complex computer programming instructions. Under the leadership of IBM scientist John Cocke, the 801 approach was to simplify the range of instructions used to per-

Figure I.1. IBM RT System. The System Unit can be seen beside the desk, and the associated display and keyboard are on the desktop.

form tasks and optimize the computer to execute this limited range of instructions with extreme efficiency. Born of this approach is the name "*R*educed *I*nstruction *S*et *C*omputer," or RISC.

In January 1986, IBM announced the first product to utilize the RISC approach in the IBM Personal Computer RT (for *R*ISC *T*echnology) shown in Figure I.1. At the same time, IBM introduced its own version of the UNIX operating system to run on the Personal Computer RT, called the *A*dvanced *I*nteractive e*X*ecutive (AIX) operating system. Later, IBM released versions of the AIX operating system for the smaller IBM Personal System/2 computers and the larger S/370 mainframe computers.

In early 1986, IBM hardware and software engineers in Austin, Texas, took on the task of designing a new product family. It would represent IBM's second-generation RISC technology, combining the RISC philosophy with more traditional concepts with a goal of achieving balanced performance. The result of that effort is the RISC System/6000 family of products and AIX version 3 — both introduced on February 15, 1990. The remainder of this book will focus on the current RISC System/6000 family and the AIX operating system.

1

IBM RISC System/6000—
A New Beginning

This chapter first provides an overview of the RISC System/6000 family of computers, covering the highlights of these new systems. The latter part of the chapter then moves in for a closer look at the design details of the RISC System/6000 family.

MEET THE FAMILY

The IBM RISC System/6000 (RS/6000) family is IBM's second generation of computers based on the **Reduced Instruction Set Computing (RISC)** architecture developed by IBM in the late 1970s. With this concept, a very simple set of programming instructions is used to perform all work within the computer system. Since the instructions are very simple, they can be executed at very high speed, and they also lend themselves to a more efficient implementation of the program being executed. The RISC architecture was first introduced in the IBM RT® Personal Computer, later renamed the IBM RT System. The RS/6000 family is based on a second-generation RISC architecture, called the **Performance Optimized With Enhanced RISC (POWER)** architecture. The POWER architecture combines the concepts of the original RISC architecture with a sprinkling of more traditional concepts to create a system with optimum overall system performance.

The RS/6000 family is designed to address the computing needs of engineering/scientific users as well as those of more general commercial applications. The engineering/scientific user will perform such tasks as designing mechanical devices on the computer screen (computer-aided design), simulating physical stresses on the object to test the strength of the design (computer-aided engineering), and then automatically generating the programming necessary to manufacture the part with numerical control machine tools (computer-aided manufacturing). Other examples of engineering/scientific applications of the RS/6000 family include statistical analysis, geological analysis, and artificial intelligence. Engineering/scientific users can be found in business, government, and academic environments, and they often have an RS/6000 system as their own personal workstation with a large display and various input devices (like the IBM 3-Button Mouse) and output devices (like printers and plotters). These standalone workstations are often networked to allow the user community to share programs, data, and peripheral equipment.

Another type of environment addressed by RS/6000 computers is that of traditional commercial applications — also found in business, government, and academic organizations. In these environments, a single RS/6000 system is usually shared by multiple users, each having a low-cost terminal or Personal System/2 computer attached to the system. Terminals are usually attached directly to the RS/6000 system using the EIA-232D type of communications. Personal System/2 computers can be attached in the same way, or alternately via a local area network. Typical applications in commercial environments include general accounting, word processing, and business graphics.

There is also another type of user becoming commonplace as technological advances make more powerful computer systems affordable: more technical business users who, like the engineering/scientific user, need their own RS/6000 system dedicated to their demanding applications. These applications include publishing, financial analysis, economic simulations/analysis, securities analysis and trading, and business statistical analysis. These users will often be part of a communications network, allowing them to share programs, data, and peripheral equipment with other technical business users as well as exchange information with the more traditional commercial computing systems.

The RS/6000 family uses the *A*dvanced *I*nteractive e*X*ecutive (AIX) operating system. The AIX operating system is IBM's version of the UNIX operating system, which was originally developed by AT&T Bell Labs in 1969. In the AIX operating system, IBM has combined the basic functions of the UNIX operating system with enhancements made by many other companies and academic institutions. IBM has also included many of their own enhancements to the AIX operating system and has adhered to the mainstream industry standards developed to make the systems from various vendors more compatible. Because the AIX operating system conforms to many industry standards, the RS/6000 family is considered an **open system.** This term simply means that the AIX operating system conforms to standards (programming interfaces, communications protocols, etc.) defined by independent standards bodies rather than utilizing an IBM proprietary set of standards not generally adhered to by other computer manufacturers. The advantage of the open system strategy comes when an independent software development company writes an application program conforming to these industry standards. Since many computer manufacturers offer "open system" computers conforming to these industry standards, the software development company can offer its application program on many different brands of computers. The advantages to computer users are (1) that after selecting the application program that best meets their needs, they have more flexibility as to which brand of computer system to buy, and (2) that after the user has purchased an "open system" computer, he or she can choose from the large body of open application programs to meet new needs as they emerge.

The open system concept is not without its difficulties, however. First, there are multiple standards organizations simultaneously defining standards for the same "open system" environment. This leads to conflicts and incompatibilities. Further, while "open system" manufacturers conform to industry standards, they also offer proprietary extensions to help differentiate their computer systems from the others. The more a software development firm exploits these proprietary extensions, the more we diverge from the spirit of the open system concept. Even with these difficulties, the open system approach provides the most widely compatible environment today and shows great promise for the future.

System Unit Frame	RISC System/6000	Processor Speed	Key Point Offered by Model
Desktop/Deskside	Model 320	20 MHz	Low cost desktop system
(some expansion)	Model 320H	25 MHz	Best performing desktop system
Deskside	Model 520	20 MHz	Low cost deskside system
(More expansion)	Model 530H	33 MHz	Larger Data Cache/wider Memory bus (better performance)
	Model 550	41 MHz	Most powerful deskside system
Rack-mounted frame	Model 930	25 MHz	Low cost rack-mounted system
(Most expansion)	Model 950	41 MHz	Most powerful rack-mounted system

Figure 1.1. IBM RISC System/6000 at a glance.

There are seven current models that make up the RS/6000 family: Models 320, 320H, 520, 530H, 550, 930, and 950. Figure 1.1 shows the RS/6000 family at a glance and the upgrade paths offered (indicated by arrows). Let's briefly look at each of these models along with the Xstation 130, which is a close cousin of the RS/6000 family.

The RS/6000 Model 320 (Figure 1.2) is based on a 20 MHz Main Processor and provides 8 MB of Main Memory and 160 MB of disk storage as standard equipment. The Model 320 is designed to sit on the user's desktop, but is also capable of operating while sitting on end alongside a desk. It features low cost and a compact design. Another, more powerful version of the Model 320 (called the Model 320H) is based on a 25 MHz Main Processor and provides 16 MB of standard memory.

The RS/6000 Models 520, 530H, and 550 are all packaged in the same type of mechanical enclosure, shown in Figure 1.3. The System Unit is sitting on the floor beside the desk in the center of the photo, with the associated display on the desktop.

Figure 1.2. IBM RISC System/6000 Model 320 or 320H in an office setting.

Figure 1.3. IBM RISC System/6000 Model 520, 530H, or 550 in a typical office environment. Notice that more than one user is sharing the single System Unit seen beside the desk.

The larger enclosure of these models is designed to sit on the floor and allows these models to accommodate more Main Memory, more disk storage, and more I/O adapters than the desktop models. Since the Model 520 uses the same processor used in the Model 320, performance of the two systems is comparable. However, the Model 520 offers greater expansion capabilities and can be upgraded to larger models. The Model 530H has 32 MB of Main Memory as standard and offers improved performance over the Models 320 and 520. This is due mostly to the faster processor and the more efficient memory design used in the 530H. The Model 550 is one of the most powerful systems in the RS/6000 family due to its faster processor (41 MHz).

The Models 930 and 950 use a completely different approach to physical packaging. The Model 930/950 System Unit is the large floor-standing rack, shown in Figure 1.4. These systems offer performance comparable to that of a Model 530 and 550 respectively, but offer more disk expansion capability than any other member of the RS/6000 family. The Models 930 and 950 are designed to be shared by multiple users, each provided with a low-cost terminal directly connected to the system or an intelligent workstation (e.g., PS/2 or Xstation 130) attached to the system via a LAN.

Figure 1.4. IBM RISC System/6000 Model 930 or 950 in an office setting.

The Xstation 130, also shown in Figure 1.3 on the leftmost desktop, is not formally an RS/6000 computer. However, it bears mentioning here because it is such a close friend of the RS/6000 family. The Xstation 130 is a graphics terminal that provides access to RS/6000 computer systems (as well as other open systems) in a local area network environment. It provides a low-cost alternative to providing each user with an individual RS/6000 computer system.

The RS/6000 family of computers offers systems designed to meet the needs of either technical users (engineers, scientists, economists, etc.) or general-purpose commercial users (executives, accountants, clerks, secretaries, etc.). The various models along with the options covered in Chapter 2 offer many different levels of performance, capacity, and function.

IBM offers several pre-configured RS/6000 systems varying in the amount of

Main Memory, the size of the disk, and the adapters/peripherals included as standard equipment. Some preconfigured systems are considered POWERstations suitable for use as a single-user workstation, while others are POWERserver configurations geared more for use in local area networks or as multiuser systems.

Model 320/320H Specifics

The 7012 RS/6000 Model 320 and 320H System Unit, along with a display, keyboard, and mouse, is shown in Figure 1.5. The Models 320 and 320H are housed in a mechanical frame designed to reside on the user's desktop or beside the desk on the floor. A row of vents on the front of the System Unit allows an internal fan to force air through the structure, cooling the internal components. Like the Model 220, small building blocks such as 3.5-inch diskette drives, 3.5-inch disk drives, and surface-mounted chips minimize the overall size of the Model 320/320H. This smaller size is important since Model 320/320H also is designed to sit on a desktop. Otherwise, the pedestal under the System Unit (not visible) can be mounted on the side of the System Unit, providing secure footing for setting the system on its side for those wishing to move the System Unit onto the floor beside their desk. The LED operator display can be rotated to accommodate this sideways orientation.

Although the Models 320 and 320H use the same mechanical structure, they offer different levels of performance. The Model 320 is based on a 20 MHz processor and the Model 320H is based on a faster 25 MHz processor.

The Model 320 comes standard with 8 MB of Main Memory and 160 MB of disk storage. The 8 MB of Main Memory is packaged on a single Memory card. This card can be replaced with the 16, 32, or 64 MB Memory card. Further, you can add a second Main Memory expansion card in the provided memory adapter slot, for a maximum of 128 MB. The standard 3.5-inch 160 MB drive comes installed in one of the two disk bays provided in the Model 320 System Units. You can choose to replace the 160 MB disk with a larger 320 MB disk. Further, you can add a second disk of either 160 or 320 MB. This allows a Model 320 to have up to 640 MB of internal disk storage. The 160 MB configuration offers four available Micro Channel slots, while configurations with the 320 MB disk drive consume one of these slots (with the SCSI I/O Controller required with the 320 MB drive), leaving three available. The Model 320 can be upgraded to a Model 320H (which is then called a Model 320E to designate that it is an upgraded system rather than a factory-built Model 320H) at any time.

The Model 320H comes standard with 16 MB of Main Memory and 400 MB of disk storage. The 16 MB of Main Memory is packaged on a single Memory card. This card can be replaced with the 32 or 64 MB Memory card. You can add a second Main

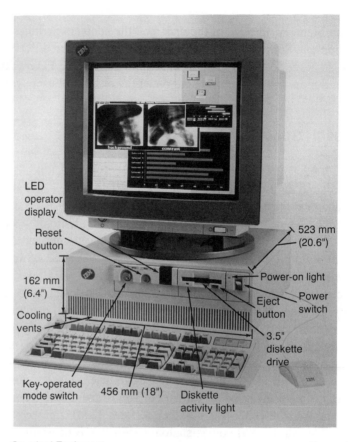

LED
operator
display

Reset
button

523 mm
(20.6")

162 mm
(6.4")

Power-on light

Power
switch

Eject
button

Cooling
vents

3.5"
diskette
drive

Key-operated
mode switch

456 mm (18")

Diskette
activity light

Standard Equipment		*Expansion*

Main Processor:
  320 = 20 Mhz
  320H = 25 Mhz
Memory:
  320 = 8 MB (128 MB max)
  320H = 16 MB (128 MB max)
8 KB Inst. Cache
32 KB Data Cache
64-bit Memory Bus
Disk:
  320 = 160 MB (800 MB max internal)
  320H = 400 MB (800 MB max internal)
	* SCSI Controller Adapter/port
	  (1) 3.5" 1.44 MB diskette
	  (1) Parallel port
	  (2) Async ports
	  Horizontal/vertical pedestal
	  Mouse Port
	  Tablet Port
	  Keyboard/Speaker port
	  Key-operated mode switch
		Micro Channel slots:
		  320 = 4 slots
		  320H = 3 slots
		x (2) Memory slots
		+ 160 MB disk drive
		  320 MB disk drive
		  400 MB disk drive
		+ Model 320 to 320H
		  upgrade

x Although one of these slots is used in the standard configuration, the memory card that is provided
   in a standard configuration can be replaced with an optional memory card that contains more
   memory if necessary.
* Model 320H only.
+ Model 320 only.

Figure 1.5. RS/6000 Models 320 and 320H specifics.

Memory expansion card in the provided memory adapter slot, for a maximum of 128 MB. The standard 3.5-inch 400 MB drive comes installed in one of the two disk bays provided in the Model 320H System Units. You can add a second 400 MB disk drive, providing a total of 800 MB of disk storage. Since the 400 MB disk drive requires a SCSI I/O Controller which is provided as standard with the Model 320H and comes pre-installed in one of the four Micro Channel slots. This SCSI I/O controller is also used to control the second 400 MB disk drive if installed. This leaves three Micro Channel slots to house other optional adapter cards (covered in Chapter 2).

Either model comes standard with a 1.44 MB diskette drive and provides a 32 KB Data Cache and a 64-bit-wide path between Main Memory and the Data Cache. A key lock provided on the operator panel helps discourage unauthorized tampering with the system. The Model 320/320H System Unit can also be tied down with the optional RS/6000 Security Cable to help protect against unauthorized movement.

Model 520/530H Specifics

The 7013 RS/6000 Model 520/530H System Unit is shown in Figure 1.6. The mechanical frame used with these models is significantly larger than that of the desktop models (Model 320H) and is designed to rest on the floor beside a desk or table. This means that only the display and keyboard need occupy your desk space. The air vents visible on the side and front allow the internal fan to draw air through the System Unit for cooling. The larger size of these models allows them to accommodate more Main Memory, disk storage, and optional adapter cards than in the desktop RS/6000 models.

The Model 520 is based on a 20 MHz processor and provides 16 MB of Main Memory, a 32 KB Data Cache, and a 64-bit-wide path between Main Memory and the Data Cache. The Model 520 can be upgraded to a Model 530H (which is then called a 530E to indicate that it was upgraded to a 530H from a 520) or a 550 (called a 550E) at any time.

The Model 530H, which replaces the original Models 530 and 540, offers higher system performance than the Model 520 in the same mechanical package. The processor used in the 530H operates faster (33 MHz), the Data Cache is twice as large (64 KB), and the path between Main Memory and the Data Cache (called the **memory bus**) is twice as wide (128 bits). The Model 530H also comes standard with 32 MB, while the smallest 520 configuration comes with 16 MB of Main Memory. A Model 530H can be upgraded to a Model 550 (called a 550E, designating that it was upgraded) at any time.

The Model 520 comes standard with one 1.44 MB diskette drive and a 355 MB disk drive. This standard drive comes installed in one of the three full-high disk bays

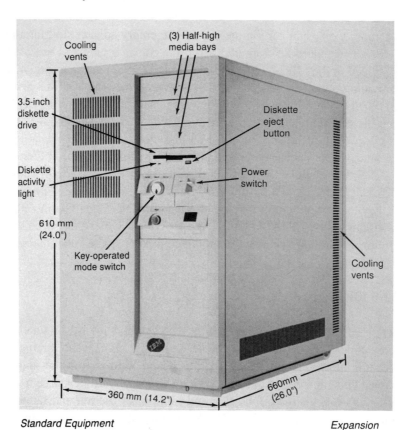

Standard Equipment		Expansion
Main Processor:	8 KB Inst. Cache	(7) Micro Channel
520 = 20 Mhz	64 KB Data Cache	slots
530H = 33 Mhz	128-bit Memory Bus	x Memory slots:
Memory:	400 MB disk (2.5 GB max. internal)	520 = 8
520 = 16 MB (512 MB max)	SCSI Adapter Card/port	530H = 8
530H = 32 MB (512 MB max)	(1) 3.5" 1.44 MB diskette	+ (2) 5.25" disk bays
Data Cache:	(1) Parallel port	# (3) 1/2-high Media bays
520 = 32 KB	(2) Async ports	Model Upgrades
530H = 64 KB	Mouse Port	520 to 530
Memory bus:	Tablet Port	520 to 550
520 = 64-bit	Keyboard/Speaker port	530 to 550
530H = 128-bit	Key-operated mode switch	
Disk:		
520 = 355 MB (2,571 MB max internal)		
530H = 400 MB (2,571 MB max internal)		

x Although one (Model 520) or two (Model 530H) of these slots are used in the standard configuration, the memory card(s) provided in a standard configuration can be replaced with an optional memory card that contains more memory if necessary.

+ Each bay can support one 5.25" disk option or two 3.5" disk options.

See Chapter 2 for description of devices supported by the Media Bays.

Figure 1.6. RS/6000 Models 520 and 530H specifics. These models are designed to stand on the floor.

provided in the Model 520 System Unit. You can choose to replace this 5.25-inch disk with a larger 5.25-inch disk (670 or 857 MB) or two 3.5-inch disks of 320 MB each (640 MB total). Further, each of the two remaining disk bays can accept either one 5.25-inch disk or two 3.5-inch disks, to yield up to 2,571 MB of internal disk storage. The larger mechanical structure of the Model 520 also provides three 1/2-inch-high media bays just above the standard diskette drive. These media bays provide mounting locations for internal CD-ROM Drives or 2.3 GB 8mm Tape Drives, both described in Chapter 2.

The Model 530H comes standard with one 1.44 MB diskette drive and a 400 MB disk drive. This standard drive comes installed in one of the three disk bays provided in the Model 530H System Unit. You can replace this 3.5-inch disk with a 857 MB 5.25-inch disk to provide more disk storage in the standard configuration. Further, each of the two remaining disk bays can accept either one 5.25-inch disk or two 3.5-inch disks, to yield up to 2,571 MB of internal disk storage. Like the Models 520 and 530, the Model 530H provides three 1/2-inch-high media bays just above the standard diskette drive. These media bays provide mounting locations for internal CD-ROM Drives or 2.3 GB 8mm Tape Drives, both described in Chapter 2.

A 16 MB Main Memory card is provided as standard with the Model 520; however, you can choose to substitute this card with a 32 or 64 MB Memory card. Further, you can add Main Memory expansion cards in the remaining seven memory adapter slots, for a maximum of 512 MB. The Model 530H comes standard with two 16 MB Main Memory cards, for a total of 32 MB, and provides six available Main Memory adapter slots. This model requires at least two Main Memory cards to support the more efficient 128-bit path between Main Memory and the Data Cache. These two 16 MB Main Memory cards can be replaced with two 32 or 64 MB Main Memory cards to provide more standard Main Memory. In either model, the remaining six memory adapter slots can each support additional Main Memory adapters, allowing for up to 512 MB of Main Memory.

The Models 520 and 530H have eight Micro Channel expansion slots, which can accommodate the I/O adapter cards (covered in Chapter 2). The SCSI High-Performance I/O Controller (covered later in this book) comes standard with either model, leaving seven Micro Channel slots available for expansion. The key lock provided on the operator panel discourages unauthorized tampering with the system.

Model 550 Specifics

The mechanical frame used by the 7013 RS/6000 Model 550 (shown in Figure 1.7) is identical to that used by the RS/6000 Models 520 and 530H. Like these models, the Model 550 provides a 64 KB Data Cache and a 128-bit-wide path between Main

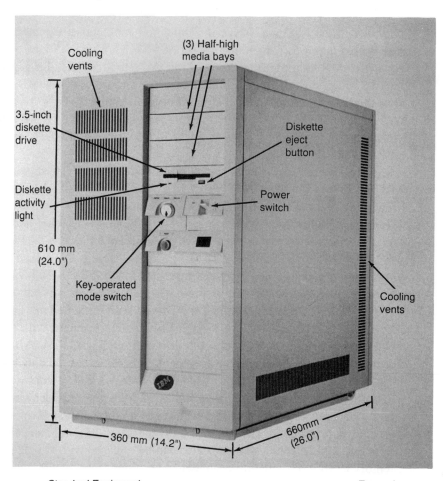

Figure labels:

Cooling vents

(3) Half-high media bays

3.5-inch diskette drive

Diskette eject button

Diskette activity light

Power switch

610 mm (24.0")

Key-operated mode switch

Cooling vents

360 mm (14.2")

660mm (26.0")

Standard Equipment		*Expansion*
41 MHz Main Processor	400 MB disk (2.5 GB max. internal)	(7) Micro Channel
64 MB Main Memory (512 MB max)	SCSI Adapter Card/port	slots
8 KB Inst. Cache	(1) 3.5" 1.44 MB diskette	x (8) Memory slots
64 KB Data Cache	(1) Parallel port	+ (2) 5.25" disk bays
128-bit Memory Bus	(2) Async ports	# (3) 1/2-high Media
800 MB disk (2,571 MB max)	Mouse port	bays
8 KB Inst. Cache	Tablet port	
64 KB Data Cache	Keyboard/Speaker port	
128-bit Memory Bus	Key-operated mode switch	

x Although two of these slots are used in the standard configuration, the memory card(s) provided in a standard configuration can be replaced with an optional memory card that contains more memory if necessary.

+ Each bay can support one 5.25" disk option or two 3.5" disk options.

See Chapter 2 for description of devices supported by the Media bays.

Figure 1.7. RS/6000 Model 550 specifics.

Memory and the Data Cache. However, the Model 550 provides improved system performance over the Models 520 and 530H because of its 41 MHz processor.

The Model 550 comes standard with 64 MB of Main Memory, consisting of two 32 MB Main Memory adapters. Like the Model 530H, the Model 550 requires at least two Main Memory cards to support the more efficient 128-bit path between Main Memory and the Data Cache. The two 32 MB Main Memory cards provided as standard with the Model 550 can be replaced by two 64 MB Main Memory cards to provide 128 MB of Main Memory in two slots. The Model 550 has six additional memory adapter slots with which to further expand Main Memory. A Model 550 can have up to 512 MB of Main Memory.

Also provided are a 1.44 MB diskette drive and three 1/2-inch-high media bays. These media bays provide mounting locations for Internal CD-ROM Drives or 2.3 GB 8mm Tape Drives, both described in Chapter 2. The Model 550 comes standard with 800 MB of disk storage, consisting of two 400 MB 3.5-inch disk drives. In any case, these drive pairs fit into one of the three disk bays provided in the Model 550 System Unit. Either drive pair can be swapped for a single 857 MB disk unit.

Each of the two remaining disk bays can accept either one 5.25-inch disk or two 3.5-inch disks. This means that a single Model 550 can have up to 2,571 MB (2.5 GB) of internal disk storage.

The Model 550 has eight Micro Channel expansion slots that can accommodate the I/O adapter cards (covered in Chapter 2). The SCSI High-Performance I/O Controller (covered later in this book) comes standard, leaving seven Micro Channel slots available for expansion. The key lock provided on the operator panel discourages unauthorized tampering with the system.

Model 930/950 Specifics

The 7015 Models 930 and 950 System Unit, shown in Figure 1.8, represents a departure from the physical packaging concepts we have seen so far in the RS/6000 family. The models 930 and 950 are housed in an industry-standard 19-inch rack that stands 1.6 meters (5.3 feet) tall. The processor is housed in a "drawer" that is installed in the rack. Other drawers in the rack house the Power Distribution Unit, the disks, and the tape drives. An optional battery backup option provides standby power for up to three drawers for at least ten minutes in the event of a power failure.

The 930 Processor Drawer provides a 25 MHz processor and 32 MB of Main Memory as standard equipment. The 32 MB of Main Memory consists of two 16 MB Main Memory adapters. These two 16 MB Main Memory cards can be substituted by two 32 or 64 MB Main Memory cards, to provide up to 128 MB of Main Memory in two slots. The remaining six memory adapter slots provided in the Pro-

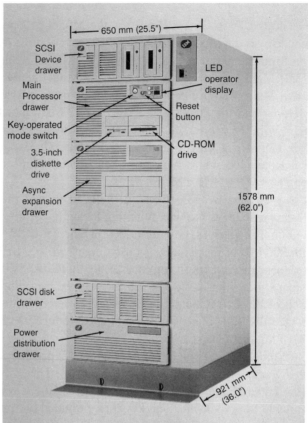

Standard Equipment		Expansion
Main Processor: 930 = 25 Mhz 950 = 41.6 Mhz Memory: 930 = 32 MB (512 MB max) 950 = 64 MB (512 MB max) Disk: 930 = 670 MB (11.9 GB max internal) 950 = 1.7 GB (11.9 GB max internal) 8 KB Inst. Cache	64 KB Data Cache 128-bit Memory bus CD-ROM Drive 2.3 GB 8mm Tape Drive SCSI Adapter Card/port (1) 3.5" 1.44 MB diskette (1) Parallel port (2) Async ports Audio speaker? Key-operated mode switch 1.6 m (63") rack enclosure	(7) Micro Channel slots x (8) Memory slots # (1) 1/2-inch high media bay # (2) 5.25" media bays * Optional Drawers Model upgrade from 930 to 950

x Although two of these slots are used in the standard configuration, the memory cards that are provided in a standard configuration can be replaced with an optional memory card that contains more memory if necessary.

* See Chapter 2 for description of devices supported in optional drawers.

See Chapter 2 for description of devices supported by the Media Bays.

Figure 1.8. RS/6000 Models 930 and 950 specifics. These models are specifically designed to be shared among a group of users.

cessor Drawer can each support an 8, 16, 32, or 64 MB Main Memory adapter, allowing for up to 512 MB of Main Memory.

The 950 Processor Drawer provides a 41.6 MHz processor and 64 MB of Main Memory as standard equipment. The 64 MB of Main Memory consists of two 32 MB Main Memory adapters. These two 32 MB Main Memory cards can be substituted by two 64 MB Main Memory cards, to provide up to 128 MB of Main Memory in two slots. The remaining six memory adapter slots provided in the Processor Drawer can each support an 8, 16, 32, or 64 MB Main Memory adapter, allowing for up to 512 MB of Main Memory.

The Model 930/950 Processor Drawer also has one 1.44 MB diskette drive, the standard ports, a power supply, a SCSI I/O Controller card, a CD-ROM drive, and a 1/2-inch-high media bay that can support a second diskette drive, a second CD-ROM drive, or a tape drive. There are also eight Micro Channel slots, one of which is taken up by the SCSI I/O Controller card.

In addition to the Processor Drawer, a SCSI Device Drawer is provided with all Model 930 or 950 systems. The SCSI Device Drawer in a Model 930 comes with a 5.25-inch 670 MB disk drive and a 2.3 GB 8mm Tape Drive. These two devices come installed in two of the four 5.25-inch bays provided in the SCSI drawer. Alternatively, you can choose to substitute the 670 MB disk with a larger, 857 MB disk unit. The two remaining bays can accept other SCSI devices, including another disk (either 670 or 857 MB), a second tape drive, or a CD-ROM drive.

The SCSI Device Drawer in a Model 950 comes standard with two 5.25-inch 857 MB disk drives and a 2.3 GB 8mm Tape Drive. As with the Model 930, the two remaining bays can accept other SCSI devices.

Up to two more SCSI Device Drawers can be installed in a single 930/950 system, each capable of housing up to four 5.25-inch SCSI devices. This means a single Model 930 or 950 system can have up to 11,998 MB of disk storage. All SCSI Device Drawers attach to the Processor Drawer through a SCSI adapter installed in a Micro Channel slot in the Processor Drawer. Other optional drawers (covered in Chapter 2) available for Model 930/950 systems include the Async Expansion Drawer and the 1/2-inch 9-Track Tape Drive Drawer.

Xstation 130 Specifics

Figure 1.9 shows a 7010 Xstation 130 and associated display, keyboard, and mouse. This device can be thought of as a high-powered "window" into a local area network (covered in Chapter 6). This network can consist of RS/6000 computers as well as other types of "open system" computers that support the industry-standard "X Windows" communications protocol. When an Xstation 130 is attached to the network, a user can sign on to any "X Windows compatible" computer on the network and run programs on that computer as if he or she were directly using that computer. In fact, the Xstation 130 user can sign on to many different computers on the network and simultaneously work with independent application programs on each. The Xstation 130 handles this multiapplication environment by dividing the display screen into sections called **windows**. Each window shows the display for its particular program. These windows can quickly be enlarged, reduced, moved, or overlaid to provide the most convenient arrangement. With Xstation 130s, multiple users can share one or more RS/6000 systems or other computers that comply with Xwindow standards.

The Xstation 130 is not a diskless version of an RS/6000 computer in that it can't run any RS/6000 application program by itself. The concept of the Xstation 130 is to provide low-cost (but graphics-capable) workstations with which to interact with RS/6000 systems and other open systems. With an Xstation 130, the program(s) and data being accessed by the user are resident on one or more computers in the network. Unlike low-cost ASCII terminals, Xstation 130 workstations can display and manipulate full graphics images like an RS/6000 workstation can. However, it is less expensive to provide each user with an Xstation 130 attached to a local area network than to provide each user with a fully capable RS/6000 computer system attached to that network.

The displays originally designed for the IBM PS/2 family (e.g., IBM 8503, 8507, 8513, and 8514) can be used with the Xstation 130, as can those used with the RS/6000 family (e.g., IBM 6091). The 1 MB Video Memory provided as standard on an Xstation 130 is capable of displaying very respectable images (e.g., 1024 × 768 resolution with up to 256 colors out of a palette of 16.7 million colors). This Video Memory can be expanded to a maximum of 2 MB to provide higher image resolution (e.g., 1280 × 1024 resolution with up to 256 colors).

Though not capable of running RS/6000 programs on its own, the Xstation 130 is a computer in its own right with a 12.5 MHz Intel 80C186 Microprocessor, 512 KB of I/O Memory, a 32 MHz Texas Instruments TMS 34020 Graphics microprocessor, 1 MB of Video Memory, and 2 MB of System Memory. The two microprocessors used in the Xstation 130 are specialized to handle the communications with other more powerful computers over the network and to handle the presentation of graphics on the Xstation 130 display respectively.

The System Memory is used to store many different types of information. First, it stores the logistical information necessary to create the images seen on the screen (window templates, bit maps for fonts and icons, background color data, etc.). For applications that support panning of large images within a window, for example, the System Memory can locally store the excess pixel information not currently displayed on the screen so that when the window is panned, pixels are immediately available for display without having to retrieve the excess pixel information over the network.

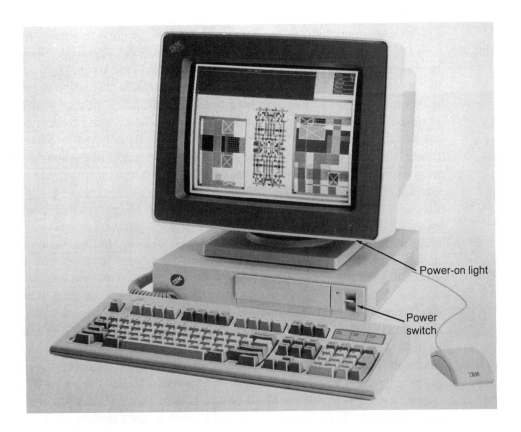

Power-on light

Power switch

Standard Equipment

TMS 34020 Graphics Processor (32 Mhz)
1 MB Video memory (2 MB max)
80C186 I/O Processor (12.5 Mhz)
2 MB System memory (16 MB max)
512 KB I/O Memory
(2) Async ports
(1) Parallel port
Integrated Ethernet Controller/port
Integrated Display Adapter/port
Mouse
Enhanced Keyboard
Audio Speaker

Expansion

* (1) Expansion Slot
Video memory upgrade
30 MB Disk drive
System memory upgrades

* This slot can support either a Token-Ring Network 16/4 Adapter/A, a second
Ethernet adapter, or a Dual Async Adapter/A.

Figure 1.9. The IBM Xstation 130. This intelligent workstation cooperates with RS/6000 systems attached over a LAN.

Another optional use for System Memory is to provide a temporary holding area (local caching) for information necessary to redraw areas of the display that are momentarily covered up by pop-up windows (called **save under**) or that are hidden due to overlapping windows (called **backing store**). If this space is not available within the Xstation 130 System Memory, the information must be sent to and later retrieved from a host computer over the network. While using System Memory for save under and backing store sounds like an automatic boost in Xstation performance, that may not always be the case. This is especially true when the Xstation is receiving ASCII codes or high-level graphics commands over the network from its host computer system.

The Xstation 130 comes with 2 MB of System Memory, which can be expanded up to 16.5 MB. When the optional disk drive is installed, it serves as a low-cost and somewhat slower extension to the System Memory. In this capacity, the information stored on the disk drive is lost when the system is turned off, just like the information stored in the System Memory. However, the optional disk drive can also be used to store information such as a boot image and fonts, which will be preserved even when the Xstation is turned off.

Generally speaking, the more System Memory (including disk storage used as System Memory) available in an Xstation 130, the less often the need arises to store information to and retrieve it from a host on the network. Thus, more System Memory will typically result in faster system response times for the Xstation user and an overall reduction in the workload on the communications network and associated host computers. This is especially true if many windows are being used on the Xstation 130.

The Xstation 130 comes standard with an Ethernet adapter, allowing the Xstation to participate in any network conforming to Ethernet Version 2 or the closely related IEEE 802.3 standards. You can also install an optional Token-Ring Network adapter for participation in an IBM Token-Ring Network. Both adapters can be used simultaneously to allow a single Xstation 130 to participate in two different networks at the same time. Alternately, you can install a Dual Async Adapter/A, which adds two more async ports to the Xstation.

The programming used by an Xstation 130 must be sent from an RS/6000 also participating in the network every time the Xstation 130 is turned on. To perform this initialization for the Xstation 130, the RS/6000 must be running the AIX Xstation Manager/6000 extension to the AIX operating system.

The Xstation 130 also comes standard with a mouse, two async ports (19.2 Kbaud), and a parallel printer port. These ports can be used to attach local ASCII printers (e.g., IBM Personal Printer Series II). The Xstation Manager program can then redirect RS/6000 print jobs to printers attached to the Xstation 130. Also provided is 2 KB of battery-backed memory to preserve configuration information and network error logs even when the Xstation 130 is turned off.

Performance Overview

One important aspect of a computer system is the speed at which the computer can perform work. This speed is known as the **performance** of the computer. The higher the performance, the more work the computer can do. Many things, such as the processor, Main Memory, disk storage, and program efficiency, affect the performance of a computer system. It is difficult and often misleading to predict the overall performance of a computer system by looking at selected specifications of the individual components that make up the computer system. While things such as disk access times and system clock speeds are important, they do not give the whole picture in terms of overall system performance.

A better way to compare the overall performance of different computers is to perform **benchmark testing**. This testing involves running various programs and measuring how each computer system behaves under the workload. Through this benchmark testing, all elements of the computer system come into play, and the overall performance of selected computer systems can be meaningfully compared.

IBM has conducted benchmark testing to document the performance of the various RS/6000 models. This testing was done by loading the computers with specially written programs, each designed to exercise the RS/6000 computers as they would be used in various environments. It should be understood that to perform benchmark testing, the test group must make assumptions about the kind of work being done and the behavior of the users and programs. For this reason, the performance measurements in this benchmark may vary significantly from what one finds if one's specific environment is not the same as the assumptions made in the testing. However, since all assumptions are the same for all computers included in the benchmark testing, one can get a good feeling for the relative performance of the computer systems. Since the RS/6000 system is designed for use in both technical and commercial environments, we will examine benchmark test results for each.

In a technical environment, RS/6000 systems are typically used as single-user workstations and are called upon to perform millions of floating-point mathematical calculations per second. In these environments, RS/6000 systems are doing things like drawing mechanical designs on the screen, performing stress and thermal analysis, merging high-resolution images and text onto a single page for publication, or performing statistical analysis on large amounts of information. Due to the numerically intensive applications found in technical environments, numerically intensive benchmark programs are used to compare the performance of technical workstations. Figure 1.10 shows the results of benchmark testing designed to show the relative performance of the various RS/6000 models and other selected computer systems. The number shown for each model is called the model's **SPECmark**. This number represents the composite result of benchmark testing using a series of ten programs written in C and FORTRAN programming languages. This group of programs makes up the Systems Performance Evaluation Cooperative (SPEC) Suite 1.2 set of benchmarks and is designed to test the computer's ability to perform numerically intensive and highly precise mathematics. They do little to test the computer's

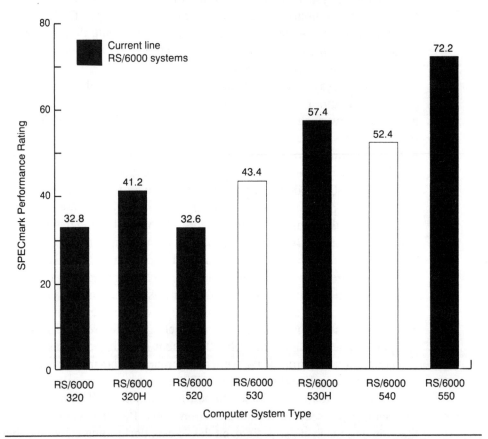

Figure 1.10. Overall performance comparison measured by benchmark testing geared toward the technical workstation environment. Data shown are based on a series of programs designed to test the performance of computers in technical applications. This testing is not representative of a specific user environment. Results in other environments may vary significantly.

graphics capability or the performance of the disk subsystems. RS/6000 graphics subsystem performance is covered later in the chapter, and disk subsystem performance is reflected more in the commercial environment benchmark testing, discussed next. However, these programs test the processing power of the RS/6000 Main Processor and are representative of highly technical environments.

Notice that the RS/6000 Models 320 and 520 offer roughly the same performance with SPECmarks of 32.8 and 32.6 respectively. This is because they are each based on the same Main Processor running at the same system clock rate (20 MHz). The Main Processor used in the RS/6000 Model 320H is 25% faster (25 MHz) than those used in Model 320/520 systems, which results in a SPECmark of 41.2 — a 25% improvement over the SPECmarks of the Model 320/520. The Model 530H is an enhanced version of the older Model 530 with a Main Processor running at 33 MHz. Again, the faster processor accounts for a correspondingly higher SPECmark of the Model 530H (57.4). Finally, the Model 550 is built around the fastest Main Processor (41.67 MHz), making it the most powerful RS/6000 system in the family (SPECmark of 72.2).

In typical commercial environments, one finds application programs like order entry, accounts payable, accounts receivable, and so on. In these environments, RS/6000 systems are usually shared by more than one user, either in a traditional multiuser or in a LAN configuration. Commercial applications typically move large amounts of information between disk and Main Memory. To evaluate the relative performance of the various RS/6000 models and other selected computers, the **Transaction Processing Performance Council Benchmark – A (TPC-A)** benchmark can be used. This TPC-A benchmark testing collectively considers two performance parameters: **interactive throughput** and **interactive response time**. Interactive throughput measures the amount of work the computer system performs for active users in a given period of time. The amount of work is defined as the number of user requests for activity (or **transactions**) a computer system can perform per second. Since businesses buy computers to perform work, this is an important indicator.

Interactive response time is a measurement of the amount of time an individual user would have to wait from the time he or she hits the Enter key initiating a transaction until the computer responds. Response time, usually measured in seconds, is important because it has a direct effect on users' productivity and satisfaction. A slow response time makes the user wait every time the Enter key is hit, which can affect concentration and cause frustration.

Response time and throughput are not only each important in their own right, but they are also related to one another. As the throughput of a computer system is increased by adding more users or having each user perform more work, the response time will increase. (The system will appear to slow down.) For consistency, the TPC-A benchmark requires that 90 percent of all transactions be completed within two seconds. That is, the computer's **utilization** in this benchmark testing will not be driven beyond the point where the response time is greater than two seconds.

Figure 1.11 shows the maximum throughput (number of transactions per second) that the various RS/6000 models can deliver without driving the systems beyond the point where response time is degraded. The Model 520 can deliver up to 23 transactions per second without degrading response time beyond TPC guidelines. The Models 530H and 550 each rate at 32 transactions per second, or over about 40% more than the Model 520. The performance advantage of the Models 530 and 550 is due to a combination of faster Main Processors, a larger Data Cache, and a more efficient path between the processor and memory. One would think that the Model 550, with its faster Main processor, should be capable of handling more transactions per second than the Model 530H. The reason that the Models 530H and 550 are rated the same in the TPC-A benchmark test is because of a rule in the testing methodology that requires the systems under test to support at least 10 terminals per transaction/second. Since IBM-supported configurations for both the 530H and 550 are limited to a maximum of 320 terminals, the maximum transaction/second rating for the 530H and 550 is 320/10 = 32. While the Models 530H and 550 are probably capable of handling more than 32 transactions per second, the maximum terminal limitation prevails according to TPC testing rules. Since the Model 950 (based on the same Main Processor as the Model 550) can have more than 320 terminals attached, it achieves a rating of 38 transactions/second—a more accurate reflection of the true processing capability of the system itself. Under each bar in the graph in Figure 1.11 is listed a number labeled K$/TPS. This number represents the cost (in thousands of dollars)/performance rating (TPC transactions/second) established according to TPC rules. That is, K$/TPS is a value rating based on the estimated cost of owning and operating the entire computer system configuration over a five-year period (K$) and on the performance offered by that system (transactions per second). The smaller the number, the better the value.

More detailed information about the SPECmark and TPC-A benchmark testing is provided in Appendix B.

A CLOSER LOOK

There are many elements that together provide the functions and performance of RS/6000 computers. Not only must each element be highly efficient, but each must be able to "keep up" with all other elements that make up the computer system. It doesn't matter how fast a processor is if, for example, the disk subsystem is the "bot-

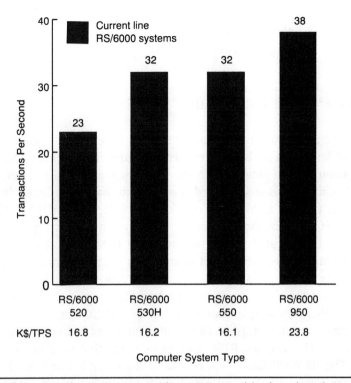

Figure 1.11. Overall performance comparison measured by benchmark testing geared toward the commercial data processing environment. Data shown are based on a series of programs designed to test the performance of computers in commercial applications. This testing is not representative of a specific user environment. Results in other environments may vary significantly.

tleneck" that limits the overall speed at which the computer can perform work. A high-speed graphics adapter will be handicapped if the expansion slot in which it resides is unable to keep up with information flow rates. RS/6000 designers utilized computer modeling and other tools to simulate various design approaches with the goal of achieving a computer system with **balanced performance**. The remainder of this chapter will provide a closer look at some of the elements of the RS/6000 design:

- ❑ Hardware architecture
- ❑ Graphics
- ❑ Auxiliary storage
- ❑ Micro Channel expansion slots
- ❑ Standard ports

□ Enhanced keyboard

□ Packaging technology

RS/6000 Hardware Architecture

The internal organization of the hardware elements comprising the RS/6000 system is known as its **hardware architecture**. The architecture of RS/6000 computers contributes a great deal to the performance offered by these systems. The RS/6000 architecture is an enhanced version of the earlier ***Reduced Instruction Set Computing* (RISC)** architecture originally developed by IBM in the 1970s. As the name RISC implies, the instruction set or total number of programming instructions that can be executed within the computer is reduced compared with more traditional ***Complex Instruction Set Computers* (CISC)**. Since the instructions in RISC systems are very simple, they can be executed using high-speed computer hardware within the computer system in a very short period of time (e.g., one clock cycle). Further, the simple instruction set of a RISC computer typically can be carefully employed to perform even complex functions in a more efficient manner.

This original RISC architecture was first used in the earlier IBM RT system. The RS/6000 family introduces IBM's second-generation RISC architecture, called the ***Performance Optimized With Enhanced RISC* (POWER)** architecture. This architecture utilizes a blend of the original RISC architecture and some traditional CISC concepts with an emphasis on doing multiple operations at the same time. The POWER architecture, coupled with the high-speed circuitry and the RS/6000 system's **multiprocessor** approach, provides the foundation for the entire family of high-performance computer systems. By using multiple processors in a single RS/6000 system, each specialized for a specific job, overall system performance is enhanced. For example, the SCSI I/O Controller used in most RS/6000 configurations has its own microprocessor which handles the detailed processing associated with moving information to and from disk and tape units. Similarly the 64-port Async Adapter and the associated terminal concentrators are each equipped with microprocessors used to handle the heavy communications traffic between the RS/6000 system and the many ASCII terminals and printers that may be attached. This multiprocessor approach allows the RS/6000 Main Processor to concentrate on running the user's application programs rather than handling system overhead processing. The result is improved overall system performance.

To understand the POWER architecture, it is necessary to look at two key pieces of RS/6000 systems. These are the **Main Processor** and the **Main Memory system.** The Main Processor and the Main Memory system, along with other circuits, make up the **Central Processing Unit (CPU)** circuit board found inside the RS/6000 chassis.

The smallest piece of information the Main Processor and Main Memory can use is called a **bit.** These bits are grouped into **bytes** (8 bits), **half-words** (16 bits), and **words** (32 bits) to form the computer's representation of numbers, letters of the alphabet, instructions in a program, and so on. With this basic knowledge, let's take a closer look at the RS/6000 system's Main Processor and Main Memory.

The Main Processor

The main processor is the heart of a computer system because it is the control center for information flow inside the computer. It is the main processor that does the data manipulation or "thinking" necessary to perform tasks for the user. The speed of the circuits making up the main processor, along with the architecture of the Main Processor, determines the overall processing speeds achievable by the computer system.

There are five basic elements in RS/6000 Main Processors, each made up of thousands of circuits packaged in one or more specially designed chips:

1. Instruction Cache/Branch Processor
2. Fixed-Point Processor
3. Floating-Point Processor
4. Data Cache
5. I/O Unit

Figure 1.12 is a block diagram showing how these elements are organized to make up the RS/6000 hardware architecture. To see how this architecture can do multiple operations at the same time, let's quickly trace the flow of information through the system. It all starts when the user executes a command to start a program, which causes the instructions of that program to be retrieved from disk storage and loaded into Main Memory (shown at the bottom of the diagram). After the program is loaded into Main Memory, the RS/6000 Main Processor requests the very first instruction (4 bytes) in the program. In compliance with the request, the first instruction (4 bytes), along with the next several instructions (a total of 64 sequential bytes), is retrieved from the Main Memory and loaded into the *Instruction Cache Unit* (ICU). The Instruction Cache is a group of very high speed memory circuits contained in the ICU chip. It is used as a temporary holding area (8 KB in size) for programming instructions that are likely to be next in line to be executed. When the Main Processor requests the next instruction, it will first look in the ICU. Most of the time, the next instruction needed will already have been loaded into the ICU, eliminating the delay

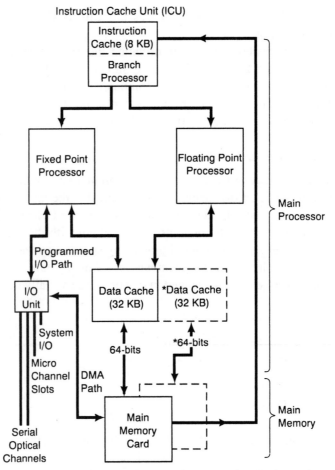

Instruction Cache Unit (ICU)

*The second 32 KB Data Cache and the second 64-bit data path
are only provided on the larger RS/6000 Models.

Figure 1.12. RS/6000 POWER architecture block diagram.

associated with getting the instruction from slower Main Memory. This is called a **cache hit.** Since the Instruction Cache can respond much more quickly than the system's Main Memory, the system's performance is dramatically improved with every cache hit. If the needed instruction has not already loaded into the ICU (called a **cache miss**), another 64 bytes starting with the needed instruction are automatically loaded from the Main Memory into the ICU. In the case of a cache miss, loading the ICU takes longer than simply getting the needed instruction from Main Memory. That is, a cache miss results in a penalty to RS/6000 system performance. So it is a game of statistics. Since most computer programs will experience many more cache hits than misses during normal operation, the cache technique usually increases overall RS/6000 system performance significantly.

So far, then, we have gotten the first few programming instructions loaded into the 8 KB of Instruction Cache memory located in the ICU. Next, the **branch processor** component of the ICU examines each programming instruction in turn and independently executes any **condition register** instructions or **branch** instructions. Condition register instructions manipulate the contents of working storage locations (a condition register) within the main processor that store information about the results of calculations performed earlier in the program. Branch instructions are a commonly used type of programming instruction that directs the flow of the program, usually taking different paths depending on the contents of the condition register. Branch instructions that are executed completely within the ICU while other operations are happening in the other, more traditional processor elements are said to occur in zero system clock cycles. These branches are therefore said to be **zero cycle branches**.

While the branch processor intercepts and executes branch and condition register instructions, the remaining instructions are simultaneously fed to and executed by the **fixed-point processor** and the **floating-point processor**. The fixed-point processor performs mathematical and logical operations with things that don't have decimal points, like whole numbers (e.g., the integers 1, 5, and −6) and numeric representations of text (e.g., ASCII codes). These fixed-point instructions are common in almost any computing environment. The floating-point processor performs mathematical and logical operations (IEEE 754-1985) with things that do have a decimal point (i.e., real numbers like 53.254376, 4.6, and 3.1313). These floating-point instructions are common in engineering/scientific applications and others requiring sophisticated computer graphics.

For those who aren't counting, that makes four independent operations going on inside the RS/6000 at the same time:

1. A branch instruction
2. A condition register instruction
3. A fixed-point instruction
4. A floating-point instruction

In fact, if the floating-point instruction happens to be the multiply-add (A×B+C) or the multiply-subtract instruction, these can be counted as two floating-point operations, making a total of five operations being performed at once. This architecture is therefore said to be a **superscaler** implementation or a **parallel processing** implementation.

The instruction cache and parallel processing units in the Main Processor allow the RS/6000 system to execute a great many programming instructions in a very small amount of time. However, that's not enough to make a Main Processor architecture that offers high performance. You must also be able to efficiently move the data on which the programming instructions are to operate between the RS/6000 Main Processor and Main Memory. This is where the **Data Cache Unit** comes in. The Data Cache Unit operates much like the Instruction Cache Unit, only the Data Cache Unit provides a temporary holding area for data needed during program execution rather than programming instructions. When a program instruction requires data on which to operate, the Data Cache Unit is first checked to see if the needed data has already been loaded. If the Data Cache Unit contains the needed data (a cache hit), the Data Cache Unit can very quickly provide the needed information and dramatically boost RS/6000 system performance. If the Data Cache Unit does not have the requested data, a cache miss occurs, which negatively impacts system performance. In the event of a cache miss, the needed data plus the next few words of data are automatically loaded from the slower Main Memory to the Data Cache Unit. In this way, the Data Cache Unit continuously accumulates the data most likely to be needed during upcoming calculations, increasing the likelihood of cache hits. As with the ICU, the more cache hits, the better the system performance. Statistically speaking, the larger the Data Cache, the higher the percentage of cache hits, thus the higher the overall system performance. The base models of the RS/6000 family have a Data Cache 32 KB in size while the larger models have a 64 KB Data Cache, accounting in part for their higher performance. Those models with the 64 KB Data Cache are also designed to move twice as much information between Main Memory and the Data Cache. That is, the models with the 64 KB Data Cache provide a more efficient path (i.e., 128-bit-wide data path vs. 64-bit-wide data path on models with the 32 KB Data Cache) between Main Memory and the Data Cache, which also serves to boost system performance. All RS/6000 models use a scheme called **set associativity** to reduce the number of instruction and cache misses by allowing for more efficient sharing of the Data Cache among multiple programs running simultaneously.

Finally, the **_Input/Output_ Unit (I/O Unit)** element of the RS/6000 Main Processor manages data transfers between all input/output devices and the rest of the RS/6000 system. These include things like the disks, communications adapters installed in the Micro Channel slots, and any devices attached to Serial Optical Channels. Often, the information will flow directly between the I/O device and Main Memory. This is called **Direct Memory Access (DMA)**. Other times, the program may directly control the information between the Main Processor and the I/O device. This is called **Programmed I/O.**

The activities of the five RS/6000 processor elements are coordinated by an electronic signal called the **system clock.** The system clock is the heartbeat of the computer system. It steps the Main Processor through each step in the execution of a program. It is the time reference of the Main Processor and sets the pace for all Main Processor activity. The speed at which the system clock runs is called the **system clock rate** and is measured in millions of clock steps per second, or **megahertz (MHz).** For example, the RS/6000 Models 320 and 520 run at 20 MHz, while the Models 550 and 950 run at 41 MHz. All other things being equal, the performance of the computer system is directionally proportional to the system clock rate. However, there are many other things inside a computer (i.e., main processor architecture, instruction sets, memory system speeds, disk speeds, I/O bus speeds, etc.) that together define the overall performance of a computer system. Therefore, comparing individual specifications (e.g., system clock rate) of computer systems can be very misleading, as was discussed earlier in the chapter.

The Main Memory

The Main Memory is also a very important part of a computer. Main Memory is the set of electronic chips that provide a "workspace" for the main processor. That is, it holds the information (program instructions and data) being used by the main processor. The Main Memory is called **Random Access Memory (RAM)** because it can store and retrieve information independent of the sequential order in which it was originally stored.

The smallest RS/6000 systems come standard with 8 MB (about 8 million bytes) of Main Memory. The largest systems can have up to 512 MB of Main Memory. When you have this much Main Memory in a system, schemes to detect and correct memory defects become necessary to protect the integrity of the information stored in the computer system's Main Memory. The RS/6000 uses several techniques to protect the integrity of its Main Memory. The **Error Checking and Correction (ECC)** technique used by all members of the RS/6000 family can detect single- and double-bit errors and correct single-bit errors. This is done by appending seven additional bits (called **ECC bits**) onto every word (32 bits) in Main Memory. The seven ECC bits are automatically generated by the ECC circuitry based on the value of the associated word and then stored in Main Memory alongside that word. New ECC bits are calculated and stored every time a word is written to Main Memory. Later, when that word is read back from Main Memory, the value stored in the corresponding ECC bits is checked to make sure that the word didn't somehow get corrupted through some type of Main Memory failure. The most common type of failure is to have a single bit in the word accidentally get changed to the wrong value. In this case, the ECC circuitry can use the value stored in the ECC bits to actually correct the error on the fly and allow normal operations to continue undisturbed. On rare occasions, a Main Memory failure will cause two bits in a single word to be changed. In this case, the ECC circuitry can only detect and report the error. In addition to monitoring all read/write activity in Main Memory, the ECC circuitry periodically scans all of Main Memory to ensure the integrity of the information. This is called **memory scrubbing**. The RS/6000 Main Memory employs some other techniques to ensure the integrity of the system: **bit scattering, memory bus parity**, and **bit steering**.

Bit scattering means that memory chips used to make up the memory system are organized in a way that minimizes the impact of a single chip failure. Memory bus parity refers to an extra bit appended to the parallel group of wires (called a **bus**) used to transfer information to and from Main Memory. This extra bit, called a **parity bit**, is used to detect any errors that may occur as the information is transferred along the memory bus. In fact, parity bits are used on chip-to-chip data busses and throughout most internal chip data paths. Finally, bit steering is a concept in which extra memory bits designed into the memory system can be used to replace failing bits in many cases without disrupting normal operation. The extra bit is "steered" onto the memory bus in place of the failing bit. All of these things help protect the integrity of the information in an RS/6000 system and allow the RS/6000 to recover from errors without disrupting the user(s).

In any computer system, there is a great deal of information moving in and out of Main Memory. For this reason, the design of the Main Memory can significantly affect overall system performance. Why is so much time spent moving information in and out of the Main Memory? There are two major reasons: First, the programming instructions of the active program(s) reside in the Main Memory. Therefore, every instruction in the program must at some point be retrieved from the Main Memory. Secondly, the Main Memory holds and accepts data used in the program(s) being executed. If the overall information flow to and from Main Memory (assisted by the Instruction Cache Unit and the Data Cache Unit) cannot keep pace with the Main Processor, the Main Processor will be delayed and system performance will suffer. For this reason, the Main Memory must be designed to keep up with the speeds achievable by the Main Processor. The design of the RS/6000 Main Processor and its Main Memory are balanced through the use of separate Data and Instruction caches and the wide path between Main Memory and the caches, as discussed earlier. To further balance the system, the path or "bus" between the caches and Main Memory (which can operate at up to 660 MB/sec) is independent from the Micro Channel bus used for input/output activity (e.g., disk information transfers). This prevents interference between Main Memory activity and input/output activity, which can decrease the overall performance of the system.

Finally, the RS/6000 Main Memory design uses a technique called **interleaving**. This is a way of subdividing the memory chips to allow an overlap of multiple transfers to and from memory. That is, two words of data (64 bits) can be read from a Main Memory card in a single system clock cycle (two-way interleaving). The wider data path of the more powerful RS/6000 models allows the two Main Memory cards to each provide two words per cycle for a total of four words (128 bits) per cycle (four-way interleaving). Interleaving increases the effective transfer rate between Main Memory and the caches, ultimately feeding the RS/6000 Main Processor with the necessary programming instructions and data.

Memory Management

The way in which a computer system utilizes available Main Memory and disk storage is called the computer's **memory management** scheme and is basic to the capabilities of the computer. Understanding the basics of this memory management will give insight into one of the features of RS/6000 computers. Figure 1.13 shows conceptually what the memory in RS/6000 systems looks like. The Main Memory is contained inside the computer's System Unit. The disk storage may be inside the System Unit or in a separate box cabled to the System Unit.

When the RS/6000 computer is first turned on, information vital to an orderly startup and smooth operation is automatically copied from the disk to the Main Memory. Once normal system operation is established, users can begin to do their work. During the course of this work, the users will start various computer programs. As the user starts each program, it is copied from the disk to Main Memory and then executed. Based on the work being done by the user, the computer programs manipulate various sets of data which are also loaded from the disk to Main Memory as needed. It doesn't take long to realize that the Main Memory in a computer can quickly become filled up with programs and data as the system is called upon to do more and more work. In earlier days of computing, the Main Memory size limited the amount of work a computer could manage at any one time. This limitation capped the size of programs, the number of programs that could be run concurrently, the number of users who could share the system, and so on. In today's environment, a technique called **virtual memory** alleviates the need to squeeze all active programs and data into Main Memory. In computers that support virtual

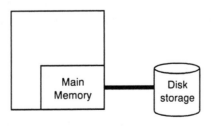

Figure 1.13. Conceptual view of RS/6000 Main Memory and disk storage.

memory, the computer basically fakes out the computer programs and users and appears to have much more Main Memory than it actually has. The largest of today's RS/6000 systems can have 512 MB of Main Memory. The POWER architecture can support future systems that can address up to 2 GB (2^{32}, or over 2 billion bytes) of Main Memory. The virtual memory supported by all RS/6000 systems is a whopping 4 petabytes (PB) in size (2^{52}, or over 4500 trillion bytes), which is over 1000 times larger than that provided on the IBM RT System (1 terabyte). The RS/6000 system's 4 PB of addressing capability is enough to keep track of the information contained on over 2 trillion pages of single-spaced computer output. That's a stack of paper over 200,000 miles high — almost reaching the moon.

Virtual memory therefore allows more programs, data, and users to be simultaneously active on the system than could be supported in real Main Memory without virtual memory. That is, it allows you to make the most out of whatever size Main Memory you actually have.

Here's how virtual memory works. Say a user tells the computer to start a word-processing program. The computer would first attempt to load the needed portion of the word-processing program into Main Memory. If there is no space left in Main Memory, some space will be made available by overwriting an inactive portion of some program or by "swapping out" some inactive data to a temporary space on the disk. The needed portion of the word-processing program can then be loaded into the available space and the user can begin typing. If the program that was overwritten or the data that was swapped out is again needed, it will be reloaded from disk to some other available Main Memory area. So a virtual memory computer system is constantly swapping programs and information between Main Memory and disk storage (robbing Peter to pay Paul and then vice versa). Virtual memory allows the maximum size program or combination of all programs and data to be limited only by the combined amount of Main Memory and disk space rather than by the amount of Main Memory alone. The advantage of having this virtual memory hocus pocus built into the RS/6000 hardware and AIX operating system is that neither the programmer nor the user of any RS/6000 system need be concerned with Main Memory size. To them, the system seems to have as much Main Memory as they need, and they are never made aware that information is constantly being swapped from Main Memory to disk and back again. The computer hardware and AIX operating system efficiently manage **paging** automatically.

While virtual memory is a powerful system feature, it comes at a price. The paging between disk and Main Memory is processing overhead that can reduce the overall system performance. While a little paging will not appreciably hurt performance, the more paging, the more system performance will be reduced. When the paging performed by a virtual memory system gets excessive, the system is said to be **thrashing**, or spending too much time paging information between disk and Main

Memory. Thrashing can be reduced by increasing the amount of Main Memory in the RS/6000 system through the installation of Main Memory expansion options described in Chapter 2. Increasing the Main Memory in the system will provide more room for programs and data, reducing the amount of virtual memory paging.

The virtual memory concept is implemented in many of today's computer systems to some degree. RS/6000 systems implement their virtual memory scheme through a concept called **single-level storage**. This term simply means that in RS/6000 systems, there is no distinction made between disk storage and Main Memory. All storage appears to be one homogeneous sea of Main Memory which is accessed in exactly the same way. This consistency provides for a simple and efficient virtual memory implementation that is the same for programs, data, temporary holding areas, and so on. Other virtual memory implementations must create and manage separate address spaces, and they often treat programs differently from data, for example. The simplicity of single-level storage results in a consistent and more complete virtual memory system than that of most other implementations.

Graphics

Images presented on a computer's display are used to present information to the user. The quality of these images can directly affect the user's productivity, effectiveness, and enjoyment during a work session. Graphics image quality is especially important in applications such as computer-aided design (CAD), publishing, visualization of large data sets, and others that revolve around computer-generated images.

Users accessing an RS/6000 system from an ASCII terminal have no graphics capabilities. That is, they can only see letters, numbers, or other special characters predefined in the ASCII standard. Users accessing an RS/6000 through a high-function display or an Xstation 130, however, have a powerful graphics capability. Let's take a closer look at RS/6000 graphics.

Graphics Basic Training

There are two hardware elements that work together to generate computer graphics: the **display** and the **graphics adapter**. The display is the device that resembles a small television set and actually transforms the electronic signals from the computer system into light images discernible by the human eye. We will examine the displays supported by the RS/6000 systems in Chapter 2.

Graphics adapters are circuit boards (or independent boxes known as **graphics subsystems**) that contain circuitry that converts the bits and bytes inside the computer system to the electrical signals that are used by the display to create the image you see. The images generated by the graphics adapters are made up of patterns of many individual dots on the display, called *Picture Elements* **(PELs)** or **pixels,** that blend together to form the desired image. This technique is depicted in Figure 1.14.

All RS/6000 graphics subsystems generate images using the *All-Points Addressable* **(APA)** technique. With APA each individual PEL on the display screen can be independently turned on or off by writing the appropriate bit pattern to its associated location within the special-purpose memory area called the **frame buffer** (often called the **graphics memory**).

The number of individual PELs represented in the frame buffer determines the number of PELs that make up the image (or **resolution**) of the image seen on the surface of the computer's display. The more PELs represented in the frame buffer, the higher the resolution of the image (assuming the display can also support that resolution). All RS/6000 graphics adapter/subsystems support resolutions up to 1280 × 1024 PELs.

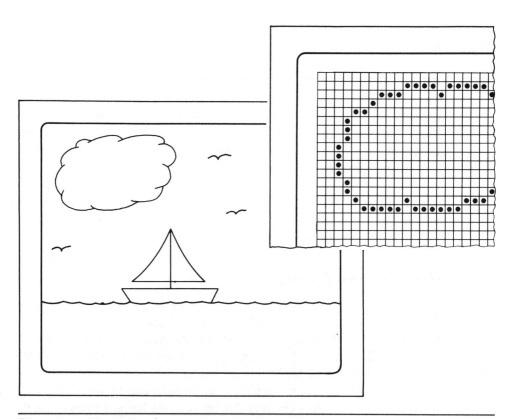

Figure 1.14. Mechanics of a computer-generated image.

The number of bits associated with a single PEL determines how many different colors or brightnesses it can have. RS/6000 graphics adapters/subsystems support from 1 bit/PEL (2^1=bright or dark) to 24 bits/PEL (2^{24}=over 16.7 million different colors). That is, RS/6000 computer images can have from 2 (black and white) to 16.7 million different colors in them. With black-and-white displays, the graphics adapters translate the different colors that appear in a display into brightness levels, also called **shades of gray**. Using up to 16.7 million colors in a single image is called **true color** and results in extremely lifelike images.

A frame buffer of a given size can be used to represent different numbers of PELs (i.e., different resolutions) with different numbers of bits per PEL (i.e., different number of maximum colors) under the control of the graphics software. Some graphics subsystems have two full-frame buffers. This allows one frame buffer to be displayed undisturbed while the second is updated by the application program. When it is time to display the updated image, the second frame buffer is displayed, allowing the first frame buffer to be updated, and so on. The results of this dual frame buffer technique is a smoother transition from one image to another. Because less unnecessary screen is displayed as images are updated, this is especially useful for applications that employ animation.

There are some other bits associated in each PEL that should be mentioned here. The **overlay frame** is a separate part of the frame buffer used to more quickly overwrite portions of the display screen. If the overlay frame is empty, the image in the normal part of the graphics memory will be displayed in its entirety. If an image (e.g., some text, a pop-up window, etc.) is written to the overlay frame, it takes precedence over what is in the normal part of the frame buffer and is displayed on the screen. Once the overlay frame is reset, the original image is restored automatically. This allows an application program to quickly overwrite sections of the display screen and then restore the original image without having to recreate it. **Multiple overlay frames** means that each PEL has multiple bits in the overlay frame, which allows the image to be overwritten using more colors.

All computer images are represented on a flat two-dimensional display screen. However, computers can internally model an object in three dimensions and create an image that appears to be three-dimensional on the computer's display, as shown in Figure 1.15.

A memory area used in the generation of three-dimensional graphics is called the **Z-buffer**. While not actually part of the frame buffer itself, it is a special-purpose memory area that is used for **hidden-line** and **hidden-surface removal**. As you rotate a solid pyramid, for example, some of the lines and surfaces that make up the pyramid will begin to fall behind the pyramid itself (Figure 1.16). With the hidden-line and hidden-surface removal function afforded by the Z-buffer, these lines and surfaces automatically disappear as they fall behind the pyramid and reappear on the

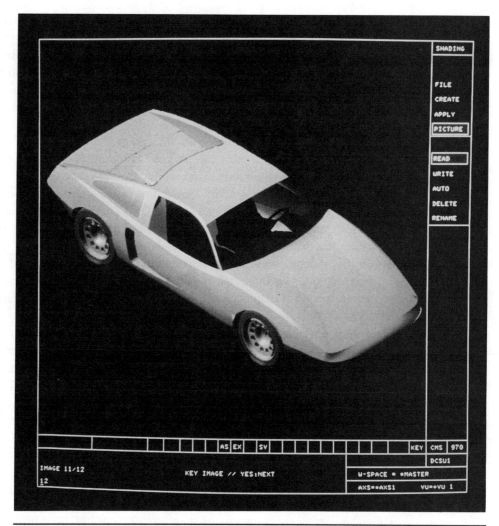

Figure 1.15. Example of a three dimensional image created by the RS/6000 system.

other side as the rotation continues. The Z-buffer keeps track of what PELs are in front of what other PELs so that only the top PELs appear on the screen at any instant in time.

Finally, there are **mask bits** that are primarily used by the microcode to improve performance when managing the logistics of creating images. These mask bits simply prevent areas of the frame buffer from being displayed. Alternately, they can be used to modify the colors displayed.

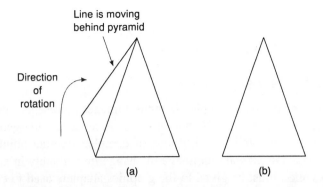

Figure 1.16. Example of hidden line removal. (a) Three edges of the pyramid are visible. (b) As the pyramid rotates clockwise, one of the edges disappears behind the pyramid. The hidden line removal function of the graphics circuitry automatically removes the hidden line.

When generating, moving, or otherwise manipulating a three-dimensional object on the display screen, many complex (floating-point) calculations must be performed. The speed at which these calculations can be performed determines how quickly and smoothly the object appearing on the screen can be rotated, moved, enlarged, reduced, and so on. Performance limitations in this area can paralyze a computer system and make it ill suited for graphics-intensive applications such as computer-aided design and publishing. There are several different graphics subsystems for RS/6000 systems that can be used in three-dimensional graphics environments. Some rely heavily on the RS/6000 Main Processor for some calculations while others have their own specialized microprocessors to speed up such calculations and reduce the workload of the Main Processor.

Another need in the three-dimensional world is an extremely large number of colors. These colors are needed to provide the proper **shading**. Shading is a technique, commonly used in paintings and drawings, that helps create the illusion of depth. The more colors available, the more realistic the image appears. The shading technique can be seen in Figure 1.15.

There are different techniques used for shading images including **flat shading, smooth shading (Gourad shading)**, and **dithered shading**. Each of these shading techniques uses a different approach to creating the illusion of depth. Flat shading uses the simplest technique, and while quite effective, is perceivably less realistic than the other two. Smooth shading, also called "Gourad shading," breaks the image into many triangles and gradually makes the transition of color across the triangle using interpolation. Dithered shading, the most realistic of all, breaks the image into more complex shapes and makes for a more realistic color transition.

All RS/6000 models, except the Models 930 and 950 which are exclusively designed for use with terminals, can be configured to support an array of graphics adapters varying in function and performance. Chapter 2 examines the specific graphics options available for RS/6000 systems.

Graphics and Performance

The need to create and manipulate complex computer images represents a significant workload on a computer system. Every time an image is reduced, enlarged, rotated, moved, and so on, thousands and even millions of complex floating-point calculations must be done. Since users want an image to change immediately in an interactive way, special attention must be given to the graphics adapters used to create and manipulate the images.

The speed with which these images can be created and manipulated is known as the **performance** of that graphics subsystem. RS/6000 systems' graphics adapters offer a range of function and performance. This allows the users to select the appropriate level of graphics capability needed for their specific environment. The functional details of each graphics adapter/subsystem are covered in Chapter 2.

In order to document the performance differences between the various RS/6000 system graphics adapters, IBM performed benchmark testing specifically designed to reveal these performance differences. The results of these tests are shown in Figure 1.17. These performance benchmarks measure the speed at which the graphics circuitry can create and manipulate images. Each computer tested is called upon to generate a simple image over and over again. The rate at which these images can be created is then measured and used for performance comparisons. The first performance test is simply to move a series of pixels from one part of the screen to another as fast as possible. This test is called the **bit-blit** and is representative of how quickly the graphics circuitry can, for example, move a window across the screen as you drag it using a mouse.

Another test conducted measured the rate at which the various graphics adapters could generate lines (also called **vectors**) in two- and three-dimensional space. Two-dimensional vectors are lines that can be oriented in any direction on a single plane. Conceptually, any way that you can lay a pencil down on a desktop represents a two-dimensional vector in the plane defined by the desk surface. Three-dimensional vectors are lines that can be oriented in any direction in free space. For example, if you now hold the pencil above the desktop and rotate it freely in any direction, any orientation represents a specific three-dimensional vector.

To generate the more complex three-dimensional vectors, the 3D Graphics Processor Adapter, POWER Gt4x, POWER Gt4, and 7235 POWER GTO subsystem are equipped with specialized processors designed to handle the more complex calculations associated with three-dimensional modeling. Since the other adapters are

	Bit-blit (screen to screen)	2D vectors	3D vectors	Shaded triangles
Grayscale Adapter	16 M/second	75 K/second	N/A	N/A
Color Graphics Adapter	13 M/second	125 K/second	N/A	N/A
POWER Gt3	not available	650 K/second	N/A	N/A
POWER Gt4	not available	650 K/second	400 K/second	20 K/second
POWER Gt4x	not available	800 K/second	800 K/second	80 K/second
7235 POWER GTO	not available	990 K/second	990 K/second	120 K/second

Figure 1.17. Graphics circuitry performance comparison.

not designed for three-dimensional graphics applications, they are not equipped with such specialized circuitry.

Finally, the most demanding test of three-dimensional capabilities that we will examine is the rapid generation of **shaded triangles**. For the purposes of this test, these three-sided two-dimensional surfaces can be oriented along any plane in three-dimensional space. To visualize this test, first draw a triangle on a piece of paper. Then pick up the paper and rotate it in any direction. Any orientation you choose represents a specific triangle oriented in three-dimensional space. To further test the capabilities of the graphics circuitry, each triangle is also shaded—a technique commonly used to give an image a more realistic three-dimensional appearance on a two-dimensional computer screen.

Notice that the Grayscale Graphics Display Adapter is the fastest in the bit-blit test. This is not a surprise since each pixel in a grayscale image is represented by fewer bits of frame buffer (4 bits versus 8 bits per pixel) since no color information is needed. Fewer bits per pixel means pixels can be moved more quickly. However, the Grayscale Graphics Display Adapter is the slowest at generating two-dimensional vectors.

The POWER Gt3 graphics adapter shows a dramatic performance improvement in the 2D vectors test due to the two on-board graphics processors that form the heart of this adapter.

Like the Gt3, the POWER Gt4 has two on-board processors. These processors allow the Gt4 to match the Gt3's 2D vector performance. However, the Gt4 is designed to create and manipulate 3D images as well. In order to improve the performance of the Gt4x, six on-board graphics processors are used in the generation and manipulation of images.

When we get to the 7235 POWER GTO, performance is again improved in every benchmark test. There are several reasons for this performance advantage. For one thing, the 7235 POWER GTO has many specialized processors working in concert to create graphics images quickly. Among them are 18 proprietary floating point processors specially designed by IBM. This powerful array of processors allows the 7235 to perform many of the graphics calculations more quickly. Another thing that accounts for the 7235's performance advantage is the increased use of high-speed electronic circuitry to perform graphics functions. That is, many of the functions performed through the programming of the processors in other adapters are done more quickly through dedicated circuitry in the 7235 POWER GTO.

Auxiliary Storage

Auxiliary storage, commonly used in all computers, provides a relatively inexpensive way to store computer data and programs. The information stored on auxiliary can be easily modified or kept unchanged over long periods of time as an archive. Since all auxiliary storage is **nonvolatile**, the information stored remains intact whether the computer is turned on or off. The RS/6000 systems use four types of auxiliary storage: **diskettes, disks, Magnetic Tape**, and **CD-ROM**. Let's look more closely at each type of auxiliary storage.

Diskette Storage

Diskettes are a portable magnetic storage medium that can be used to record and later retrieve computer information via a **diskette unit**. The diskette consists of a flexible disk with a magnetic surface permanently enclosed in a square, protective outer jacket. The diskettes are manually inserted into a diskette unit, which spins the circular disk inside the jacket. The **read/write head** inside the diskette unit makes contact with the spinning disk much as a record player's needle contacts a record. As the disk spins, the head magnetically reads and writes information on the disk's surface.

All RS/6000 systems use the 3.5-inch diskettes shown in Figure 1.18. The 3.5-inch diskette, also used in the IBM PS/2 family, has a rigid outer case that completely encloses the magnetic material. A sliding metal cover, which protects the magnetic material, is only retracted while the diskette is inside the diskette drive. These characteristics protect the 3.5-inch diskettes from damage that may result from normal handling. Further, the new 3.5-inch diskettes are small enough to conveniently fit into a shirt pocket or purse. The write-protect switch (not visible) in the lower left corner on the back of the diskette allows you to prevent accidental overwriting of information. When the switch is positioned so that the square hole in the lower left corner is open, the diskette is write-protected. When the switch is blocking the square hole, information can be written to the diskette.

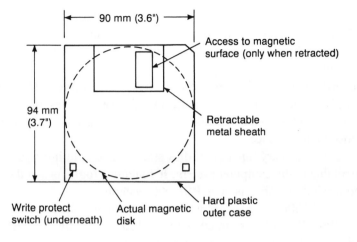

Figure 1.18. All RS/6000 systems use a 3.5-inch diskette.

One of the primary functions of the diskettes is to provide portable storage, allowing for the transfer of programs and data between computers. To this end, all RS/6000 computer systems can freely exchange programs and data via diskettes. Further, information can also be exchanged between RS/6000 systems and IBM Personal System/2 (PS/2) computers. This is because RS/6000 systems can read or write diskettes (either 720 KB, 1.44 MB, or 2.88 MB) in a format compatible with PS/2s running either the DOS or AIX operating system.

In RS/6000 systems, the diskette drive controller electronics is packaged on the standard I/O board inside the RS/6000 System Unit. An internal cable connects this circuitry to the diskette drive. There are optional 5.25-inch diskette drives available for RS/6000 systems. Although larger, the 5.25-inch diskettes have less capacity (1.2 MB) than the 3.5-inch diskettes supported as standard on RS/6000 systems. However, the 5.25-inch format is still in wide use today and is supported on the RS/6000 for the sake of compatibility with 5.25-inch based systems. Chapter 2 will examine optional 5.25-inch diskette drives that can be used with RS/6000 systems.

Disk Storage

RS/6000 systems use another kind of auxiliary storage—**disks** or **Direct Access Storage Devices (DASD).** These are high-capacity magnetic storage devices commonly used in all types of computers from PS/2s to the largest mainframe computer systems. The basic anatomy of a disk drive is shown in Figure 1.19. It consists of a drive mechanism with metallic disks (called **platters** because their shape is like that of a dinner plate). These platters have a magnetic surface that can store information. A single disk drive usually has multiple platters in order to store more information. The platters constantly spin at very high speeds while a built-in **read/write head** records or recalls information on the disk's surface. The arm that positions the read/write head is called the **actuator.** Unlike diskettes, the read/write heads in disks never actually touch the platter's magnetic surface but are positioned extremely close to that surface.

The primary function of disk storage is to hold information that must be readily available to the computer system. It contains programs and data, and provides a temporary holding area used by RS/6000 systems.

RS/6000 systems are available with many different disk configurations. The smallest RS/6000 system comes with 160 million bytes (MB) of fixed-disk storage, while the largest system can have over 12 billion bytes (11.9 GB) of internal disk storage. Figure 1.20 shows the internal disk configurations supported by the various RS/6000 models.

While most disks in RS/6000 systems are internal to the System Unit, there are two optional disk drives that reside outside the RS/6000 System Unit and are attached via a cable. These disk drives will be covered in Chapter 2.

Disk subsystem performance is important to the overall performance of a computer in most applications. This is especially true in virtual storage and/or LAN server environments where there is heavy transfer of information between the fixed-disk and Main Memory. The performance of a disk refers to the rate at which information can be located and transferred between the disk and the Main Memory. As with traditional record albums, information on disk is stored in concentric rings on the disk platter surface. Each ring is called a **track**. To read information from a disk, the actuator first must move the read/write head to the proper track. The time it takes (on the

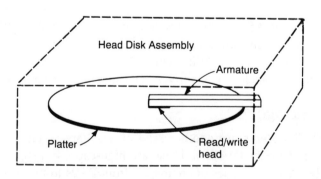

Figure 1.19. Anatomy of a disk drive.

RS/6000 System	Standard Configuration	*Maximum Internal Configuration	Internal Disk Devices	Average Seek Time	Average Latency	Data Transfer Rate
Model 320	160 MB	640 MB	3.5" drives 160/320 MB	16/12.5 ms	8.3/7 ms	1.5/2 MB/Sec
			3.5" drive 400 MB	11.5 ms	7 ms	2 MB/Sec
Model 320H	400 MB	800 MB	3.5" drives 320/400 MB	12.5/11.5 ms	7/7 ms	2/2 MB/Sec
Model 520	355 MB	2,571 MB	5.25" drives 355/670/857 MB	16/18/11.2 ms	8.3/8.3/6.0 ms	1.9/1.9/3 MB/Sec
			Dual 3.5" drive assemblies 640 MB			
Model 530H	400 MB	2,571 MB	3.5" drive 400 MB	11.5 ms	7 ms	2 MB/Sec
			5.25" drive 857 MB	11.2 ms	6.0 ms	3 MB/Sec
Model 550	800 MB	2,571 MB	5.25" drive 857 MB	11.2 ms	6.0 ms	3 MB/Sec
			Dual 3.5" drive assemblies 800 MB	11.5 ms	6.95 ms	2 MB/Sec
Model 930	670 MB	11,998 MB	5.25" drives 670/857 MB	18/11.2 ms	8.3/6.0 ms	1.9/3 MB/Sec
Model 950	1.7 GB	11,998 MB	5.25" drives 670/857 MB	18/11.2 ms	8.3/6.0 ms	1.9/3 MB/Sec

* Table indicates internal Disk configurations.
  External Disk Drive Options are also available.

Figure 1.20. Internal disk drive configurations supported by RS/6000 systems.

average) for the actuator to move the read/write head over the proper track (or seek the track) is called the **average seek time** — usually expressed in milliseconds (1/1000 of a second). Once the read/write head is located over the right track, it must wait until the disk rotation brings the right part of the track under the head. The time it takes for this to happen (on the average) is called the **average latency** of the drive, also expressed in milliseconds. Finally, after the proper track and proper part of the track are positioned under the read/write head, the information is transferred between the disk controller circuitry and the disk one bit at a time in a continuous stream as the disk surface passes underneath the read/write head. The speed at which this is done is called the **data transfer rate** and is expressed in millions of bytes per second (MB/sec). The shorter the access time and latency, the better. The higher the data transfer rate, the better. All of these factors (and more) determine how the disk subsystem will contribute or hinder overall system performance. Figure 1.20 shows the average seek, average latency, and data transfer specifications for the disk drives used in RS/6000 systems.

Each disk device effects transfers to and from RS/6000 systems through control circuitry located on adapter cards in the RS/6000 System Unit. The 160 MB disk used in the Model 320 has control circuitry built into the drive unit itself. An internal cable from the drive unit directly to the standard I/O board allows information transfers to and from the 160 MB drive. All other disk drives used with RS/6000 systems attach to a **Small Computer System Interface** (SCSI) I/O Controller. SCSI is an industry-standard way of connecting devices (disks, tape, CD-ROM drives, etc.) to computer systems. The SCSI High-Performance I/O Controller is IBM's implementation of the industry standard for the RS/6000 family. This I/O Controller resides in a Micro Channel slot and has its own on-board high-speed microprocessor and memory system. The SCSI I/O Controller comes standard with all RS/6000 systems except those using the 160 MB disk drive, as mentioned earlier.

Figure 1.21 shows how devices are attached to the SCSI I/O Controller. Each SCSI-compatible device is attached to a shared cable or bus in a **daisy-chained** fashion. Up to eight SCSI devices can share a single SCSI bus. In addition to the SCSI I/O Controller, these devices can be a single disk unit, a single tape unit, or a controller with up to eight other devices attached. To improve system performance, however, IBM recommends placing no more than four disk drives on any single SCSI I/O Controller. Further, tape backup operations can be accomplished more quickly if the tape backup device and the disk unit being backed up do not share the same SCSI I/O Controller.

When a controlling device called an **initiator** (e.g., the SCSI I/O Controller) wants to perform an information transfer with another device called a **target** (e.g., a disk unit), the initiator arbitrates for control of the SCSI bus. Once the initiator has control of the bus, it issues one of the commands defined in the SCSI standard protocol. While the target device processes the command, the SCSI bus is available for any other SCSI command traffic. When the target device is ready, it gains control of the bus and supplies the requested information along with a completion status to the original initiator.

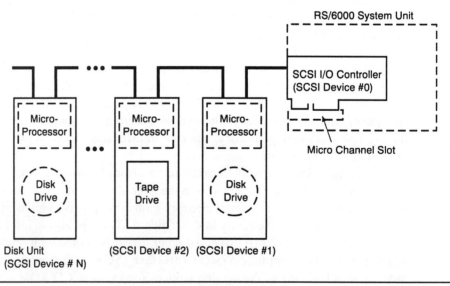

Figure 1.21. Devices are attached to the SCSI Controller via a daisy-chained cable scheme.

One of the primary differences between SCSI and earlier disk interfaces is that each SCSI device must have local processing capability to participate in the SCSI command protocol. That is, each SCSI device attached to the bus is responsible for doing much of its own processing (e.g., error checking, error correction, and retry of failed operations). Earlier disk interface standards put the responsibility for managing the various devices in a centralized I/O Controller rather than distributing the responsibility among the various connecting devices.

The advantage of the SCSI approach is that work (e.g., error correction and error retries) is distributed over the processing capabilities of all SCSI devices, which off-loads the main computer system and puts the work where it can be done most efficiently. Also, things like the **read-ahead** function used in RS/6000 systems can be implemented completely in the disk unit itself, making it transparent to the RS/6000 system and SCSI I/O Controller. "Read-ahead" means that the SCSI disk unit loads extra information read from the disk platter to a buffer area in anticipation of the next request from the SCSI I/O Controller. When the next request comes, if the needed information is already available in the buffer area, it can be sent to the SCSI I/O Controller immediately, eliminating the mechanical delays associated with disk drive seek time, latency, and so on. The result is highly efficient transfer of information between the SCSI I/O Controller and the disk units. Maximum instantaneous transfer rates over the SCSI bus can exceed 4 million bytes/second (4 MB/sec).

The disadvantage of SCSI is that each device must have local processing capability, which often implies higher cost. However, current technology usually makes this additional cost modest, and future technology advances promise to further diminish the importance of this issue.

High-performance disk units and efficient SCSI interface implementations will provide high information transfer rates between the disk units and the SCSI controller. However, the information being transferred must also flow between the RS/6000 system and the SCSI Controller. Efficient transfer between the RS/6000 and the SCSI Controller is just as important as disk seek times and SCSI bus transfer rates. To this end, the SCSI I/O Controller exploits the Bus Master and Streaming Data Procedure functions of the Micro Channel architecture to achieve burst information transfer rates of up to 40 MB/second (18 MB/sec on average). Finally, Main Memory in RS/6000 systems acts much like a giant **disk cache** due to the concept of single-level storage (discussed earlier in this chapter). In the spirit of the RS/6000 system's Instruction and Data caches, a disk cache is a temporary holding area that contains information likely to be requested next by the active program. When the requested information is in the disk cache, delays associated with a traditional I/O access are eliminated, improving system performance. Single-level storage eliminates the need for a disk cache on the SCSI I/O Controller, reducing costs and further eliminating I/O access delays associated with such a disk cache. Chapter 2 will look more closely at the specific fixed-disk options available for RS/6000 systems.

Tape Storage

The next type of auxiliary storage we will cover is **magnetic tape,** or simply **tape.** One primary use of tape storage is to keep a backup copy of the information stored on the computer's disks. In the event of a disk failure, the backup tape can be used to restore the lost information on a new disk unit.

The low cost and high recording densities inherent in tape also make it ideal for some other applications. These include archiving information to which immediate access is no longer needed, distributing programs, and transferring information from one computer system to another. Diskettes can often be used for all these functions, but the higher storage capacity of tapes is preferred if you are dealing with a large amount of information.

Tape consists of a long flexible strip coated with magnetic material, rolled on a reel and placed into a cartridge. In addition to industry-standard 1/2-inch tape reels, there are two types of cartridges used with RS/6000 systems — the 1/4-inch tape cartridge, which can hold 150 MB of information, and the 8mm tape cartridge, which holds up to 2.3 GB of information.

In either case, a **tape unit** reads and writes information on the tape much as a cassette recorder records and plays music on audio cassette tapes. The tape unit runs the tape across the read/write head, which is in contact with the tape surface. Electrical impulses in the read/write head are used to transfer information to and from the tape surface. Chapter 2 will explore some of the tape units used with RS/6000 computer systems.

CD-ROM Storage

The final type of auxiliary storage we will discuss is the **Compact-Disk Read-Only Memory (CD-ROM).** This storage medium uses the same technique to store information as audio compact disks do. Rather than using magnetics, as with disks, diskettes, and tape, CD-ROM systems use optical techniques to achieve their much higher recording density. A single disk used in RS/6000 CD-ROM drives can hold about 600 MB of information. That's enough storage to hold over 300,000 sheets of computer output (or a stack over 90 feet high). The optical disks used with RS/6000 systems are **read only.** That is, RS/6000 users can view the information but they can't change it. The information is prerecorded on the disk using specialized equipment and then distributed to RS/6000 users for their use. The primary use of CD-ROM storage is to distribute large amounts of information in a convenient package. For example, the entire library of RS/6000 and AIX user manuals is stored on a single CD-ROM disk. Not only is this a much easier way to distribute and store RS/6000 manuals, but RS/6000 electronic methods of looking up information in these electronic manuals is much more convenient—as we will see in Chapter 3. Other potential uses for CD-ROM include distribution of program libraries, financial reports, operations manuals, phone directories, or any large (and relatively stable) database.

The extremely high storage capacity of CD-ROMs can be attributed to the technique used to store the information. When the CD-ROM is first recorded, a laser beam is used to burn tiny patterns on the reflective surface of an optical disk according to industry standards. Later, by bouncing the low-power laser beam in the RS/6000 CD-ROM Drive off the optical disk's surface, a series of mirrors and sensors can read back the information burned into the disk. While this optical technology lends itself quite well to the information distribution applications mentioned earlier, the limited speed (compared with RS/6000 disks) and inability to record information preclude usage of CD-ROM disks as normal RS/6000 disk storage.

There are two CD-ROM drives that can be used with RS/6000 computers: the IBM Internal CD-ROM Drive and the IBM 7210 External CD-ROM Drive. These will be covered in Chapter 2.

Micro Channel Expansion Slots

In order to meet the needs of widely varying environments, computer systems must be flexible in terms of configuration. To this end, the RS/6000 family provides expansion slots that accept a wide variety of optional feature cards or adapters that provide additional function and expansion beyond the standard features of the RS/6000 system. The RS/6000 expansion slots are an enhanced version of the **Micro Channel** slots originally introduced with the IBM PS/2 family of computers in April 1987. In fact, some of the feature cards originally designed for the PS/2 family are used with RS/6000 systems. However, some of the feature cards designed specifically for the RS/6000 family are larger (4.5 inches tall) than those used by PS/2s (3.5 inches tall). These larger feature cards, along with their greater electrical power and cooling requirements (15 to 25 watts), were necessary to package the function-rich and higher performing feature cards needed in RS/6000 systems.

It is the job of the Micro Channel bus to provide a highway for information flow between the RS/6000 system elements and the optional I/O feature cards (e.g., SCSI adapters and Token-Ring Network adapters) that are plugged into the Micro Channel expansion slots. In most PS/2 designs, the Micro Channel slots are used for both I/O devices (e.g., communications cards) and Main Memory expansion. In the RS/6000 family, however, a separate and completely independent set of adapter slots is used for Main Memory expansion. This separate Main Memory and I/O bus design eliminates contention between I/O activity and Main Memory data transfers while providing more overall expansion capability. Another advantage of this dual-bus design is that the design of the Main Memory expansion bus need not be compromised for the sake of compatibility with earlier I/O adapters originally designed for the PS/2 family. That is, the RS/6000's Main Memory expansion bus can be optimized for improved system performance while the Micro Channel slots provide compatibility with previous I/O adapters.

The data path on the Micro Channel slots used in RS/6000 systems is 32 bits wide to match the data bus used by the RS/6000 Main Processor. This allows the Main Processor to efficiently move information directly to and from devices in the Micro Channel slots. In many cases, the desired transfer of information over the Micro Channel bus is not between a feature card and the Main Processor; quite often it is necessary to transfer information directly between a feature card and Main Memory. An efficient way of performing information transfers directly between a feature card and memory is through **Direct Memory Access (DMA) channels**. The RS/6000 Micro Channel design supports these information transfers directly between memory and the feature card, freeing the Main Processor for other activity. The Micro Channel design also supports a high-function feature card called a **bus master** which can temporarily take complete control of the Micro Channel bus and transfer information without the assistance of the microprocessor or the DMA circuitry.

DMA transfers require information to be first read from the feature card and then written to the PS/2 systems memory—a two-step process. Bus master feature cards, however, can directly transfer their own information to the PS/2 system's memory in one step, effectively reducing the traffic on the Micro Channel and often improving overall system performance. This bus master capability is a building block on which the RS/6000 multiprocessor architecture is built. For example, the RS/6000 SCSI Controllers use this bus master feature of the Micro Channel architecture to effect an improved interface between disks and the rest of the RS/6000 system. The Micro Channel architecture's **arbitration** mechanism is the traffic cop that grants control of the Micro Channel bus to the Main Processor, bus masters, and DMA circuitry. Since the same arbitration method is used to control all Micro Channel bus activity, all devices are assured access to the Micro Channel bus in an effective manner. Through this arbitration mechanism, the Micro Channel architecture allows up to 15 masters to efficiently share control of the system with the microprocessor.

In order to support the demanding RS/6000 family, the optional **Streaming Data Procedure** defined in the Micro Channel architecture has been fully implemented. The Streaming Data Procedure is a way of performing multiple data transfers during a single bus cycle, thus significantly increasing the rate at which information can be transferred over the Micro Channel bus. With the Streaming Data Procedure, a 40 MB/sec (about 40 million bytes per second) peak transfer rate is achieved, which is twice as fast as the Micro Channel bus's standard peak data transfer rate (20 MB/sec). Depending on the amount of information being moved, the Streaming Data Procedure can sustain an average transfer rate of 20 to 25 MB/sec, again about twice as fast as the normal rate. The Streaming Data Procedure is implemented in feature cards that demand maximum performance (e.g., graphics adapters and the SCSI Adapter).

The 32-bit data path, bus masters, DMA, and the Streaming Data Procedure all work together to increase the speed at which information can be moved around inside the computer system. Since the lion's share of the work done by a computer is often just that, overall system performance is improved.

Aside from performance, other elements of the Micro Channel architecture are worth mentioning. The **Address and Data Parity** and **Synchronous Exception Signaling** functions of the Micro Channel architecture are implemented in the Micro Channels of RS/6000 systems.

The Address and Data Parity function, when exploited by feature cards, provides error checking of information being moved across the Micro Channel bus. This improves overall system integrity by quickly detecting problems such as poorly seated feature cards or those caused by electrical noise.

Synchronous Exception Signaling is designed to detect errors (also called "exceptions") on the RS/6000 Micro Channel bus and report them to the system right when they are detected. That is, the reporting of the problem is synchronized with the actual error event. In earlier designs, errors were detected and reported, but the system would not know exactly when the error occurred, so the system would simply stop rather than trying to fix the problem. With Synchronous Exception Signaling, the RS/6000 knows what event caused the error and can often recover from the error without interrupting normal system operations.

In addition to those items, the **interrupt signals** differ from those used by earlier systems. Interrupt signals are used by feature cards to get the Main Processor's attention when they require service. The interrupt structure used on the Micro Channel bus allows each interrupt signal to be shared among several feature cards. This sharing allows more feature cards to operate simultaneously without interfering with one another. In IBM's original personal computers, for example, most interrupt signals could only support a single feature card each. The "handshake" protocol used on the Micro Channel bus's interrupt structure provides for more reliable interrupt processing.

The *Programmable Option Select* (**POS**) mechanism built into the Micro Channel architecture allows for electronic switches that can be set by computer programs. Before POS, users often had to manually set mechanical switches, depending on the technical details of their operating environment. These switches often caused confusion and frustration. With POS, this is not necessary. The same POS function also provides a mechanism to isolate any one of the Micro Channel slots and determine if the slot is occupied or empty. This capability aids in testing the health of the system and in problem determination. No switches also means that the costs associated with setting up the system (maintenance contracts, product documentation, etc.) are reduced.

The **audio signal** in all Micro Channel slots gives feature cards access to the speaker provided in all RS/6000 System keyboards. This means that feature cards can produce sounds (e.g, telephone call progress tones, music, voice messages, etc.).

Another design point for the Micro Channel bus includes reducing unwanted radio frequency emissions that are associated with computers. U.S. and foreign governments regulate the amount of such emissions and the laws become more difficult to obey as computers speed up. The Micro Channel's compact pin layout, grounding, and connectors help keep these emissions down. This will facilitate the development of even faster computer systems in the future.

Standard Ports

With the exception of the Models 930 and 950, all RS/6000 computer systems come standard with five types of **ports**. Ports are connectors accessible from outside the RS/6000 covers that are electrically connected to support circuitry that interacts with the rest of the RS/6000 elements. These ports provide a means of attaching external devices (e.g., printers, mouse, keyboard) to computers via cables between the port and the external device.

The RS/6000 Models 930 and 950 come standard with two async ports and one parallel port. All other RS/6000 systems come standard with the following ports:

- ❑ Two async ports
- ❑ Parallel printer port
- ❑ Keyboard port
- ❑ Mouse port
- ❑ Tablet port

Since the Models 930 and 950 are exclusively designed to be shared by multiple users, the additional ports provided as standard with the other RS/6000 systems typically are not required.

The **async port** is accessible through a 25-pin D-shell connector. This port transfers bytes (one bit at a time) using the asynchronous communications protocol at a rate of up to 19.2 Kb (19,200 bits) per second. This port can be used to connect many varying devices to RS/6000 systems, such as ASCII terminals, printers, plotters, and external modems. This port can also be used to communicate with other computer systems, as we will see in Chapter 6.

The **parallel port** is accessible via the 25-pin D-shell connector. It is called a "parallel" port because it transfers bytes of information one byte at a time, or eight bits in "parallel." This port is an implementation of a widely used industry standard often used to communicate with a printer.

The **keyboard, mouse**, and **tablet ports** provide for the attachment of the Enhanced Keyboard, the 3-Button Mouse, and the 5083 Tablet, all covered in Chapter 2.

The Enhanced Keyboard

RS/6000 systems use the IBM Enhanced Keyboard shown in Figure 1.22. This keyboard is needed only when RS/6000 systems are being used as a workstation. However, this keyboard has the same layout as the enhanced keyboard used by IBM's ASCII displays, the PS/2 family, and the InfoWindow family of displays used with other IBM computer systems. This means that once familiar with this layout, the user will not have to adapt to different keyboard layouts when using other IBM computer equipment. This same keyboard is available in different languages to fill the needs of many different users around the world

The keyboard cable plugs into the keyboard port provided on RS/6000 systems. Small retractable legs on the bottom of the keyboard can be extended to change the angle of the keyboard if desired.

Mechanical Packaging

The overall physical size of the RS/6000 systems has been kept to a minimum. Several things have contributed to the compactness of the design. At the electronic circuit level, the use of **Very Large Scale Integration (VLSI)**, and **Surface Mount Technology (SMT)** reduced the overall size of the systems. VLSI is an electronic fabrication technology that allows literally thousands of electronic circuits to be packaged on a single electronic chip. The type of VLSI circuitry used in most RS/6000 circuits is **1-micron CMOS**. CMOS stands for *C*omplementary *M*etal *O*xide *S*emiconductor, which is a type of VLSI circuitry. CMOS is fairly high speed

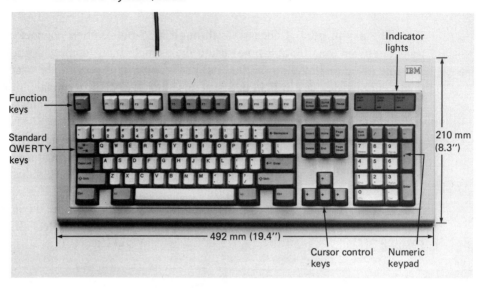

Figure 1.22. The IBM Enhanced Keyboard supported by RS/6000 systems as well as PS/2s and other IBM systems.

circuitry with low power requirements, which reduces overall system power supply and cooling requirements. Part of the power used by the CMOS chips is turned into heat as it is with all electronic circuitry. Ironically, this heat can reduce the reliability of the circuitry that generates it. Even though CMOS circuitry creates very little heat compared with most other VLSI technologies, the heat that is generated must be eliminated from the computer. This is done though the use of **heat sinks** that draw heat from the VLSI chips and fans that draw room-temperature air through the RS/6000 enclosure. The heat sinks are small radiators mounted directly on top of the VLSI chips residing on the RS/6000 CPU circuit board shown in Figure 1.23. The heat sinks used in RS/6000 systems help reduce the size and speed of the fan needed. This makes for a quieter computer system.

The term "1-micron" means that the circuitry and wiring in the chips are built from elements that are one micron (1×10^{-6} meters) in size. This allows for densely packaged circuitry with from 60,000 to 3.8 million transistors in a single chip. The IBM-designed processor chips as well as the four-megabit (4 Mb) memory chips used in RS/6000 systems utilize this CMOS technology. The chips used in the high-end RS/6000 models are built using the still more advanced 0.5-micron CMOS technology.

Since VLSI allows more circuits to fit on a single chip, there are fewer interconnections between chips. Also, the VLSI chips go through a ***Built-In Self-Test*** **(BIST)** in which all logic and memory circuity are extensively tested and all errors

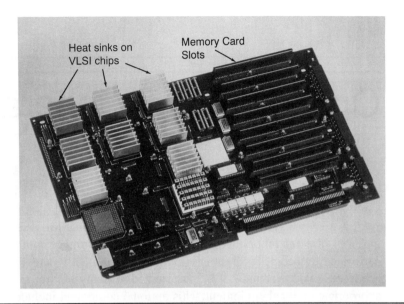

Figure 1.23. Processor board used in the RS/6000 system.

are recorded. This BIST testing automatically occurs every time an RS/6000 system is turned on. For these reasons, the use of VLSI in RS/6000 systems provides the additional benefit of increased reliability.

VLSI chips must be placed in a mechanical package in order to be mounted on a circuit board and connected to other VLSI chips. Many different package types are used in RS/6000 systems. One package style that helped keep the size of RS/6000 systems down is the industry-standard SMT mechanical package type.

There are several mechanical enclosures used to house the various elements of RS/6000 systems. The Models 320 and 320H use a desktop enclosure type similar to that used by the IBM PS/2 family. The RS/6000 desktop enclosure can sit on a desktop or rest on its side beside a desk. The Models 520 through 550 all use a floor-standing enclosure similar to that used by some of the low-end IBM AS/400 models. This larger enclosure, called a **deskside** design allows for more expansion in Main Memory, disk storage, I/O adapters, and peripheral devices.

The RS/6000 Models 930 and 950 use yet another enclosure that complies with industry standards. This structure is a 1.6-meter **rack** similar to that used by the high-end IBM AS/400 and low-end IBM S/390 models. This enclosure style uses various **drawers** to hold the main processor, disk drives, and other devices. Multiple drawers are installed in a single 1.6-meter rack to build a complete system.

2

Options and Peripherals

RS/6000 systems are likely to be found in many diverse environments ranging from research laboratories to fish markets to insurance companies. The activities performed by people in these environments vary widely, and so do their computing needs. RS/6000 systems can be customized to many environments by selecting the appropriate optional equipment. This optional equipment includes **feature cards** and **peripherals**. Feature cards are circuit boards containing electronics that provide some additional capacity or function(s) to the RS/6000 systems in which they are installed. They can be installed in the Micro Channel slots provided in all RS/6000 systems.

Peripherals are devices that are installed in or attach to RS/6000 computers and perform functions under the computer's control. Things like disks, tape drives, printers, and plotters fall into this category. In this chapter, we will cover:

- Graphics displays
- Graphics options
- ASCII terminals
- Printers
- Plotters
- Memory expansion options
- Auxiliary storage options
- Communications options
- Other options

This chapter does not provide comprehensive coverage of all optional equipment that can be used with RS/6000 systems. It will, however, introduce the reader to many devices that are representative of those most commonly used with RS/6000 systems.

Peripheral devices have specific **product numbers** associated with them (e.g., 6091 Display and 4019 LaserPrinter). Optional features installed in RS/6000 System Units are identified by **feature numbers** (e.g., the 640 MB SCSI Disk Drive Pair is feature number 2542, and the 32 MB HD1 Memory Card is feature number 4032). Either product numbers or feature numbers are provided for options covered in this chapter.

GRAPHICS DISPLAYS

A computer's **display** is the "TV-like" device that converts the computer's electrical signals into light images that convey information to the user. Displays rest either on top of the System Unit (e.g., Model 320) or on a desktop immediately adjacent to the System Unit. They are attached to the RS/6000 System Unit via a cable between the display and a graphics adapter located inside the RS/6000 System Unit. Graphics adapters contain the circuitry necessary to create the images seen on the display. Here we will look at the displays themselves. Graphics adapters/subsystems will be covered later in the chapter.

Displays should not be confused with **terminals** (e.g., 3151 ASCII Display Stations) are devices that include a display and a keyboard and do not support graphics applications. The purpose of a terminal is to provide a user with a self-contained device with which to interact with an RS/6000 system. Terminals typically are used in commercial environments where a single RS/6000 system is being shared by many users equipped with similar terminals. They are attached to an RS/6000 system via a communications line (e.g., the EIA-232D).

Displays can be used with any RS/6000 system (except the Model 9XX systems, which are designed exclusively for use in multiuser environments through attached terminals). There are many types of displays that can be used with RS/6000 systems. Let's examine three displays that meet most needs:

- IBM 5081 Color Display
- IBM 6091 Color Display
- PS/2 Displays

5081 Color Displays

The IBM 5081 Color Display Model 16, shown in Figure 2.1, provides a full-color image. Working in cooperation with various RS/6000 graphics adapters, it can display images with resolution of 1280 × 1024. The screen of this display measures 16

Screen size: 16 inches
Type: Full color

Figure 2.1. 5081 Display Model 16.

inches diagonally. The viewable area on the screen is 9.3 inches (236 mm) × 9.3 inches (236 mm).

In the 5081, images are generated by focusing a beam of electrons on the appropriate areas of the phosphor deposited on the glass screen through a shield called a **shadow mask**. A shadow mask is basically a sheet of metal containing many small holes through which the electron beam is focused. It is the job of the shadow mask to improve the sharpness of an image by helping prevent stray electrons from impacting the phosphor. The closer the holes in the shadow mask are spaced, the more finely detailed the image. This spacing, called the **shadow mask pitch**, is one way color displays are compared. The 5081 offers a shadow mask pitch of 0.26 mm, which allows for a sharp image.

Signals that drive the display are redriven to output connectors on the display to allow for the attachment of other displays, screen printers, or projection systems. The tilt/swivel pedestal is standard and allows the user to position the display for comfortable viewing. An anti-reflective coating on the screen helps reduce any reflections on the face of the display.

6091 Color Displays

The IBM 6091 Color Display, shown in Figure 2.2, provides a full-color image. There are two different 6091 models used with RS/6000 systems. The 6091 Model 19 offers a 19-inch screen, and the 6091 Model 23 offers a 23-inch screen. While both models offer the same resolution (1280 × 1024 pixels), the larger screen offered by the Model 23 provides for greater image magnification.

Like the 5081, 6091 images are generated by focusing a beam of electrons on the appropriate areas of the phosphor deposited on the glass screen through a shadow mask. Both 6091 models offer a shadow mask pitch of 0.31 mm and provide a front operator panel with controls such as the On/Off switch, brightness, mode selection, and centering. Signals that drive the display are re-driven to output connectors

	Model 19	Model 23
Screen size:	19 inches	23 inches
Type:	Full color	Full color

Figure 2.2. 6091 Display (shown resting on an Xstation 120 System Unit).

Screen size: 19 inches
Type: White on black (gray shades)

Figure 2.3. Monochrome Display 8508. Other low-cost PS/2 displays can also be used with some RS/6000 configurations.

on the display to allow for the attachment of other displays, screen printers, or projection systems. The tilt/swivel stand is standard and allows the user to position the display for comfortable viewing. The antiglare screen helps reduce any reflections on the face of the display.

8508 Monochrome Display

The IBM 8508 Monochrome Display originally offered for the IBM PS/2 family, can be used with RS/6000 systems. It has a 19-inch screen and provides a white-on-black image. This low-cost display is shown in Figure 2.3. This display does not provide full-color images, but rather images consisting of different brightness levels or **shades of gray** — similar to the technique used in a black-and-white television set or a black-and-white photograph. When attached to the required IBM Grayscale Graphics Display Adapter, the 8508 can produce images with a resolution of up to 1280 × 1024 pixels.

The 8508 has an antiglare screen and an independent On/Off switch along with controls for contrast and brightness. These controls are located on the front of the display for easy access. The standard tilt/swivel stand allows the user to adjust the viewing angle.

XSTATION 130

The Xstation 130 with a display is a cross between a display and a terminal in that it provides a user with graphics capabilities while attaching as a terminal in a multiuser environment. The Xstation 130 can be used as a graphics workstation in a local area network (Token-Ring or Ethernet) to give a user access to one or more RS/6000 systems in the network. Xstation 130s can also be used to access other types of computers in the network supporting X Windows standards. Chapter 1 covers the Xstation 130 in more depth.

PS/2 displays, including the 8503, 8507, and 8508 monochrome displays as well as the 8512, 8513, 8514, and 8515 color PS/2 displays, can be used with an Xstation 130.

GRAPHICS OPTIONS

In order to support the displays discussed earlier in this chapter, an RS/6000 system must be equipped with graphics adapter circuitry. This circuitry translates the information stored in an RS/6000 system into the electronic signals necessary to create images on the displays used with RS/6000 systems. Those unfamiliar with computer-generated graphics terminology may want to refer to the "Graphics Basic Training" section in Chapter 1 before reading about the graphics adapters described next.

Since the RS/6000 Models 930 and 950 are not designed to be used with graphics displays, they cannot use any of the graphics adapters discussed in this section. The Models 930 and 950 are exclusively designed to support a pool of ASCII terminals or to act as a server in a LAN environment. All other RS/6000 models can support any of the following graphic adapters:

- ❑ Grayscale Graphics Display Adapter
- ❑ Color Graphics Display Adapter
- ❑ POWER Gt3 Graphics Feature
- ❑ POWER Gt4/Gt4x Graphics Feature
- ❑ 7235 POWER GTO

Option	Type	Max Colors	On-Board Graphics Processor(s)	3-Dimensional Functions
Grayscale Adapter	White on Black (shades of gray)	16 (shades of gray)	No	No
Color Graphics Adapter	Color	16 to 256	No	No
POWER Gt3	Color	16 to 256	Yes	No
POWER Gt4	Color	16.7 Million	Yes	Yes
POWER Gt4x	Color	16.7 Million	Yes	Yes
7235 POWER GTO	Color	16.7 Million	Yes	Yes

Figure 2.4. Summary comparison of the RS/6000 graphics adapters/subsystems.

Figure 2.4 summarizes the differences between these graphics adapters/subsystems. For performance comparisons of these graphics adapters/subsystems, see Chapter 1.

Grayscale Graphics Display Adapter

The IBM Grayscale Graphics Display Adapter (#2760) is a low-cost graphics adapter for the RS/6000 family. It can generate a black-and-white image with a resolution of 1280 × 1024. It can only be used with the 8508 Monochrome Display covered earlier in this chapter.

The Grayscale Graphics Display Adapter can simultaneously display 16 different brightnesses (4-bit pixels) from a library of the 256 brightness levels. The eye interprets these brightness levels, resulting in an effect similar to that of a simple black-and-white photograph. This adapter can take advantage of the Micro Channel architecture's bus master and Streaming Data Procedure to effect highly efficient transfers of information between the adapter and the other RS/6000 elements. Up to two Grayscale Graphics Display Adapters can be installed in a single RS/6000 System Unit.

Color Graphics Display Adapter

The IBM Color Graphics Display Adapter (#2770) is a low-cost color graphics adapter for the RS/6000 family. It can generate a color image with a resolution of 1280 × 1024. It can be used with any of the color displays covered in this chapter.

The Color Graphics Display Adapter can simultaneously display from 16 (4-bit pixels) to 256 colors (8-bit pixels) from a library or palette of 16.7 million colors. (Two hundred fifty-six colors are enough to allow effective color shading to enhance the realism of an image.) Like the Grayscale Graphics Display Adapter, this adapter can take advantage of the Micro Channel's bus master and Streaming Data Procedure to effect highly efficient transfers of information between the adapter and the other RS/6000 elements. Up to two Color Graphics Display Adapters can be installed in a single RS/6000 System Unit.

POWER Gt3 Graphics Feature

The POWER Gt3 Graphics Feature (#2777), like the Color Graphics Adapter, is designed primarily for two-dimensional applications like drafting and technical publishing, and it offers 1280 × 1024 resolution. However, the Gt3 can generate graphics images many times faster than the Color Graphics Adapter can. This makes it better suited for graphics-intensive two-dimensional applications. The improved graphics performance offered by the Gt3 is due to the two on-board IBM-designed processors that form the heart of the Gt3. A single 8-bit frame buffer provides up to 256 colors in an image. The two 8-bit color maps provided aid in things like simple animation. Two overlay plains also provided allow applications to more quickly overlay one image on top of another (e.g., overlaying text on an X-ray image or a grid over an image of a map). The Gt3 has circuitry designed to speed up the generation and manipulation of windows, which is commonplace today. The Gt3 consumes one Micro Channel slot and uses the bus master and Streaming Data Procedure defined in the Micro Channel architecture.

POWER Gt4 and Gt4x Adapter

The POWER Gt4 and Gt4x Graphics features offer higher performance than the Gt3. Both the Gt4 and the Gt4x are designed for applications that utilize three-dimensional graphics such as mechanical solids modeling, animation, and molecular modeling. They offer 1280 × 1024 resolution, double-frame buffers, five-color maps, and a 24-bit Z-buffer (see Chapter 1). Specialized programming is included on the Gt4 and Gt4x to provide the advanced graphics primitives that cooperate with things like PHIGS, GL, and X windows programming interfaces (see Chapter 5). Specialized circuitry is also provided to speed up tasks associated with windowing.

The Gt4 has two on-board processors that perform the calculations associated with generating three-dimensional images. It comes in two versions: the POWER Gt4 8-bit feature (#2795) which offers up to 256 colors in an image and the POWER Gt4 24-bit feature (#2796). The 8-bit feature consists of two cards that consume two Micro Channel slots. The 24-bit feature consists of three cards (the third being the additional graphics memory for 24-bit **true color** support) and consumes three Micro Channel slots. The Gt4 8-bit to 24-bit Upgrade (#2792) can be installed on a POWER Gt4 8-bit feature at any time, bringing it up to a POWER Gt4 24-bit feature. Further, the Gt4 can be upgraded to a Gt4x by installing the POWER Gt4 Performance Upgrade (#2794).

The Gt4x is a faster version of the Gt4. The Gt4x has six on-board processors (rather than the two in the Gt4) that provide a significant performance improvement over the Gt4. The Gt4x also comes in two versions: the POWER GT4x 8-bit feature (#2790) which offers up to 256 colors in an image and the POWER Gt4x 24-bit feature (#2791). The 8-bit feature consists of two cards that consume two Micro Channel slots. The 24-bit feature consists of three cards (the third being the additional graphics memory for 24-bit true color support) and consumes three Micro Channel slots. The Gt4 8-bit to 24-bit Upgrade (#2792) can be installed on a POWER Gt4x 8-bit feature at any time, bringing it up to a POWER Gt4x 24-bit feature.

7235 POWER GTO

The 7235 POWER GTO is a standalone box that houses the most powerful graphics hardware available for the RS/6000 family. That is, the speed at which images can be created and manipulated or the performance of the 7235 is the highest of all graphics options available for the RS/6000 family. It can be used with any RS/6000 model except the 9XX model.

There are two models of the 7235. Model 001 is an 8-bit model able to display up to 256 colors in a single image and providing two frame buffers. It consists of four circuit cards: a Micro Channel interface card, a Graphics Processor card, a Drawing Processor card, and an 8-bit Frame Buffer card. The latter three cards are housed in their own mechanical frame designed to rest near the RS/6000 System Unit. A 7235 Model 001 can be upgraded to a Model 002 at any time.

The 7235 Model 002 has these same four cards and an additional Shading Processor and full 24-bit "true" color. The Shading Processor handles the many calculations associated with adjusting colors over an area on the screen to provide a three-dimensional appearance. Several types of shading are supported including flat shading, smooth shading (Gourad shading), and dithered shading. Each of these shading techniques uses a different approach to create the illusion of depth. The Shading Processor also handles the automatic hidden line and hidden surface removal as objects are moved about on the screen.

Either 7235 model is optimized to work very efficiently with applications that use the PHIGS graphics language. While the 7235 is also optimized for application programs that use the GL language, some incompatibilities exist that may require modifications to the application program. The 7235 POWER GTO provides capability and performance equivalent to that of the powerful 6096 Graphics Processor used with the largest IBM computers and the Supergraphics Subsystem provided standard with the older RS/6000 Model 730.

The 7235 attaches to an RS/6000 system via the POWER GTO Accelerator feature (#4250).

5086/5085 Attachment Adapters

The 5086 Attachment Adapter (#2801) and the 5085 Attachment Adapter (#2802) allow RS/6000 systems to communicate with the 5086 Graphics Processor and the 5085 Graphics Processor, respectively. These graphics processors are small, self-contained boxes about the size of a floor-standing IBM PS/2 that efficiently perform the calculations necessary to display and manipulate complex graphic images on a computer display. They replace the function of the graphics adapter/subsystem and provide performance and function much like that of the RS/6000 7235 POWER GTO.

The RS/6000 attachment adapters allow RS/6000-based application programs to utilize the graphics circuitry in the 5086/5085. The adapters also support a switching function that allows S/370 or S/390 application programs to utilize the 5086/5085 circuitry when proper communications are established.

The adapters have a 64 KB memory, used as temporary storage for information being transferred between the graphics processor and the RS/6000, which makes for more efficient communications. They use the Micro Channel architecture's bus master function to efficiently transfer information to and from other RS/6000 elements.

These 5085 and 5086 Graphics Processors were originally designed to be used as graphics workstations with IBM's large S/370 and S/390 host computers.

Xstation 130 1 MB Video Memory Upgrade Kit

The Xstation 130 comes standard with 1 MB of Video Memory, which allows the Xstation 130 to display respectable images (e.g., 1024 × 768 resolution with up to

PEL resolution and maximum number of colors	1 MB Video Memory (Standard)	2 Mb Video Memory
640 x 480 x 256 gray/colors	X	X
1024 x 768 x 256 gray/colors	X	X
1280 x 1024 x16 gray/colors	X	X
1600 x 1200 x 2 gray (with 8508 display)	X	
1280 x 1024 x 256 gray/colors		X
1600 x 1200 x 4 gray (with 8508 display)		X

Figure 2.5. The video capabilities of the Xstation 130 depend on the amount of video memory installed. This table shows the different resolutions and maximum number of colors supported by the various Xstation 130 video memory configurations.

256 colors out of a palette of 16.7 million colors). This Video Memory can be expanded to its maximum size of 2 MB by installing a 1 MB Video Memory Upgrade Kit (#4201). With 2 MB of Video Memory, the Xstation 130 can provide for many colors on higher resolution displays (e.g., 1280 × 1024 resolution with up to 256 colors). Figure 2.5 shows the video modes supported by the various Video Memory sizes.

ASCII TERMINALS

The devices people typically use to interact with RS/6000 systems in a multiuser environment are known as **ASCII terminals**. Terminals provide the user with a display and a keyboard for interaction with a shared RS/6000 system. Like the high-function graphics displays discussed earlier in the chapter, the display component of a terminal is a TV-like device that converts the computer's electrical signals into light images that convey information to the user. However, unlike the high-function graphics displays discussed earlier in the chapter, the displays on ASCII terminals are designed to display alphanumeric text and related symbols.

Terminals also come equipped with a keyboard that allows the user to send information back to the computer. **ASCII** stands for the *American Standard Code for Information Interchange* and refers to the way in which alphanumeric characters are encoded in the computer system and terminal. While some of the ASCII characters can be used to create simple line drawings, ASCII terminals are not capable of displaying full computer graphics.

If a terminal is near the computer system, say in the same building, it can be **locally** attached to the RS/6000 computer system via a cable between the async port provided on the terminal to an async port in the RS/6000 system. This can be one of the standard async ports provided with the RS/6000 or an async port located on an optional asynchronous adapter (discussed later in this chapter) installed in an RS/6000 Micro Channel slot. The physical connectors and the electrical signals in the async ports provided on all these terminals (and in the RS/6000 system) conform to the RS-232-C (compatible with RS/6000 system's EIA-232D) or the RS-422-A (compatible with EIA-422A) industry standards.

If the terminal is not near the computer, say in another state, it can be **remotely** attached over communications lines. Either way, the function provided to the terminal user is the same. Some type of terminal (or an Xstation) is required to allow the user to interact with an RS/6000 system when being used in a multiuser environment.

There are many types of ASCII terminals (both IBM and non-IBM) that can be used with RS/6000 systems. In this chapter, we will look at the following:

❑ 3151 Terminals

❑ 3164 Terminals

❑ PS/2s terminal emulation

A list of terminals that were tested with the RS/6000 computers is provided in Appendix A. Further, since the RS/6000 supports industry-standard communications, other workstations not listed may also work with RS/6000 systems.

3151 Terminals

The IBM 3151 family of ASCII terminals all have a similar appearance (Figure 2.6). There are five basic members of the 3151 family used with RS/6000 systems: the Models 110, 310, 410, 510, and 610. All models have a 14-inch monochrome display, a separate keyboard, and a tilt/swivel stand. The displays have a flat screen, etched to reduce glare, and can display 24 or 25 lines of text plus a line at the bottom for operator messages. They can be either green-on-black or amber/gold-on-black displays. Which you choose is purely a matter of individual taste. There are several different types of keyboard offered in the 3151 family, and all have an adjustable slope to accommodate the user. All models provide an auxiliary async port for attaching printers or other devices.

All models can also **emulate** ten non-IBM ASCII displays. These modes are mostly used when the 3151 is attached to systems other than the RS/6000 family. Optional cartridges can be installed in a 3151 to emulate additional terminal types.

The 3151 Model 110 is compatible with the older IBM 3161 and 3162 ASCII displays. It offers an 84-key keyboard and can display up to 25 rows of 80 characters each (2000 characters) plus a one-line operator message. The display presents a green-on-black image.

The Models 310 and 410 are also compatible with the older IBM 3161 ASCII displays and have 102-key keyboards just like those used with the 316X family. These models can display up to 25 rows of 132 characters (3300 characters) plus the operator message line at the bottom. RS-232-C communications is provided as standard and an option supports the RS-422-A standard at speeds up to 38.4 Kb/sec. The Model 310 creates a green-on-black image, and the Model 410 creates an amber/gold-on-black image.

The 3151 Models 510 (green-on-black display) and 610 (amber/gold-on-black display) come with a 102-key keyboard almost identical to that used with RS/6000 workstations and PS/2 systems. Like the 310 and 410, the 510 and 610 can also display either 80 or 132 characters per row and are compatible with the IBM 3161 and

Model:	110	310	410	510	610
Type:	14" Monochrome (green/black)	14" Monochrome (green/black)	14" Monochrome (amber/black)	14" Monochrome (green/black)	14" Monochrome (amber/black)
Features:	Tilt/swivel 84-key Keyboard 80 characters Aux Async Port	Tilt/swivel 102-key Keyboard 80/132 characters Aux Async Port	Tilt/swivel 102-key Keyboard 80/132 characters Aux Async Port	Tilt/swivel 102-key Keyboard 80/132 characters Aux Async Port	Tilt/swivel 102-key Keyboard 80/132 characters Aux Async Port
Standard interface:	RS-232	RS-232	RS-232	RS-232 & RS-422	RS-232 & RS-422
Optional interface:		RS-422	RS-422		

Figure 2.6. 3151 ASCII terminal.

other earlier ASCII displays. The 510 and 610, however, come standard with both RS-232-C and RS-422-A communications capability selectable by the user or host computer. Further, PS/2 computer-type operating modes that support things like windowing and a mouse attached to the auxiliary port are also provided with the 510 and 610.

3164 Color Terminals

Figure 2.7 shows an IBM 3164 Color Terminal. The 3164 can display 24 rows of 80 characters in up to eight different colors. The twenty-fifth row is used to display operator messages. It comes with a 14-inch glare-resistant display that can be tilted to allow a comfortable viewing angle. The 3164 terminal can be set up to go blank after a few minutes of keyboard inactivity to help preserve the display phosphors.

Model:	110	120
Type:	14" Color	14" Color
Features:	Tilt/swivel	Tilt/swivel
	102-key Keyboard	102-key Keyboard
	80 characters	80 characters
	Split screen	Split screen
	Printer port	Printer port
Standard interface:	RS-232	RS-232 & RS-422

Figure 2.7. 3164 Color Terminal.

The blanked image is restored by pressing any key. An adjustable audio alarm is provided. The separate keyboard has an adjustable slope to allow for comfortable positioning.

Color can be used to effectively highlight and associate information on a display, making the information more clear. While some highlighting capability is provided on most monochrome terminals, color provides additional flexibility in this area as well as providing a more pleasing image. Both the foreground and the background can display up to eight different colors. A **split screen** capability allows the screen to be divided into two sections to support such functions as view ports, paging, and partitioning.

The 3164 Color Terminals are compatible with the IBM 3161 and 3163 ASCII displays while providing additional capabilities. One notable difference is that the 3164 Color Terminals have the ability to attach a local printer (via an auxiliary RS-232-C) that can be used to print the contents of the display screen.

The 3164 Model 110 provides an EIA RS-232-C interface, and the Model 120 offers an EIA RS-232-C or an RS-422-A interface selectable under program control. In either case, data rates of up to 19,200 bits/sec are supported.

PS/2 ASCII Terminal Emulation

With the proper programming, an IBM Personal System/2 (Figure 2.8) can also be used as an ASCII terminal with RS/6000 systems. In this case, the PS/2 computer is said to be emulating an ASCII terminal. In the simplest case, the PS/2 computer appears to the RS/6000 computer as any other ASCII terminal with no special capabilities. Either Operating System/2 Extended Edition (OS/2 EE) or the *Disk Operating System* (DOS) and AIX Access for DOS Users will provide the necessary programming to perform ASCII terminal emulation. The user can then interact with the RS/6000 in the same manner as with any other ASCII terminal discussed so far.

Since the PS/2 system is a computer, not just a terminal, it has its own **intelligence**. It is therefore called an **intelligent workstation**. This intelligence can be used to run PS/2 programs independently of the RS/6000 interaction just mentioned, or it can be used to work with RS/6000 systems. The PS/2 computer's intelligence also provides for direct interaction between specially written programs running on the PS/2 computer and those running on RS/6000 computers. This type of interaction can be done without user intervention to perform functions from simply transferring a file between the PS/2 computer and the RS/6000 system to more complex program-to-program communications. You can also concurrently interact with multiple RS/6000 systems with a single PS/2 computer, or sign on to a single system at

Figure 2.8. Properly configured Personal System/2 computers can be used as terminals with RS/6000 systems.

more than one terminal. Chapter 6 will further discuss interaction between PS/2 computers and RS/6000 systems. For more information about PS/2 computers, refer to *IBM PS/2 — A Business Perspective* (published by John Wiley & Sons, Inc., IBM form #G325 — 0400), which is a book similar to this one, only dedicated to the PS/2 family.

PRINTERS

Printers are electromechanical devices that print a computer's electronically encoded information onto paper. There are many printers that work with RS/6000 systems, and exhaustive coverage of these printers is beyond the scope of this book. We will limit our discussion here to some representative printers that fit the needs of many environments:

	Series II Impact Printer	Quickwriter	Quietwriter III	4226 Printer	4224 Printer
Type	Near Letter Quality	Letter Quality	Letter Quality	Near Letter Quality	Near Letter Quality
Technique	9-wire Dot Matrix	24-wire Dot Matrix	Resistive Ribbon	9-wire Dot Matrix	9- or 18-wire Dot Matrix
Speeds	65 to 320 cps	55 to 330 cps	80 to 160 cps	100 to 533 cps	50 to 600 cps
PEL res.	144 x 144	180 x 360	240 x 240	Not avail.	144 x 144
Interface	Parallel or Async	Parallel or Async	Parallel	Parallel or Async	Async

Figure 2.9. Summary comparison of various printers used with RS/6000 systems.

- ❑ Personal Printer Series II
- ❑ 5204 Quickwriter
- ❑ 5202 Quietwriter III
- ❑ 4226 Printer
- ❑ 4224 Printer
- ❑ 4234 Printer
- ❑ 6252 Impactwriter
- ❑ 4019 LaserPrinter
- ❑ 3816 Page Printer
- ❑ 6262 Printer

Figure 2.9 summarizes the differences among these printers. A list of other printers originally tested with the RS/6000 systems is provided in Appendix A. Since the RS/6000 systems's async and parallel ports are compatible with industry standards, many other printers not listed may also work with RS/6000 systems.

Personal Printer Series II

The IBM Personal Printer Series II (PPS II) family consists of two low-cost printers differing only in carriage width. The PPS II Model 2380 is a narrow-carriage printer, and the Model 2381 is a wide-carriage printer (Figure 2.10). Either of these printers can produce draft-quality documents at speeds up to 320 CPS at a **character pitch** of 10. Character pitch refers to the size and spacings of the characters. A character

	4234 Printer	6252 Impactwriter	4019 LaserPrinter	3816 Page Printer	6262 Printer
Type	Near Letter Quality	Letter Quality	Letter Quality	Letter Quality	Letter Quality
Technique	Dot-band Matrix	48 to 128 char. Print Band	Laser/EP	Laser/EP	Print Band
Speeds	200 to 800 lines/min	365 to 800 lines/min	5 to 10 pages/min	24 pages/min	1200 to 2200 lines/min
PEL res.	variable	N/A	300 x 300	240 x 240	N/A
Interface	Async	Parallel or Async	Parallel or Async	Async	Async

Figure 2.9. *(Continued).*

Type:	Near letter quality
Technology:	9-wire dot matrix
Printing speed: (pitch of 10)	320 cps (FastDraft mode)
	270 cps (Draft mode)
	65 cps (Near letter quality mode)
APA resolution:	144v x 240h PELs per square inch
Print line:	2380 = narrow carriage, 2381 = wide carriage
Interface:	Parallel or Async port
Print buffer:	11 KB standard (additional 32 KB optional)

Figure 2.10. The IBM Personal Printer Series II family.

pitch of 10 means that 10 characters can be printed in one inch. Either PPS II printer supports six different pitches ranging from 10 to 20 plus **proportional spacing** in which the distance between characters is automatically adjusted to provide an over-all uniform appearance. In "draft" mode and "near-letter-quality" mode, the clarity of the document produced is improved at the cost of reduced printing speed.

The PPS II family is based on the **dot-matrix** printing technique. With this technique, the image is created by causing a series of small pins contained in the print head to impact a ribbon which in turn strikes the paper. By selecting the proper pins, a fine dot pattern is generated. As with the dot pattern illuminated on a comput-er's display, the human eye naturally blends these printed dots to form the desired image. PPS II printers can operate in **alphanumeric mode** or **all-points-address-able (APA) mode**. In alphanumeric mode, the printer can generate any alphanumer-ic character and a number of special symbols from a predefined library called the character set. In APA mode, complex images can be generated by allowing virtually any combination of dots to be generated.

PPS II printers are compatible with the earlier Proprinter line of printers and come standard with four different type styles (or **fonts**). The ribbon used in these printers can print up to 3.5 million draft characters before it needs to be replaced. The printer can be controlled directly by the user through the printer's operator panel or by a program. The printer comes standard with the ability to handle either contin-uous forms, single precut sheets, or single envelopes. An optional automatic sheet feed (#3646 for 2380 and #3658 for 2381) allows the printer to hold a stack of precut single sheets and automatically feed them into the printer one at a time.

A feature of the PPS Series II called **paper park** allows continuous-forms paper to be disengaged so that single cut sheets of paper or an envelope may be fed into the printer through the front slot. You can then go back to using the continuous forms without having to reload them.

The standard 11 KB buffer holds information waiting to be printed, freeing the computer for other tasks. This buffer can be expanded by adding an additional 32 KB (#5220). PPS Series II printers come standard with a parallel printer port. For serial attachment, the optional Serial Interface Module (#5261) must be installed.

5204 Quickwriter

The IBM Quickwriter (5204) shown in Figure 2.11 is software-compatible with the Personal Printer Series II (PPS II) family just discussed. Like the PPS II family, the Quickwriter uses the dot-matrix printing technique. The 24-wire implementation of dot matrix used in Quickwriter supports three different print qualities: Draft, Letter Quality, and Selectric Font. In Draft mode 330 characters per second (cps) can be printed, while Letter Quality mode is limited to 110 cps. Selectric Font mode allows

Type:	Letter quality
Technology:	24-wire dot matrix
Printing speed:	330 cps (Draft mode)
(pitch of 10)	110 cps (Letter-quality mode)
	55 cps (Selectric font mode)
APA resolution:	Up to 180 x 360 PELs
	per square inch
Print line:	335 mm (13.2")
Interface:	Parallel or Async port
Print Buffer	8 KB standard

Figure 2.11. The Quickwriter printer. This printer can print on forms up to five sheets thick.

printing at 55 cps with print quality equal to that of the IBM Selectric III Typewriter. However, to achieve this quality you must have the optional film ribbon and Selectric Font cartridge.

Eight different fonts and five different pitches are provided as standard with the Quickwriter, providing a variety of print styles. Optional font cartridges can be plugged into the Quickwriter to provide additional fonts, yielding a total of twelve fonts (eight standard and four in a cartridge) accessible at any one time. A downloadable font feature is also available to allow still further type style flexibility. Other options include a dual-drawer sheet feed that allows two different paper types (e.g., white bond and company letterhead) to be available for printing. This option, when used in conjunction with the envelope feed, allows a document with two different paper types and an envelope to be printed with no manual intervention required. While the Quickwriter is designed to print on forms up to five sheets thick (five-part forms), users should test their multipart forms before buying to ensure satisfactory results. The Quickwriter can be attached to the RS/6000 via a parallel and an async port. The standard 8 KB print buffer can be expanded to 40 KB through an expansion option.

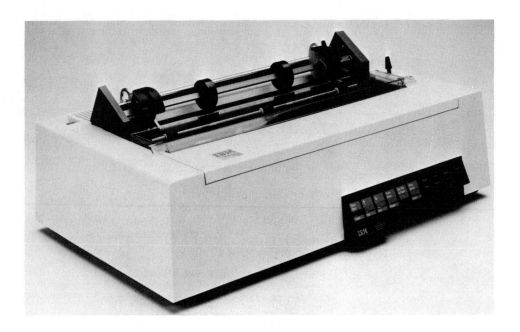

Type:	Letter quality
Technology:	Resistive ribbon
Printing speed:	160 cps (Draft mode)
(pitch of 10)	100 cps (Quality mode)
	80 cps (Enhanced mode)
APA resolution:	Up to 240 x 240 PELs
	per square inch
Print line:	335 mm (13.2")
Interface:	Parallel port only
Print Buffer	16 K standard

Figure 2.12. The Quietwriter printer. This printer uses "resistive ribbon," making for high-quality printing with very little noise.

5202 Quietwriter III

The IBM Quietwriter III (5202), shown in Figure 2.12, provides three different print-quality modes of operation: Draft, Quality, and Enhanced. Draft mode produces near-letter-quality print at a rate of from 160 to 274 cps depending on the character spacing being printed. Quality mode produces letter-quality print at rates of from 100 to 171 cps. Enhanced mode prints at a rate of from 80 to 136 cps. Enhanced mode is used when high-quality printing needs to be maintained under special conditions (e.g., high humidity, textured paper, etc.).

The Quietwriter III uses the **resistive ribbon** technique of producing a printed image. Unlike the impact technique used in dot-matrix printing, this technique uses electric current to actually melt selected portions of the ribbon onto the paper. This makes for high quality and very quiet printing (45 DBA), which is where the printer got its name.

The Quietwriter III comes standard with four different fonts. Proportional spacing is available with the addition of the optional font cartridge. A total of eight fonts can be active. Also, a special download cartridge can be installed and loaded with still other fonts with the download package. Fonts can be selected by programs or by the operator through the switches on the front of the printer.

The Quietwriter III also supports APA graphics commands compatible with the PPS II and Proprinter families and provides some enhanced capabilities as well. Images with a resolution of up to 240 PELs per inch horizontally and 240 PEL lines per inch vertically can be generated.

With the standard configuration, individual cut sheets are manually loaded into the printer. With optional equipment, cut sheets, continuous forms, and envelopes can be fed automatically. The resistive ribbon technology used by this printer also allows it to print directly on some transparencies used for overhead projection. The standard 16 KB print buffer holds information waiting to be printed, freeing the computer for other tasks.

4226 Printer

Figure 2.13 shows the IBM 4226 Printer Model 302. This printer, based on the dot-matrix technology, is designed to be shared by multiple users. It is a low-cost/heavy duty printer that can handle multiple print jobs without the need for user intervention, i.e., **unattended operation**. It can print up to 533 characters/second in **Fast Draft Mode**, 400 characters/second in **Draft Mode**, and 100 characters/second in **Near Letter Quality Mode**. The 4226 is compatible with the Proprinter III XL

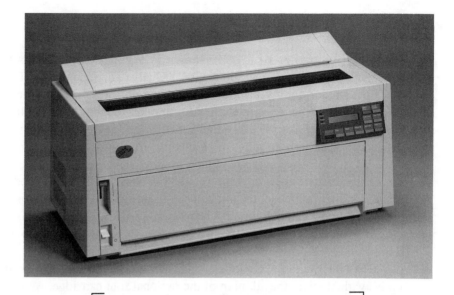

Type:	Near letter quality
Technology:	9-wire dot matrix
Printing speed:	533 cps (FastDraft mode)
(pitch of 10)	400 cps (Draft mode)
	100 cps (Near letter quality mode)
APA resolution:	144v x 240h PELs per square inch
Interface:	Parallel or Async port
Print buffer:	22 KB standard

Figure 2.13. The 4226 printer.

(4202-003) and can also emulate an Epson DFX-5000 printer. Multi-part forms up to six pages thick can be used. Four resident fonts, both serial and parallel interfaces, and a 22 KB print buffer are provided as standard equipment.

4224 Printer

The 4224 Printer is shown in Figure 2.14. This tabletop printer can produce data-processing-quality (DP mode) documents at a speed of 200 to 600 cps depending on the model. In Data-processing text (DP text) or near-letter-quality mode, the clarity of the documents produced is improved at the cost of reduced printing speed.

Type:	Near letter quality
Technology:	Dot matrix (9 or 18-wire head)
Printing speed:	200/600 cps (Data processing mode)
(pitch of 10)	100/300 cps (Data processing mode)
	50/150 cps (Near letter-quality mode)
APA resolution:	144 x 144 PELs per square inch
Print line:	335 mm (13.2")
Interface:	Async

Figure 2.14. The 4224 printer.

There are several different 4224 versions, all of which are highly compatible with IBM's older 5224 Printer. Model 301 has a maximum speed of 200 cps (DP mode) and provides a print buffer 64 KB in size. The print buffer acts as a temporary storage area, improving the efficiency of information flow between the printer and the computer system. The Models 302, 3E2, and 3C2 all produce DP mode documents at a rate of up to 400 cps. The Models 3E2 and 3C2 up the print buffer size to 512 KB. The Model 3C2 also has the capability of printing four to eight different colors depending on the ribbon used. The Model 302 can be upgraded to a Model 3E2 at any time. All models can be attached to RS/6000 systems via an async port.

Like the Personal Printer Series II family, the 4224 is also based on the dot-matrix printing technique. With this technique, the image is created by causing a series of small pins (9 on the Model 301 and 18 on the rest) contained in the print head to strike a ribbon, which in turn strikes the paper. By selecting the proper pins, a fine dot pattern is generated. As with the dot pattern illuminated on a TV set or computer's display, the human eye naturally blends these printed dots to form the desired image. The 4224 can operate in alphanumeric mode or all-points-addressable (APA) mode. In alphanumeric mode, the printer can generate any alphanumeric character (letters or numbers) and some special symbols from a predefined library called the character set. In APA mode, complex images can be generated by allowing virtually any combination of dots to be generated.

There are several options (called features) for handling paper in different ways, and at least one must be ordered with the 4224. These options can easily be changed by the printer operator to accommodate the immediate printing need. The Continuous Forms Device feature (#4001) provides a tractor feed that will move continuous forms through the printer. These continuous forms can be blank paper, preprinted forms, or multipart forms (up to six parts). Due to variations in multipart forms, however, your specific forms should be tested before you purchase the printer. This is especially true for five- and six-part forms.

The Document on Demand feature (#4002) allows you to tear off a form just printed without having to wait for the next form to be printed or having to eject a blank form, creating waste. With this feature the user can temporarily eject some blank forms, tear off the one needed, and then roll the remaining forms back into printing position with a few keystrokes. The Document on Demand feature is not available for the Model 3C2.

The Document Insertion Device feature (#4003) allows the user to insert individual sheets of paper or forms. The Document Insertion Device feature is not available for the Model 3C2. An async port is used to attach 4224 printers to the RS/6000.

4234 Printer

Figure 2.15 shows the 4234 Printer. This printer is called a **line printer** because it prints an entire line of text at one time rather than one character at a time as do the Personal Printer Series II models and the 4224 Printer just discussed. This line-at-a-time printing makes the 4234 faster than the fastest 4224. The 4234 is designed to stand on the floor and can print draft-quality documents at a speed of up to 800 lines per minute (not to be confused with characters per second). When operating in either near-letter-quality or data-processing-quality mode, the clarity of the document produced is improved at the cost of reduced printing speed. The 4234 is attached to an async or parallel port on the RS/6000.

The 4234 uses a **band-matrix** printing technique. This is similar to the dot-matrix printing technique in that the image is created by causing a series of small dots to impact a ribbon which in turn strikes the paper. With the band-matrix tech-

Type:	Near letter quality
Technology:	Dot-band matrix
Printing speed:	800 cps (Draft mode)
(pitch of 10)	600 cps (DP mode)
	200 cps (Near letter-quality mode)
APA resolution:	Variable depending on band
Print line:	335 mm (13.2")
Interface:	Async or Parallel

Figure 2.15. The 4234 printer.

nique, however, images can be printed more quickly since multiple characters (an entire line) are being printed simultaneously.

As with the 4224, the 4234 can operate in alphanumeric mode or APA mode. In alphanumeric mode, the printer can generate any alphanumeric character and a number of special symbols from a predefined character set. In APA mode, complex images can be generated by allowing virtually any combination of dots to be generated. The user can install various print bands providing different dot sizes and thus different print resolution.

6252 Impactwriter

The 6252 is shown in Figure 2.16. This printer can produce up to 800 lines per minute using the **print band** printing technique. With this technique, a metal band engraved with the character set spins at high speeds within the printer. As the needed character on the spinning print band aligns with the correct spot on the paper, an impression is made. So rather than creating the character through a series of dots, the entire character is printed, providing for high-quality printing. However, no APA graphics can be supported since only the characters on the print band being used can be printed on the paper.

Type:	Letter quality
Technology:	Print Band
Printing speed:	365 to 800 lines/minute
APA resolution:	not supported
Interface:	Async or Parallel

Figure 2.16. The 6252 Impactwriter.

There are different print bands for the 6252, providing from 48 to 128 individual characters including alphanumeric symbols, special symbols, and some graphics characters. There is also an optional bar code kit that allows the 6252 to print various types of bar code labels.

There are two different models in the 6252 Printer used with RS/6000 systems, differing only in the way they attach to the RS/6000. The 6252 Model AS8 attaches to an async port on the RS/6000 system (RS-232 or RS-422). The 6252 Model AP8 attaches to a parallel port.

Either model provides an operator panel and an 80-character LCD display for operator interaction. Words (English or other languages as necessary) are displayed in the LCD display rather than the codes found in 6252 predecessors (IBM 3262 and 5262).

4019 LaserPrinters

The IBM 4019 LaserPrinters are tabletop letter-quality printers (Figure 2.17). The printers discussed earlier print documents one character or one line at a time. The 4019 LaserPrinter produces a whole page at a time. It prints on individual sheets of paper (**cut sheets**), not continuous forms as do the other printers discussed so far. The 4019 LaserPrinter Model 001 can produce up to ten pages per minute and is designed to handle a load of up to 20,000 pages per month. The entry-level 4019 LaserPrinter E (4019 Model E01) can produce up to five pages per minute and can handle up to 12,000 pages per month. The Model E01 can be upgraded to a Model 001 at any time.

The 4019 LaserPrinters use the **laser/*Electro*Photographic** (**EP**) process to print an entire page at a time. This technique uses the laser to produce a charged image on a drum inside the printer. Ink (toner) is attracted to the charged portions of the drum and then transferred to the paper, as with a copy machine. The print cartridge containing the toner can typically print about 10,000 pages before it needs to be replaced. This EP printing technique makes for the highest quality of printing of any printer covered so far.

Either model comes standard with a 200-sheet autofeeder as well as a 100-sheet output tray and manual paper and envelope feed capability. An optional second paper-feed drawer can hold an additional 500 sheets. Paper drawers for legal-sized paper and an automatic envelope feed are also available as optional accessories.

There are three resident fonts provided with the LaserPrinters, each having multiple pitches and sizes and each able to be printed in the **portrait** (like the pages of this book) or the **landscape** orientation (which is sideways [rotated 90 degrees] on the page). Optional font cards can be installed in the two available slots to add additional fonts. Also, font diskettes are available that contain additional fonts that can be sent from the computer to the printer's memory (**downloaded**) and used.

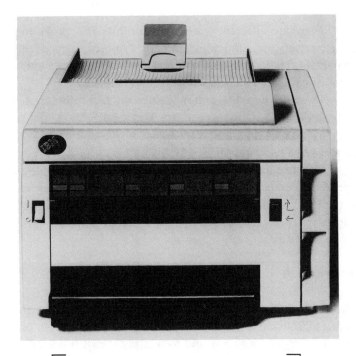

Type:	Letter quality
Technology:	Laser/EP
Printing speed:	Model E01 = 5 pages/minute
(any pitch)	Model 001 = 10 pages/minute
APA resolution:	Up to 300 x 300 PEL
Print line:	203 mm (8")
Interface:	Parallel port or Async port
Paper feed:	Friction

Figure 2.17. The 4019 LaserPrinter. Two different models are available, varying in printing speed.

The LaserPrinters come standard with the ability to receive and print data formatted in three different ways: the data format typically used by printers attached to PCs and PS/2 computers, the data format used by the popular Hewlett-Packard LaserJet Series II printers, and the format used with IBM 7372 Color Plotters and Hewlett-Packard 7475A Color Plotters. That is, programs written to print output to these devices can also print on 4019 LaserPrinters with no changes necessary. When one of the **PostScript** options is added, the LaserPrinter is able to process the flexible PostScript document formatting commands that are used in desktop publishing. PostScript documents can be generated using many different desktop publishing systems as well as high-function word-processing programs. The LaserPrinter PostScript options provide for from 17 to 39 different PostScript fonts, depending on the options selected.

An async port, a parallel port, and 512 KB of memory are standard equipment on both models. An additional 1 MB memory expansion is required to print full-page, high-resolution images. An additional 2 MB is required for printing extremely complex pages. A LaserPrinter can have up to 4 MB of memory by installing the available memory expansion options. With the addition of the Print Sharing option, a single LaserPrinter can be shared among up to six users.

3816 Page Printer

The IBM 3816 Page Printer (see Figure 2.18) is another tabletop printer based on the same laser/electrophotographic printing technique as the LaserPrinters. The 3816, however, can produce up to 24 letter-quality pages per minute and is designed to produce 40,000 to 80,000 pages per month. The High Capacity Paper Input option allows you to load 1200 sheets of paper for high-volume printing environments.

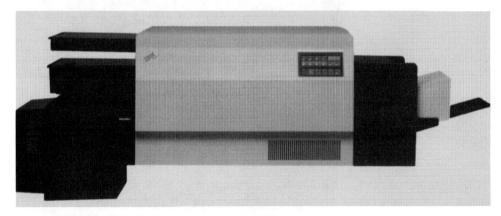

Type:	Letter quality
Technology:	Laser/EP
Printing speed: (any pitch)	24 pages/minute (max)
APA resolution:	240 x 240 PELs
Print line:	335 mm (13.2")
Interface:	Async Port
Paper feed:	Friction

Figure 2.18. The 3816 Page Printer. This printer can produce up to 24 pages per minute.

This type of printing power can be useful when shared among multiple users in a small multiuser or local area network, for example. Like the Personal Pageprinter II, this printer is also a computer in its own right with 3.5 MB of memory. While it doesn't support PostScript, it does support *Page Map Primitives* (PMP), which controls advanced functions such as font selection, rotation, and vector graphics. The 3816 attaches to an async port on the RS/6000.

Type:	Line Printer
Technology:	Print Band
Printing speed: (any pitch)	1200, 1400, or 2200 lpm
APA resolution:	Not Supported

Figure 2.19. The 6262 printer.

6262 Printer

The 6262 printer is the fastest of the printers we will cover; it is shown in Figure 2.19. This printer is based on the print band printing technique, discussed under the 6252 Impactwriter. There are different print bands for the 6262 providing different character sets, and they can print bar codes.

There are three models of the 6262 available for RS/6000 Systems: Models A12, A14, and A22. They are the same except that Model A12 prints up to 1200 lines per minute (lpm), the Model A14 can print up to 1400 lpm, and the Model A22 can print up to 2200 lpm. The Model A12 can be field-upgraded to a Model A14 at any time, but neither the A12 nor the A14 can be field-upgraded to a Model A22.

Up to six-part forms can be printed using the 6262. An 80-character display presents messages to the operator. The 6262 is attached to RS/6000 systems through a serial or an async port and uses standard 120 V electrical power.

PLOTTERS

An electromechanical device used to create drawings under computer control is called a **plotter**. Unlike a printer, which uses dot-matrix or laser technology to produce images on paper, a plotter uses a collection of pens manipulated by robot-like graspers and arms to draw, much as a human draftsman would draw. The result is highly precise drawings on a wide variety of paper sizes using many colors. The invention of plotters arose from the need to more quickly create design drawings similar to those created by a draftsman at a drafting board.

There are many plotters that can be used with RS/6000 systems. We will examine the following plotters:

- ❑ 6180 Color Plotter
- ❑ 6182 Auto-Feed Color Plotter
- ❑ 6184 Color Plotter
- ❑ 6187 Color Plotter

Figure 2.20 compares these plotters.

6180 Color Plotter

Figure 2.21 shows the IBM 6180 Color Plotter. The 6180 Color Plotter is a desktop unit that can use A (8.5" × 11") and A4 (210 mm × 297 mm) sizes of plotter paper or

	6180	6182	6184	6187
Type	Desktop	Desktop (Autofeed)	Floor-standing	Floor-standing
Plot size	A/A4	A/A4, B/A3	C/A2, D/A1	C/A2, D/A1, E/A0
Pens	8	8	8	8
Resolution	.025"	.001"	.001"	.001"
Max speed (Pen down)	16"/sec	31.5"/sec	19.7"/sec	43"/sec

Figure 2.20. Summary comparison of plotter capability.

transparency film. It provides a carousel that can hold eight pens which are automatically selected and capped after use. Two types of fiber-tipped pens are supported: those for use with paper and those designed for use with transparency film. This plotter can locate a pen anywhere on the paper to within 0.025 inches and start plotting. This is called the plotter's **addressable resolution**. The **repeatability** of this plotter is 0.1 mm, which is a measure of how accurately the plotter can plot the same thing twice. The maximum speed at which the 6180 can draw is 40 cm/sec (16 inch-

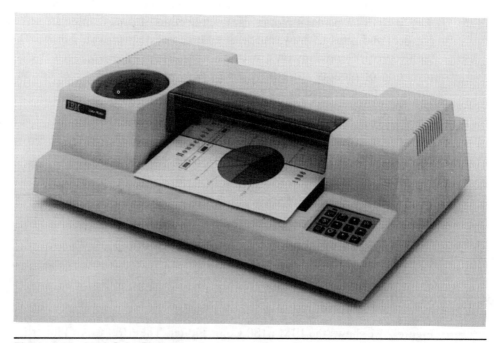

Figure 2.21. 6180 Color Plotter.

es/second). This is called the plotter's **maximum pen speed**. When the pen is not in contact with the paper, the maximum pen speed is 50 cm/sec (20 inches/second). A 60-byte buffer is provided as standard and is expanded to 1 KB with the addition of the optional Graphics Enhancement Cartridge. This cartridge also increases the number of character sets in the plotter from 5 to 19 and provides software compatibility with the IBM 7372 and Hewlett-Packard 7475A. It attaches to an RS/6000 through an EIA-232D async port.

6182 Auto-Feed Color Plotter

Figure 2.22 shows the IBM 6182 Auto-Feed Color Plotter. One of the things that sets this plotter apart from the others covered so far is its ability to automatically draw plotter paper, transparency film, vellum, or double-matte polyester film from a bin as needed. This autofeed feature eliminates the need for a person to insert the plotter paper (or other media) one by one into the plotter with each plotting job. The bin supplying the autofeed can hold up to 150 sheets of plotting paper or 100 overhead transparencies. The autofeed feature of the 6182 makes it a good plotter to be shared

Figure 2.22. 6182 Auto-Feed Color Plotter.

by multiple users — in a LAN environment, for example. It is also useful in a single-user environment when many plots need to be generated. The 6182 can create plots on A (8.5" × 11"), A4 (210 mm × 297 mm), B (11" × 17"), or A3 (297 mm × 420 mm) sizes of paper. It can plot on regular plotter paper, glossy paper, transparency film, vellum, or double-matte polyester film. It provides a carousel that can hold eight pens, which are automatically selected and capped after use. These can be fiber-tipped, rollerball, refillable drafting, or disposable drafting pens. The 6182 has an addressable resolution of 0.001 inches and a repeatability of 0.004 inches. An LCD display provides messages to ease configuration and use of the plotter functions. The maximum pen speed is 80 cm/sec (31.5 inches/second). A 1 KB buffer provided as standard holds information waiting to be printed. The buffer can be expanded to a maximum of 12 KB as necessary. This plotter also understands the IBM GL and HP-GL command sets, making it compatible with many application programs. It attaches to an RS/6000 through an EIA-232D async port.

6184 Color Plotter

The IBM 6184 Color Plotter, shown in Figure 2.23, is a drafting type of plotter capable of producing large engineering drawings. Paper sizes C (17" × 22"), A2 (420 mm × 524 mm), D (22" × 34"), or A1 (594 mm × 841 mm) are supported by this floor-standing unit. The 6184 can plot on plotter paper, vellum, or double-matte polyester film. It provides a carousel that can hold eight pens, which are automatically selected and capped after use. These can be fiber-tipped, refillable drafting, or disposable drafting pens. The 6184 has an addressable resolution of 0.001 inches and a repeatability of 0.004 inches. The maximum pen speed is 19.7 inches/second. This plotter also understands the IBM GL and HP-GL command sets, making it compatible with many application programs. It attaches to an RS/6000 through an EIA-232D async port.

6187 Color Plotter

The IBM 6187 Color Plotter, shown in Figure 2.24, is compatible with but replaces the older IBM 6186 Color Plotter models. Like the 6186, the 6187 is capable of producing full-size engineering drawings. Paper sizes C/A2 and D/A1 are supported, as is the larger E/A0 paper size, which is not supported by any other plotter covered in this chapter. However, the 6187 Color Plotter offers a 1 MB buffer as standard and has a faster maximum pen speed of 43 inches/second — the fastest of all plotters cov-

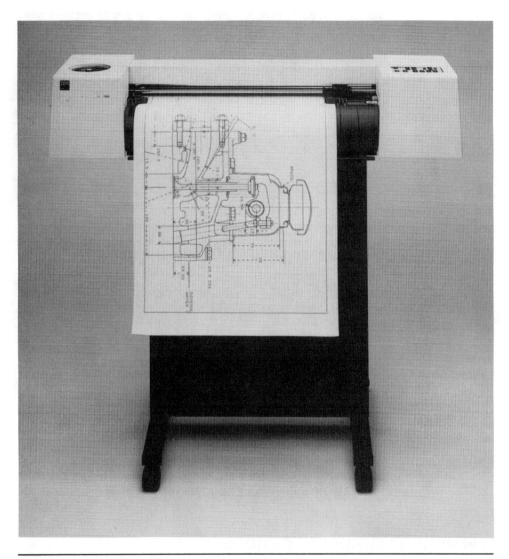

Figure 2.23. 6184 Color Plotter.

ered in this chapter. It is a floor-standing unit that comes in two different models: Model 1, which accepts precut plotter paper, and Model 2, which uses an automatic roll feed, reducing the amount of user intervention required during plotting. It provides a carousel that can hold eight pens. The 6187 has an addressable resolution of 0.00098 inches (25 mm) and a repeatability of 0.004 inches (0.1 mm). This plotter

Figure 2.24. 6187 Color Plotter.

understands the industry-standard HP-GL and the newer HP-GL/2 command sets. It attaches to an RS/6000 through an EIA-232D async port.

MAIN MEMORY EXPANSION OPTIONS

Nothing seems to grow faster than the computer user's appetite for main memory. There are several different options that allow the user to expand the Main Memory in RS/6000 computers. However, due to technical differences inside the systems, Main Memory expansion options are not necessarily interchangeable between the different RS/6000 system types. All Main Memory expansion options cards use the *Error Checking and Correction* (ECC) method to detect and often automatically correct memory problems as discussed in Chapter 1. Figure 2.25 shows the possible Main Storage sizes achievable in the various RS/6000 models.

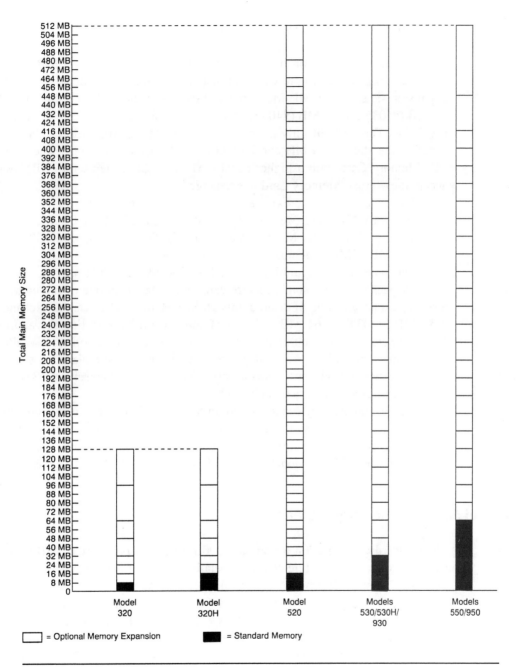

Figure 2.25. Possible RS/6000 Main Memory configurations.

Models 320/320H Main Memory Expansion

The standard configuration for an RS/6000 Model 320 provides 8 MB of memory packaged on a single feature card and installed in one of the model's two memory expansion slots. This 8 MB Memory Card can be exchanged for a 16 MB (#4010), 32 MB (#4033), or 64 MB (#4036) Memory Card by selecting the appropriate Memory Select Feature, but only at the time the system is first ordered. While those ordering the standard 8 MB configuration can later elect to replace the standard 8 MB Memory Card with a higher-density Memory Card themselves, IBM will not accept the original Memory Card in exchange.

The second memory expansion slot supports an 8 MB SD1 Memory Card (#4008), a 16 MB SD1 Memory Card (#4016), a 32 MB HD1 Memory Card (#4032), or a 64 MB HD1 Memory Card (#4035). This means a Model 320 can have up to 128 MB of Main Memory.

The standard configuration for an RS/6000 Model 320H provides 16 MB of memory packaged on a single feature card and installed in one of the model's two memory expansion slots. If desired, this 16 MB Memory Card can be exchanged for a 32 MB (#4034) or 64 MB (#4037) Memory Card by selecting the appropriate Memory Select Feature, but only at the time the system is first ordered. While those ordering the standard 16 MB configuration can later elect to replace the standard 16 MB Memory Card with a higher-density Memory Card themselves, IBM will not accept the original Memory Card in exchange.

The second memory expansion slot in Model 320H systems (including 320E versions) supports the same 8 MB SD1 Memory Card (#4008), 16 MB SD1 Memory Card (#4016), 32 MB HD1 Memory Card (#4032), or 64 MB HD1 Memory Card (#4035) used in the Model 320. A Model 320H can have up to 128 MB of Main Memory.

Model 520 Main Memory Expansion

The standard configuration for an RS/6000 Model 520 provides 16 MB of memory packaged on a single feature card and installed in one of the machine's eight memory expansion slots. If desired, this 16 MB Memory Card can be exchanged for a 32 MB (#4033) or 64 MB (#4036) Memory Card by selecting the appropriate Memory Select Feature, but only at the time the system is first ordered. While those ordering the standard 16 MB configuration can later elect to replace the standard 16 MB Memory Card with a higher-density memory card themselves, IBM will not accept the original Memory Card in exchange.

Any of the other memory expansion slots can accept an 8 MB SD1 Memory Card (#4008), a 16 MB SD1 Memory Card (#4016), a 32 MB HD1 Memory Card

(#4032), or a 64 MB HD1 Memory Card (#4035). A Model 520 system can have up to 512 MB of total system memory.

Models 530H/550 Main Memory Expansion

The standard configuration for an RS/6000 Model 530H provides 32 MB of memory packaged on two 16 MB Memory Cards and installed in two of its eight memory expansion slots. If desired, both of these 16 MB Memory Cards can be exchanged for 32 MB (#4068) or 64 MB (#4070) Memory Cards by selecting the appropriate Memory Select Feature, but only at the time the system is first ordered. As we have seen in Chapter 1, the Model 530H requires at least two memory cards to support the wider memory bus provided in these models. Further, the two memory cards must be the same type, which means you must exchange both 16 MB Memory Cards for a pair of higher-density Memory Cards, or neither. While those ordering the standard 32 MB configuration can later elect to replace the standard Memory Cards with higher-density Memory Cards themselves, IBM will not accept the original Memory Cards in exchange.

Any of the other memory expansion slots can accept an 8 MB HD3 Memory Card (#4063), a 16 MB HD3 Memory Card (#4066), a 32 MB HD3 Memory Card (#4067), or a 64 MB HD3 Memory Card (#4069). Due to the wider memory bus provided in the Model 530H, the Memory Cards must be installed in pairs. That is, you can't install one memory expansion card without installing a second identical memory expansion card in Model 530H systems.

The standard configuration for an RS/6000 Model 550 provides 64 MB of memory packaged on two 32 MB Memory Cards and installed in two of its eight memory expansion slots. If desired, both of these 32 MB Memory Cards can be exchanged for 64 MB Memory Cards by selecting the 64 MB HD3 Memory Select feature (#4071), but only at the time the system is first ordered. Like the Model 530H, Model 550s require at least two Memory Cards to support the wider memory bus provided in these models. Further, the two Memory Cards must be the same type, which means you must exchange both 32 MB Memory Cards for a pair of 64 MB Memory Cards, or neither. While those ordering the standard 64 MB configuration can later elect to replace the two standard 32 MB Memory Cards with 64 MB HD3 Memory Cards themselves, IBM will not accept the original Memory Cards in exchange.

Any of the other memory expansion slots in Model 550 systems (including 550E and 550S) can accept an 8 MB HD3 Memory Card (#4063), a 16 MB HD3 Memory Card (#4066), a 32 MB HD3 Memory Card (#4067), or a 64 MB HD3 Memory Card (#4069) in quantities of two. That is, you can't install one memory expansion card without installing a second identical memory expansion card due to the wider memory bus used on the Models 530H and 550.

By selecting the appropriate memory options, a Model 530H or 550 system can have up to 512 MB of total Main Memory.

Models 930/950 Main Memory Expansion

The standard configuration for an RS/6000 Model 930 provides 32 MB of memory packaged on two 16 MB Memory Cards and installed in two of its eight memory expansion slots. If desired, both of these 16 MB Memory Cards can be exchanged for 32 MB (#4033) or 64 MB (#4036) Memory Cards by selecting the appropriate Memory Select Feature, but only at the time the system is first ordered. The Model 930 also requires at least two Memory Cards to support the wider memory bus provided. Further, the two Memory Cards must be the same type, which means you must exchange both 16 MB Memory Cards for a matched pair of higher-density Memory Cards, or neither. While those ordering the standard 32 MB configuration can later elect to replace the standard Memory Cards with higher-density memory cards themselves, IBM will not accept the original Memory Cards in exchange.

Any of the other memory expansion slots can accept an 8 MB SD1 Memory Card (#4008), a 16 MB SD1 Memory Card (#4016), a 32 MB HD1 Memory Card (#4032), or a 64 MB HD1 Memory Card (#4035) in quantities of two. That is, you can't install one memory expansion card without installing a second identical memory expansion card, due to the wider memory bus used on a Model 930.

The standard configuration for an RS/6000 Model 950 provides 64 MB of memory packaged on two 32 MB Memory Cards and installed in two of its eight memory expansion slots. If desired, both of these 32 MB Memory Cards can be exchanged for 64 MB Memory Cards by selecting the 64 MB HD3 Memory Select Feature (#4070), but only at the time the system is first ordered. The Model 950 also requires at least two Memory Cards to support the wider memory bus provided. Further, the two Memory Cards must be the same type, which means you must exchange both 32 MB Memory Cards for a matched pair of 64 MB Memory Cards, or neither. While those ordering the standard 64 MB configuration can later elect to replace the two standard 32 MB Memory Cards with two 64 MB Memory Cards themselves, IBM will not accept the original Memory Cards in exchange.

Any of the other memory expansion slots in the Model 950 (including 930 systems upgraded to 950E systems) can accept an 8 MB HD3 Memory Card (#4063), a 16 MB HD3 Memory Card (#4066), a 32 MB HD3 Memory Card (#4067), or a 64 MB HD3 Memory Card (#4069) in quantities of two. That is, you can't install one memory expansion card without installing a second identical memory expansion card, due to the wider memory bus used on a Model 950.

By selecting the appropriate memory options, both the Model 930 and 950 can have up to 512 MB of total Main Memory.

Xstation 130 System Memory Expansion

In an Xstation 130, System Memory is used to store many different types of information, as discussed in Chapter 1. For example, it stores the logistical information necessary to create the images seen on the screen (i.e., window templates, bit maps for fonts and icons, background color data, etc.).

The Xstation 130 comes with 2 MB of System Memory which can be expanded up to 16.5 MB (with 0.5 MB used for input/output activity). System Memory expansion is accomplished by installing one or more of the following memory expansion kits: Personal System/2 1 MB Memory Expansion Kit (#4005), Personal System/2 2 MB Memory Expansion Kit (#4006), or Personal System/2 4 MB Memory Expansion Kit (#4204). These kits consist of a group of memory chips installed on a small circuit board — a SIMM. In fact, these are the same SIMMs used for Main Memory in the IBM PS/2 family. A maximum of four memory expansion kits (of any size) can be installed in an Xstation 130.

AUXILIARY STORAGE OPTIONS

As we saw in Chapter 1, there are four basic types of auxiliary storage devices for RS/6000 systems:

- ❑ Diskettes
- ❑ Fixed disks
- ❑ CD-ROM
- ❑ Tape

Let's look at the specific auxiliary storage options available for the RS/6000 family of computers.

Diskette Storage

Diskette storage is commonly used by many different types of computer systems. It provides a convenient way to transfer small amounts of information between computer systems. While diskettes can also be used for making backup copies of the information stored on the disks, diskettes lack the storage capacity to make them effective for this, especially for larger disks. As we saw in Chapter 1, all RS/6000 systems come standard with one 3.5-inch diskette drive like that used in the IBM Personal System/2 family of computers. This section will cover three diskette drive options that allow RS/6000 systems to read and write 5.25-inch diskettes used by other systems:

- ❏ Internal 5.25-inch Diskette Drive
- ❏ External 5.25-inch 1.2 MB Diskette Drive
- ❏ Internal 3.5-inch 2.88 MB Diskette Drive

Internal 5.25-Inch Diskette Drive

The Internal 5.25-inch 1.2 MB Diskette Drive (#2620) is used exclusively with the RS/6000 Model 9XX systems. It is installed in the Model 9XX Processor Drawer and is used to exchange information with other systems using 5.25-inch diskettes.

External 5.25-Inch 1.2 MB Diskette Drive

The External 5.25-inch 1.2 MB Diskette Drive (4869–002) is shown in Figure 2.26. It can be used with any RS/6000 model except the Model 9XX systems. The External 5.25-inch 1.2 MB Diskette Drive is a self-contained unit designed to rest on a desktop near the RS/6000 System Unit. It attaches to a connector provided on the RS/6000 system's standard diskette controller via a cable. It is primarily used for exchanging information with other computer systems using 5.25-inch diskettes.

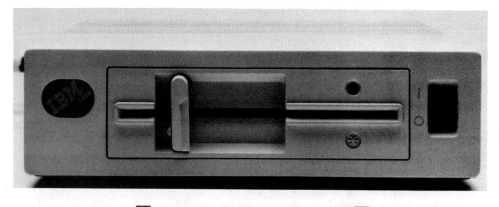

```
Diskette Type:      5.25" (from 160 to 1.2 MB)

Configuration:      Becomes "D" drive
```

Figure 2.26. External 5.25-inch Diskette Drive.

Disk Storage

All RS/6000 systems come standard with some amount of fixed-disk storage. Figure 1.20 in Chapter 1 provides information on the various RS/6000 fixed-disk configurations and compares the specifications of these disk devices. We will now look at specific disk options used with RS/6000 systems:

- 30 MB Disk for Xstation 130
- 160 MB Direct-Attach Disk Drive
- 320 MB SCSI Disk Drive
- 355 MB SCSI Disk Drive
- 400 MB SCSI Disk Drive
- 640 MB SCSI Disk Drive Pair
- 670 MB SCSI Disk Drive
- 800 MB SCSI Disk Drive Pair
- 857 MB SCSI Disk Drive
- Models 930/950 SCSI Disk Drawer
- 7204 External Disk Drive Model 320
- 7203 External Portable Disk Drive
- 9334 SCSI Expansion Unit
- 9333 Disk Drive Subsystem

30 MB Disk for Xstation 130

The System Memory in Xstation 130s can be augmented by the addition of a 30 MB Disk Drive (#2110). Chapter 1 covered the purpose of System Memory and the role the 30 MB drive can play in improving performance and providing additional function.

The disk drive itself is a 3.5-inch unit that is installed inside the Xstation 130 chassis. The control circuitry necessary to support the drive is provided as standard equipment in the Xstation 130.

The 30 MB disk has an average seek time of 19 ms, has an average latency of 8.3 ms, and transfers data at a rate of 1.27 MB/sec. Its rotational speed is 3600 rpm.

160 MB Direct-Attach Disk Drive

The 160 MB Direct-Attach Disk Drive is a low-cost 3.5-inch disk unit used exclusively with the 320. It is called **direct-attach** because its control circuitry is integrated with the disk unit itself. This distinction is necessary because most of the other

RS/6000 disks utilize the more advanced *Small Computer System Interface* (SCSI) to transfer information between the disk and RS/6000 memory. RS/6000 Model 320 systems that come standard with 160 MB utilize this disk drive. Optionally, a second 160 MB Direct-Attach Disk Drive (#2123) can be installed in a Model 320.

The disk has an average seek time of 16 ms, has an average latency of 8.3 ms, and transfers data at a rate of 1.5 MB/sec (see Chapter 1). Its rotational speed is 3600 rpm.

320 MB SCSI Disk Drive

The 320 MB SCSI Disk Drive is a high-performance 3.5-inch disk unit used exclusively with the RS/6000 Models 320 and 320H. It can be exchanged for the 160 MB disk provided as standard by specifying the 160 MB to 320 MB SCSI Disk Select (#2538) when ordering the system. It can also be used as a second disk drive in any Model 320 or 320H (#2540).

This drive is called a "SCSI" (pronounced "scuzzy") disk drive because it utilizes the *Small Computer System Interface* (SCSI) technique to transfer information between the disk and RS/6000 memory (see Chapter 1). It therefore requires the optional SCSI High-Performance Internal/External I/O Controller (#2828) covered later in this chapter.

The disk has an average seek time of 12.5 ms, has an average latency of 7 ms, and transfers data at a rate of 2 MB/sec (see Chapter 1). Its rotational speed is 4318 rpm.

355 MB SCSI Disk Drive

The 355 MB SCSI Disk Drive (#2500) is used in RS/6000 Model 520 systems. It utilizes the SCSI technique to transfer information between the disk and RS/6000 memory (see Chapter 1).

This 5.25-inch disk unit has an average seek time of 16 ms, has an average latency of 8.3 ms, and transfers data at a rate of 1.875 MB/sec (see Chapter 1). Its rotational speed is 3600 rpm.

400 MB SCSI Disk Drive

The 400 MB SCSI Disk Drive (#2560) is a high-performance 3.5-inch disk unit used with RS/6000 Model 320, 320H, and 530H systems. It requires a SCSI High-Performance Internal/External I/O Controller (#2828), covered later in this chapter.

The disk has an average seek time of 11.5 ms, has an average latency of 6.95 ms, and transfers data at a rate of 2 MB/second (see Chapter 1). Its rotational speed is 4318 rpm.

640 MB SCSI Disk Drive Pair

The 640 MB SCSI Disk Drive Pair (#2542) consists of two of the 320 MB SCSI Disk Drive options discussed earlier in this section. This disk pair unit provides 640

MB of disk storage and is used with RS/6000 Model 520 systems and its upgrades (i.e., 550E and 550S). The 640 MB SCSI Disk Drive Pair utilizes the Small Computer System Interface (SCSI) technique to transfer information between the disk and RS/6000 memory.

The disk pair has an average seek time of 12.5 ms, has an average latency of 6.95 ms, and transfers data at a rate of 2 MB/sec (see Chapter 1). The pair's rotational speed is 4318 rpm. The pair can fit into the space normally occupied by a single 5.25-inch drive.

670 MB SCSI Disk Drive

The 670 MB SCSI Disk Drive (#2510) is used with RS/6000 Model 520 and 9XX systems. This 5.25-inch drive utilizes the SCSI technique.

The disk has an average seek time of 18 ms, has an average latency of 8.3 ms, and transfers data at a rate of 1.875 MB/sec (see Chapter 1). Its rotational speed is 3600 rpm.

800 MB SCSI Disk Drive Pair

The 800 MB SCSI Disk Drive Pair (#2562) consists of two of the 400 MB SCSI Disk Drives packed together. This disk pair unit provides 800 MB of disk storage and is used exclusively with the RS/6000 Model 550 (including 550E and 550S) systems. The 800 MB SCSI Disk Drive Pair utilizes the SCSI technique to transfer information between the disk and RS/6000 memory.

The disk pair has an average time of 11.5 ms, has an average latency of 6.95 ms, and transfers data at a rate of 2 MB/sec (see Chapter 1). The pair's rotational speed is 4318 rpm. An 800 MB SCSI Disk Drive Pair can fit into the space normally occupied by a single 5.25-inch drive.

857 MB SCSI Disk Drive

The 857 MB SCSI Disk Drive (#2530) is a high-performance disk unit used with RS/6000 Model 5XX and 9XX systems. This 5.25-inch drive utilizes the SCSI technique.

The disk has an average seek time of 11.2 ms, has an average latency of 6 ms, and transfers data at a rate of 3 MB/sec (see Chapter 1). Its rotational speed is 4986 rpm.

Models 930/950 SCSI Disk Drawer

The SCSI Disk Drawer (#6100) is used exclusively with the RS/6000 Models 930 and 950. It fits into the Models 930/950 rack and occupies four EIA units vertically. The SCSI Disk Drawer can house up to four 5.25-inch disk drives. The drives can be either the 670 MB SCSI Disk Drive or the 857 MB Disk Drive—both covered earlier in the chapter. This means that a single SCSI Disk Drawer can provide up to 3428 MB of disk storage. Further, the Models 930/950 can support up to three SCSI Disk Drawers. Each drawer is attached to an SCSI High-Performance I/O Controller, which must be installed in a Micro Channel slot in the RS/6000 system's Processor Drawer. Each SCSI Disk Drawer comes with its own SCSI High-Performance I/O Controller, which plugs into a Micro Channel slot in the System Unit.

7204 External Disk Drive Model 320

Figure 2.27 shows the External Disk Drive Model 320 (7204-320), which can be used with all RS/6000 Models except the Models 930/950. This is another version of the 320 MB SCSI Disk Drive discussed earlier. This version is designed to reside outside the RS/6000 System Unit and attaches to the RS/6000 system's SCSI I/O Controller via a cable. The External Disk Drive also comes with a standard electrical power cord and plugs into a standard electrical outlet. For environments with stringent data security requirements, this drive can be detached from the RS/6000 and electrical socket nightly to facilitate storage in a vault. The drive is shock-mounted to help prevent damage as it is moved about. For use with the Model 320, the optional SCSI High-Performance Internal/External I/O Controller (#2828) covered later in this chapter is required. All other RS/6000 models come standard with the necessary SCSI I/O Controller.

The disk has an average seek time of 12.5 ms, has an average latency of 7 ms, and transfers data at a rate of 2 MB/sec (see Chapter 1). Its rotational speed is 4318 rpm.

Figure 2.27. 7204 External Disk Drive Model 320.

7203 External Portable Disk Drive

Figure 2.28 shows the 7203 External Portable Disk Drive. Like the External Disk Drive Model 320, this drive is a self-contained box designed to sit beside an RS/6000 System Unit. It plugs into a standard electrical outlet and is cabled to the RS/6000 system's SCSI I/O Controller. Unlike the External Disk Drive Model 320, the External Portable Disk Drive uses **disk drive modules**. These are actual disk drives that are shock-mounted inside a protective enclosure. They are inserted into the External Portable Disk Drive and then function as any other disk drive. These disk drive modules can be inserted and removed quickly, giving the portability of diskettes with the capacity and performance of traditional disk drives.

The External Portable Disk Drive comes standard with the 355 MB Portable Disk Drive Module. IBM will exchange this for the 670 MB Portable Disk Drive Module (#2311) if requested, but only when the drive is first ordered. Additional 355 MB (#2300) and 670 MB (#2310) Portable Disk Drive Modules can be used in the External Portable Disk Drive, but only one at a time. For environments with stringent data security needs, the disk drive modules can quickly be removed from the drive and stored in a safe overnight. These modules can also be used to make data and programs easily portable between properly equipped RS/6000 systems. The External Portable Disk Drive can be used with any RS/6000 model except the Mod-

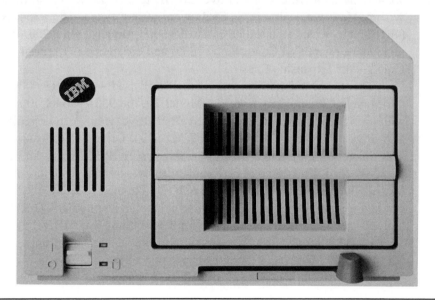

Figure 2.28. 7203 External Portable Disk Drive.

els 930/950. When used with the Model 320, the optional SCSI High-Performance Internal/External I/O Controller (#2828) covered later in this chapter is required. The 355 MB Portable Disk Drive Module has the same specifications as the 355 MB SCSI Disk Drive, and the 670 MB Portable Disk Drive Module has the same specifications as the 670 MB SCSI Disk Drive — both covered earlier in this section.

9334 SCSI Expansion Unit

The 9334 SCSI Expansion Units are designed to expand the amount of disk storage that can be attached to a single RS/6000 system. There are two types of 9334 SCSI Expansion Units: a 9334 Model 10 for use with RS/6000 Model 930 and 950 systems and a 9334 Model 500 for use with RS/6000 model 3XX and 5XX.

The 9334 Model 10 is a SCSI drawer that is installed in an Expansion Rack of a RS/6000 Model 930 or 950 system. Although it comes standard with a single 5.25-inch 670 MB SCSI Disk Drive, the 670 MB drive can be replaced with an 857 MB drive by ordering the 670 to 857 MB Disk Drive Select feature (#2533) when first ordering the system. Further, up to three more disk drives — any combination of 670 MB (#2510) or 857 MB (#2530) drives — can be installed in a single 9334 Model 10. These are the same disk drives described earlier in this section. This means that a single 9334 Model 10 can house up to 3428 MB. Since up to six 9334 Model 10 Expansion Units can be used with a single RS/6000 Model 930 or 950 system, the 9334 Expansion Units can add over 20 GB to a single RS/6000 Model 930 or 950 system. However, only six SCSI drawers of any type — e.g., 9334, SCSI Drawers (#6100), etc. — can be installed in an RS/6000 Model 930 or 950. Also, each 9334 requires its own SCSI Controller (#2835) and consumes 171 mm of space (four EIA Units) in the Expansion Rack.

The 9334 Model 500 is a standalone box used with all RS/6000 models except the Models 930 and 950. Like the Model 10, the 9334 Model 500 comes standard with a single 5.25-inch 670 MB SCSI Disk Drive, which can be replaced by an 857 MB drive by ordering the 670 to 857 MB Disk Drive Select feature (#2533) when first ordering the system. Also, up to three more disk drives — any combination of 670 MB (#2510) or 857 MB (#2530) drives — can be installed in a single 9334 Model 500, for a total of up to 3428 MB. Unlike the Model 10, the 9334 Model 500 can house up to two other SCSI devices including an internal CD-ROM drive, a 150 MB 1/4-inch Cartridge Tape Drive, or a 2.3 GB 8mm Tape Drive.

RS/6000 Model 3XX systems support the attachment of only one 9334 Model 500. RS/6000 Model 5XX systems can support up to three 9334 Model 500 Expansion Units. As with the Model 10, each 9334 Model 500 requires its own SCSI Controller (#2835).

9333 Disk Drive Subsystem

The 9333 High-Performance Disk Drive Subsystems are designed to provide a very large amount of very high speed disk storage for use with RS/6000 systems. The 9333 offers faster disk storage than that provided by the 9334 SCSI Expansion Units, as well as more total disk storage than the 9334 can provide.

There are two types of 9333 subsystems: a 9333 Model 10 for use with RS/6000 Model 930 and 950 systems, and a 9333 Model 500 for use with RS/6000 model 5XX. Either model comes standard with an 857 MB Serial-Link Disk Drive installed. There is also space for up to three more 857 MB Serial-Link Disk Drives (#3100). That means that a single 9333 can house up to 3428 MB of disk storage.

The 9333 subsystem attaches to RS/6000 computers via the required High-Performance Disk Drive Subsystem Adapter (#6210). This adapter provides an 8 MB/second data rate — twice that of the SCSI controllers used with SCSI disk drives. This improves the speed at which information can be transferred between the RS/6000 computer and the 9333 subsystem — increasing overall system performance. One High-Performance Disk Drive Subsystem Adapter has four ports that can each support a 9333 subsystem. That is, up to four 9333 subsystems can be attached to a single High-Performance Disk Drive Subsystem Adapter.

The 9333 Model 10 is a SCSI drawer that is installed in an Expansion Rack of an RS/6000 Model 930 or 950 system. Since up to 15 9333 Model 10 subsystems can be installed in a single RS/6000 Model 930 or 950 system, the 9333 subsystems can add over 50 GB to a single RS/6000 Model 930 or 950 system. Each 9333 subsystem consumes 171 mm of space (four EIA Units).

The 9333 Model 500 is a standalone box used with RS/6000 Model 5XX computers. Since up to four 9333 subsystems can be attached to a single RS/6000 Model 5XX computer, the 9333 subsystems can add over 13 GB of high-speed disk storage to a Model 5XX computer.

Either 9333 model can have two independent connections to two different RS/6000 systems. This capability, along with the mirroring support in AIX, makes **high-availability** RS/6000 configurations possible. That is, with proper application programming and by properly configuring RS/6000 systems, 9333 subsystems, and AIX, a system can be configured that can continue to function in the face of a single component failure.

CD-ROM Storage

RS/6000 systems are among the first IBM systems to make general use of *Compact-Disk Read-Only Memory* (CD-ROM). This storage medium uses the same technique to store information as do audio compact disks and can be used for many different information distribution applications. Chapters 1 and 3 cover more specifics about CD-ROM and the RS/6000 system's use of the technology. Here we will look at two CD-ROM drives that can be used with RS/6000 computers:

- Internal CD-ROM Drive
- 7210 External CD-ROM Drive

Internal CD-ROM Drive

The Internal CD-ROM Drive is designed to be installed inside the RS/6000 System Unit's frame. This 5.25-inch drive is provided as standard with the RS/6000 Model 9XX systems (in the Processor Drawer) and is supported as an option (#2600) on all other RS/6000 models except the RS/6000 Models 320 and 320H systems, which physically cannot accommodate the internal CD-ROM in their System Units. The Internal CD-ROM Drive uses a CD-ROM disk that can store approximately 600 MB of information and attaches to an SCSI I/O Controller inside the RS/6000 system. An audio output jack is provided on the bezel of the CD-ROM Drive.

The access time for this CD-ROM drive is 380 ms, and the data transfer rate is 150 KB/sec.

7210 External CD-ROM Drive

The External CD-ROM Drive (7210–001) is shown in Figure 2.29. This drive is a self-contained package designed to sit beside an RS/6000 System Unit. It is attached

Figure 2.29. External CD-ROM Drive.

to the SCSI I/O Controller via a cable and plugs into a standard electrical outlet. Multiple External CD-ROM Drives can be used with any RS/6000 model. When used with the Model 320, the optional SCSI High-Performance Internal/External I/O Controller (#2828) is required. An audio output jack is provided on the bezel of the CD-ROM Drive.

The access time for this CD-ROM drive is 380 ms, and the data transfer rate is 150 KB/sec.

Tape Storage

Computer systems are woven deeply into today's business, academic, and scientific communities and usually become the core of day-to-day operations. The information stored on the computer is a valuable asset and therefore must be protected. Magnetic tape storage provides a cost-effective and efficient means of backing up the information on the fixed disks of computer systems. Included among the tape storage options that can be used with RS/6000 systems are the following:

- 150 MB Internal 1/4-inch Cartridge Tape Drive
- 7207 150 MB External 1/4-inch Cartridge Tape Drive
- 2.3 GB 8mm Internal Tape Drive
- 7208 2.3 GB 8mm External Tape Drive
- 9348 Magnetic Tape Unit
- Models 930/950 1/2-inch 9-Track Tape Drive Drawer

Figure 2.30 summarizes the differences between these tape devices.

150 MB Internal 1/4-Inch Cartridge Tape Drive

The 150 MB Internal 1/4-inch Cartridge Tape Drive is a 5.25-inch device supported only by the Models 930 and 950. It can be installed in the Model 9XX Processor

	1/4" Cartridge Drive (Internal/External)	8mm Drive (Internal/External)	9348 Tape Unit	1/2" Tape Drawer (Models 930-950 only)
Media	1/4-Inch tape cartridge	8mm tape cartridge	1/2-inch tape reels	1/2-inch tape reels
Capacity	150 MB	2.3 GB	Variable	Variable
Data rate	90 KB/Sec	245 KB/Sec	200 to 781 KB/Sec	208 to 768 KB/Sec

Figure 2.30. Summary comparison of various tape drives used with RS/6000 systems.

Drawer (#2636) or in a SCSI Device Drawer (#2637) to provide a low-cost streaming tape drive option for data interchange with other systems and disk backup. It uses 1/4-inch tape cartridges, each capable of holding up to 150 MB of information. This cartridge capacity and its modest performance make the 150 MB Internal 1/4-inch Cartridge Tape Drive suitable for disk backup only with low-end Model 930/950 systems that have limited disk capacity. When using the Error Checking and Correction (ECC) function for tape, a single cartridge can store approximately 135 MB of information. It can read (not write) tapes created by the 6157 Model 1 (QIC 24) and it can both read and write tapes compatible with the 6157 Model 2 (QIC 150 and QIC 120). Information is transferred at a rate of 90 KB/sec. It attaches to a SCSI I/O Controller in the RS/6000 Models 930/950.

7207 150 MB External 1/4-Inch Cartridge Tape Drive

The 7207 150 MB External 1/4-inch Cartridge Tape Drive is a standalone device designed to rest beside an RS/6000 System Unit; it plugs into a standard electrical outlet. It provides a low-cost streaming tape drive option for all RS/6000 models except the RS/6000 Model 9XX systems. It can be used for data interchange with other systems and disk backup. It uses 1/4-inch tape cartridges, each capable of holding up to 150 MB of information. This cartridge capacity and its modest performance make the 150 MB Internal 1/4-inch Cartridge Tape Drive suitable for disk backup only with low-end RS/6000 systems that have limited disk capacity. It can read (not write) tapes created by the 6157 Model 1 (QIC 24) and it can both read and write tapes compatible with the 6157 Model 2 (QIC 150 and QIC 120). Information is transferred at a rate of 90 KB/sec. This tape drive is cabled to an SCSI I/O Controller. When used with the Model 320, the optional SCSI High-Performance Internal/External I/O Controller (#2828) is required.

2.3 GB 8mm Internal Tape Drive

The 2.3 GB 8mm Internal Tape Drive (#6146) is a 5.25-inch device that can be installed inside the System Unit of RS/6000 Models in the 5XX and 9XX series. It provides a high-capacity streaming tape drive option for RS/6000 systems. It is primarily used for disk backup, data archiving, and information distribution. It uses an 8mm tape cartridge like that used with 8mm video cameras. Each cartridge is capable of holding up to 2.3 GB (over 2.3 billion bytes) of information. Information is transferred at a rate of 245 KB/sec. This tape drive is cabled to an SCSI I/O Controller.

7208 2.3 GB 8mm External Tape Drive

The 7208 2.3 GB 8mm External Tape Drive is a 5.25-inch device that can be used with all RS/6000 models except the Models 930 and 950, which use the internal version. It is a self-contained device designed to rest beside an RS/6000 System Unit. It is attached to the RS/6000 via a cable to the required SCSI I/O Controller (option #2828 on the RS/6000 Model 320) and gets its power from a standard electrical socket. It is primarily used for disk backup, data archiving, and information distribution. It uses an 8mm tape cartridge like that used with 8mm video cameras. Each cartridge is capable of holding up to 2.3 GB (over 2.3 billion bytes) of information. Information is transferred at a rate of 245 KB/sec.

9348 Magnetic Tape Unit

The 9348 Magnetic Tape Unit Model 12 is an intermediate-performance streaming tape drive that uses 1/2-inch tape reels. It utilizes standard 9-track tape reels, which are automatically loaded and threaded. The 9348 is capable of reading or writing in either 1600 bpi at 200 KB/sec (PE mode) or 6250 bpi at 781 KB/sec (GCR mode). It is a tabletop device that can be attached to any RS/6000 System Unit except the RS/6000 Model 9XX systems. It is cabled to the required SCSI I/O Controller (option #2828 on the RS/6000 Model 320) and gets its power from an electrical socket. It has a 1 MB memory buffer (which will continue to accept information from the RS/6000 system while tape is being positioned). This buffer helps improve the overall performance of the 9348 Magnetic Tape Unit. The tape speed of this drive is from 123 inches per second (GCR mode) to 130 inches per second (PE mode). This tape unit can be used for disk backup and data interchange applications.

Models 930/950 1/2-Inch 9-Track Tape Drive Drawer

The 1/2-inch 9-Track Tape Drive Drawer (#6140) is used exclusively with the RS/6000 Models 930 and 950. It comes with a built-in tape drive that uses industry-standard 1/2-inch 9-track tape reels. This tape drive automatically loads and threads the tape reels and uses the IBM standard 9-track recording format (eight data bits plus a parity bit for error detection). It can record or read information at either of two densities: 6250 bpi (GCR mode at 123 inches per second) or 1600 bpi (PE mode at 130 inches per second). This allows for interchange of information with other RS/6000 systems and with many other computer types that use 1/2-inch 9-track tapes. A 1 MB buffer is provided in the tape drive to improve overall efficiency when recording or reading a tape. The nominal data throughput rate of this tape drive is 768 Kb/sec (GCR mode) or 208 Kb/sec (PE mode). The battery backup option for the Model 930/950 (discussed later in this chapter) does not support this tape drive in the event of a power failure. The 1/2-inch 9-Track Tape Drive Drawer comes with a SCSI I/O Controller that must be installed in a Micro Channel slot inside the Model 930/950 Processor Drawer.

I/O Controllers

As discussed in Chapter 1, all RS/6000 systems are based on a multiprocessor architecture that allows them to do work more efficiently. The I/O Controllers introduced in Chapter 1 manage the data flow between the computer system and other devices (e.g., auxiliary storage devices). These controllers are small, specialized processors that do most of their work independently of the main processor. They are installed in a Micro Channel slot inside the System Unit of the computer and attach via cable to the auxiliary storage.

We will cover four I/O Controllers used with RS/6000 systems:

- SCSI High-Performance Internal/External I/O Controller
- SCSI High-Performance Insternal I/O Controller
- SCSI High-Performance External I/O Controller
- High-Performance Disk Drive Subsystem Adapter

SCSI High-Performance Internal/External I/O Controller

The SCSI High-Performance Internal/External I/O Controller (#2828) is used exclusively with the RS/6000 Models 320 and 320H. It is installed in a Micro Channel slot and allows the attachment of up to four SCSI devices (e.g., disk, tape, or CD-ROM). Up to two of these devices can be installed inside the Model 320, while the other two must be external devices attached to the SCSI I/O Controller via a separate cable. Information is transferred between the SCSI I/O Controller and the SCSI device at a rate of 4 MB/sec using the parity technique to detect any errors. The SCSI I/O Controller exchanges information with the other RS/6000 components using the Bus Master and Streaming Data Procedure functions of the Micro Channel. A daisy-chain SCSI cable for the two internally supported SCSI devices is included with this SCSI I/O Controller.

SCSI High-Performance Internal I/O Controller

The SCSI High-Performance Internal I/O Controller (#2829) is used in the RS/6000 Models 520, 530, 540, and 550. It is installed in a Micro Channel slot and allows the attachment of up to seven SCSI devices (e.g., disk, tape, or CD-ROM). Up to four internal SCSI devices can be attached with the included daisy-chain cable, and up to two external devices with separately purchased cables. This SCSI I/O Controller is performance-optimized for use with six 3.5-inch disk drives. The maximum number of internal and external devices that can be attached to this SCSI I/O Controller is seven. One SCSI High-Performance Internal I/O Controller can be installed in a single RS/6000 System Unit (in addition to the one provided as standard).

Information is transferred between the SCSI I/O Controller and the SCSI device at a rate of 4 MB/sec using the parity technique to detect any errors. The SCSI I/O Controller exchanges information with the other RS/6000 components using the Bus Master and Streaming Data Procedure functions in the Micro Channel architecture.

SCSI High-Performance External I/O Controller

The SCSI High-Performance External I/O Controller (#2835) can be used with all RS/6000 models. It is installed in a Micro Channel slot and allows the attachment of up to seven external SCSI devices. Up to four SCSI High-Performance External I/O Controllers can be installed in a single RS/6000 System Unit.

Information is transferred between the SCSI I/O Controller and the SCSI device at a rate of 4 MB/sec using the parity technique to detect any errors. The SCSI I/O Controller exchanges information with the other RS/6000 components over the Micro Channel architecture using the Bus Master and Streaming Data Procedure functions.

High-Performance Disk Drive Subsystem Adapter

The High-Performance Disk Drive Subsystem Adapter (#6210) is used to attach the 9333 High-Performance Disk Drive Subsystem to RS/6000 computers. It provides four ports, each capable of supporting one 9333 subsystem. The adapter is able to exchange information with the 9333 subsystem at a rate of 8 MB/sec — twice as fast as the SCSI Controllers just covered. The adapter resides in a Micro Channel over which it exchanges information with the RS/6000 computer.

COMMUNICATIONS OPTIONS

Organizations of all kinds are placing an increasing emphasis on computer communications. This section will provide a quick communications tutorial and then an overview of some communications options (also called "feature cards," "adapters," or "subsystems") available for IBM's RS/6000 systems. These options are installed (in the case of a feature card) or attached to a card in a Micro Channel slot and add some type of communications capability to the computer system. Through these communications options, RS/6000 systems can be attached to ASCII terminals, printers, one another, larger computers (e.g., the System/390), or smaller computers (e.g., the Personal System/2). Chapter 6 is devoted to showing how to use these communications options to allow RS/6000 systems to participate in various communications configurations. If your interest is in communications environments rather than the options themselves, skip to Chapter 6. In this section, we will look at the following types of communications options:

- Asynchronous communications adapters
- LAN communications adapters
- WAN communications adapters
- Other communications options

Communications Interfaces/Protocols—A Road Map

One of the easiest areas in which to get confused in today's computer environment is communications. This section will serve as a quick communications tutorial providing you with the background necessary to understand the differences among the various communications options covered in this chapter.

A **communications line** can be thought of as a cable between two or more computer systems, or between a computer and peripheral devices such as an ASCII terminal or an ASCII printer, one other device across the room, or hundreds of devices across global distances. By using multiple communication lines, an organization can provide information from a single point to users in many locations.

In order to be attached to a communications line, the RS/6000 system must first have the proper electrical **interface.** The term "interface" refers collectively to the connector, electrical voltage levels, connector pin functions, and so on, that are provided for the attachment to a communications line. We will discuss options that use the **EIA-232D, EIA-422A, MIL-STD 188–114, CCITT X.21, CCITT V.35, Ethernet,** or **Token-Ring** interfaces. For our purposes, it is not necessary to understand exactly what all these cryptic names mean. Simply know that different types of interfaces are necessary to support different types of communications.

In addition to the different interfaces, you must also know about **communications protocols** to be conversant in computer communications. Just as there are different rules of grammar and punctuation in English, French, and other languages, there are different rules for various types of computer communications. In computer communications, a set of rules is called a communications protocol. The protocols of most interest for our purposes are the **async, bisync, SDLC, X.25, CD/CSMA (IEEE 802.3)**, and **Token-Ring (IEEE 802.5)**. Each of these different protocols has the same basic goal of moving information from one place to another efficiently and reliably. Each protocol has advantages and disadvantages, and the one you will use depends on your requirements in the areas of transmission speed, cost, and compatibility with the other device(s) in the network. At all times, however, all devices using a given communications line must be using the same protocol.

The async (short for *async*hronous) protocol is a low-speed, low-cost communications method commonly used by many devices including the ASCII terminals and printers used in multiuser RS/6000 configurations. With async, individual bytes of information are transmitted (one bit at a time) with no fixed relationship between bytes. Figure 2.31 shows one way a byte might be packaged before it is sent over an async communications line. The Start bit tells the receiving end that information is coming down the line. The user's data follows the Start Bit. The Parity bit is used by the receiving end to check for transmission errors in the user's data. Finally, the Stop bit signifies the end of the transmission of the character. This is just one example of how information might be transmitted over an async line. The user can select other organizations including eight user data bits and no parity bit, two stop bits, and so on. These different organizations exist primarily because of the many types of equipment that have used this protocol over the years. The specific organization one uses must be established at both ends of the communications link before communications can begin.

Next is the bisync protocol (short for *B*inary *S*ynchronous *C*ommunications, or BSC). The "synchronous" in "bisync" means that a special character preceding the information synchronizes the receiver with the incoming information. This synchronization allows many bytes of information to be sent as a single block, in contrast to the asynchronous protocol in which a single byte is sent at a time. The ability to send blocks of characters makes bisync more efficient than the asynchronous protocol. Bisync is an older communications protocol used by terminals and other equipment to exchange information with many different types of computers, including IBM's System 360 and 370 mainframes. As a result of its past popularity, many of today's computer systems still use this protocol.

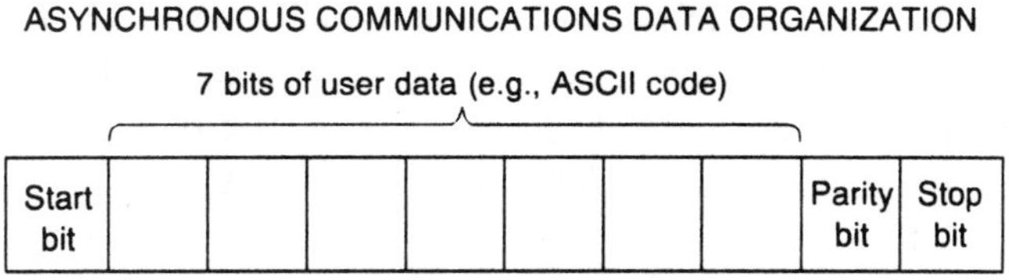

ASYNCHRONOUS COMMUNICATIONS DATA ORGANIZATION

7 bits of user data (e.g., ASCII code)

Start bit								Parity bit	Stop bit

Figure 2.31. Example data format used in ASCII asynchronous communications.

The SDLC protocol (short for *Synchronous Data Link Control*) is basically an updated version of bisync. As with bisync, SDLC is a synchronous communications protocol. SDLC, however, is a more flexible protocol that is part of IBM's *Systems Network Architecture* (SNA). SNA is a set of communications standards published by IBM that is used as a road map to ensure that compatible communications are provided for in current and future computer systems and software.

The X.25 protocol is an industry standard used in the **packet-switched** networks available to the public. While more traditional communications networks are based on **analog** (or voice-type) communications signals, packet-switched networks use **digital** (or computer-like) communications signals. Since computer information is naturally in digital form, packet-switched networks are better able to carry computer information and can move the information more quickly. The X.25 protocol used on packet-switched networks splits the information (using the SDLC protocols as a packaging format, for example) into small groups of digital data called **packets**. Each packet is then sent through the most economical and available route to its destination elsewhere in the network. Since each packet is routed in the most efficient way, overall information flow is improved over conventional techniques. X.25 is fully supported in IBM's Systems Network Architecture.

The *Carrier Sense Multiple Access/Collision Detect* (CSMA/CD) protocol is a protocol used on Ethernet local area networks to move information around the network in an orderly fashion. Its name is a mouthful, but really it's a quite simple protocol. In fact, we follow this protocol in our everyday telephone conversations. There, too, only one person can speak at a time, or neither is clearly understood. One party waits for the other to finish before beginning to speak. Thus the phone line carries only one party's voice at a time so the message is clear. This is the *CSMA* part of CSMA/CD. The *CD* part of the protocol handles the times when two nodes start transmissions simultaneously. To understand this part of the protocol, think of what you do during a telephone conversation when you begin talking at the same time as the other party. Typically, you both stop talking and begin again a few moments later, hoping that this time one of you begins sooner than the other. This is exactly analogous to the situation with CSMA/CD. If two (or more) nodes begin transmitting at the same time, the messages "collide" on the network. The nodes monitor for such a collision, and when one is detected, all nodes stop transmitting and begin again after a pause of random length. Usually, one node will begin its retransmission before the other(s), thus gaining control of the network.

The Token-Ring Network is another type of local area network. The protocol used by the Token-Ring Network is the **Token Ring** protocol. Basically, packets of information are passed around the ring from node to node in a continuous circle. These packets are called **message frames.** A unique frame, called a **token frame,** controls access to the ring. When a node receives a frame, it checks to see if it is a

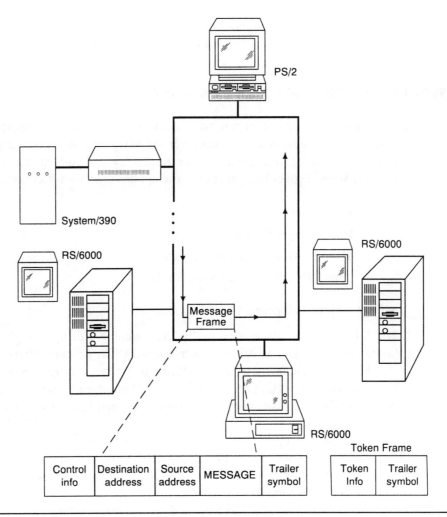

Control info	Destination address	Source address	MESSAGE	Trailer symbol		Token Info	Trailer symbol

Figure 2.32. The token-ring network uses a message frame to move information around the network in an orderly fashion.

message or a token frame. If it is a message frame, it examines the destination address (see Figure 2.32) to see if the message is intended for that node. If the message is not intended for that node, the message frame is passed on unchanged to the next node in the ring. If the frame received by a node is a token frame, the node knows that the network is idle and that it may send a message frame if it has information to transfer. After it sends a message frame, the node then sends a token frame to indicate that the ring is again inactive and ready to carry information.

With this understanding of interfaces and protocols, let's look at the specific communications options available for RS/6000 systems.

Asynchronous Communications Adapters

The async port is one of the most commonly used ports in the computer industry. The speed at which information is sent over the async port is measured in **bits/second**. Information can be transferred over the RS/6000 async ports at rates of up to 38,400 bits/sec. We will cover four types of async options used with RS/6000 systems:

- 8-Port Async Adapters
- 16-Port Async Adapters
- 64-Port Async Controller/Concentrator
- Model 930/950 Async Expansion Drawer

8-Port Async Adapters

The 8-Port Async Adapters allow for the attachment of up to eight asynchronous (async) devices, such as ASCII terminals and ASCII printers. There are three types of 8-Port Async Adapters used with RS/6000 systems, differing in the interface they provide. With the version using the EIA-232D interface (#2930), async devices can be via an EIA-232D cable up to 200 feet (61 meters) long. Another version (#2940) provides built-in surge protection circuitry and uses the EIA-422A interface, which can support cables up to 4000 feet (1200 meters) in length. A final version (#2950) provides an interface that conforms to MIL-STD 188−114, which allows cable lengths of up to 100 feet (30 meters) at 38.4 Kbits/sec (Kb/sec) and 200 feet (61 meters) when operating at 19.2 Kb/sec.

All of these adapters have the ability to transfer information at a rate of over 38,400 bits/sec (38.4 Kb/sec). They consume one Micro Channel slot and have a built-in 78-pin D-shell connector. The Multiport Interface Cable (#2995) attaches to this connector and provides eight 25-pin D-shell connectors. A cable then connects the async device to one of these connectors.

The 8-Port Async Adapters come standard with a 16-byte buffer that acts as a staging area for information just received or about to be transmitted. The adapters support a full set of modem control lines for use with external modems (discussed later in this chapter). They use the Micro Channel architecture's basic "Memory Slave" methods of transferring information (8- or 16-bit data width) to and from other RS/6000 elements. The RS/6000 Models 930/950 can have up to eight 8-Port Async Adapters installed in the Async Expansion Drawer (in addition to the async ports in the Processor Drawer). All other RS/6000 models can have as many 8-Port Async Adapters as there are available Micro Channel slots.

16-Port Async Adapters

The 16-Port Async Adapters allow for the attachment of up to 16 async devices, such as ASCII terminals and ASCII printers. There are two types of 16-Port Async Adapters used with RS/6000 systems, differing in the interface they provide. With the version using the EIA-232D interface (#2955), async devices can be via an EIA-232D cable up to 200 feet (61 meters) long. This version provides a connector that attaches to the 16-Port Interface Cable EIA-232 (#2996), which provides the 16 25-pin D-shell connectors. A cable then connects the async device to one of these connectors.

The other version (#2957) provides built-in surge protection circuitry and uses the EIA-422A interface, which can support cables up to 4000 feet (1200 meters) in length. The 16-Port Interface Cable EIA-422A (#2997) is attached to this adapter to provide the 16 25-pin D-shell connectors. A cable then connects the async device to one of these connectors.

Either of these adapters consumes one Micro Channel slot and has the ability to transfer information at a rate of over 38,400 bits/sec (38.4 Kb/sec).

The 16-Port Async Adapters come standard with a 16-byte buffer that acts as a staging area for information just received or about to be transmitted. It uses the Micro Channel's basic "Memory Slave" methods of transferring information (8- or 16-bit data width) to and from other RS/6000 elements. The RS/6000 Models 930/950 can have up to eight 16-Port Async Adapters installed in the Async Expansion Drawer (in addition to the async ports in the Processor Drawer). All other RS/6000 models can have as many 16-Port Async Adapters as there are available Micro Channel slots.

64-Port Async Controller/Concentrator

The 64-Port Async Controller (#6400) and the 16-Port Async Concentrator (#6401) work together to attach large pools of async devices (e.g., ASCII terminals and printers) to RS/6000 systems. The 64-Port Async Controller is a feature card that is installed in a single Micro Channel slot in an RS/6000 System Unit. The 16-Port Async Concentrator is a self-contained unit that resides outside the RS/6000 system. Figure 2.33 shows how these elements work together. First, the 64-Port Async Controller is installed in an RS/6000 Micro Channel slot. It is then attached to up to four 16-Port Async Concentrators using the 25-foot (7.6-meter) cable provided with each concentrator. While a 25-foot-long cable is provided as standard equipment, this RS-485 communications link can support a cable length of up to 2500 feet (762 meters). Then an RJ-45 to DB-25 Converter Cable (#6402) plugs into one of the 16 RJ-45

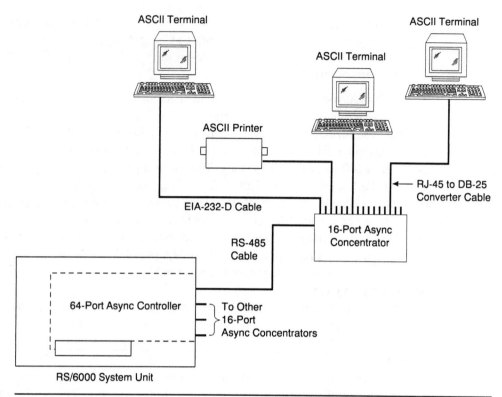

Figure 2.33. The 64-Port Asynchronous Communications Controller and the 16-Port Async Concentrator work together to attach large numbers of ASCII terminals and printers to RS/6000 systems.

connectors provided on the 16-Port Async Concentrator. This converter cable will not be necessary with terminals that directly support RJ-45 connection. The converter cable provides a 25-pin D-shell connector that allows for the attachment of the standard EIA-232D cable (up to 200 feet, or 61 meters, in length) used with async devices. Up to 16 RJ-45 to DB-25 Converter Cables can be attached to a single 16-Port Async Concentrator, which means that up to 16 async devices can be attached to a single 16-Port Async Concentrator. In turn, up to four 16-Port Async Concentrators can be attached to a single 64-Port Async Controller, which means that up to 64 async devices can be attached to a single 64-Port Async Controller feature card.

The 64-Port Async Controller has 256 KB of memory used as temporary storage for information received from and transmitted to the pool of async devices. It uses the basic "Memory Slave" method of exchanging information (16 bits of data at a time) with other RS/6000 elements over the Micro Channel bus. It provides four RJ-45 connectors to attach from one to four 16-Port Async Concentrators. Up to two 64-Port Async Controllers can be installed in an RS/6000 Model 320, while up to four can be installed in the deskside RS/6000 models. The Model 930/950 can support up to eight 64-Port Async Controllers with the addition of the optional Async Expansion Drawer used with that model.

The 16-Port Async Concentrator is a small computer system in its own right, with computing power beyond many small personal computers used today. Designed around the Intel 80186 microprocessor chip, the 16-Port Async Concentrator provides async ports capable of transferring information at up to 38.4 Kb/sec. It uses its own internal power supply and external transformer.

Together, the 64-Port Async Controller and 16-Port Async Concentrator provide the most efficient method of connecting async devices to RS/6000 systems. In situations where optimal system performance and throughput are required, the 64-Port Async Controller and 16-Port Async Concentrator are a better choice than either the 8- or 16-Port Async Adapter discussed earlier.

Async Expansion Drawer

The Async Expansion Drawer (#6002) provides eight additional expansion slots that support the installation of the 8-Port Async Adapter, the 16-Port Async Adapter, or the 64-Port Async Controller. It is used exclusively with the RS/6000 Models 930/950 and can contain various combinations of Async Adapters/Controllers with system maximum of eight. The Async Expansion Drawer attaches to the provided Async Expansion Adapter which must be installed in a Micro Channel slot in the Models 930/950 Processor Drawer.

While the expansion slots provided in the Async Expansion Drawer are based on the Micro Channel architecture, they contain only the electrical signals necessary to support the async adapters/controllers. They are not intended for use as general-purpose Micro Channel slots. For the best overall system performance, IBM recommends that async adapters/controllers be installed in any available Micro Channel slots in the Processor Drawer before installing them in the Async Expansion Drawer.

LAN Communications Adapters

All RS/6000 systems can participate in either Ethernet or Token-Ring local area networks. Each RS/6000 participating in a local area network must have the appropriate LAN communications adapters covered here.

Ethernet High-Performance LAN Adapter

The Ethernet High-Performance LAN Adapter (#2980) allows an RS/6000 system to participate in an Ethernet Version 2 or IEEE 802.3 local area network. Ethernet networks transfer information at a rate of over 10 million bits/sec (10 Mb/sec) using the CSMA/CD protocol discussed earlier. There are two different types of cable used in Ethernet networks: **thick** cable, which is 50 ohm coaxial cable, and **thin** (BNC) cable, which is RG-58A/U coaxial cable. The Ethernet High-Performance LAN Adapter comes standard with a built-in transceiver that can be used with thin Ethernet cable. However, the user must provide an external transceiver if the Ethernet network uses the thick cable type.

The Ethernet High-Performance LAN Adapter has a 16 KB high-speed buffer memory to streamline the receipt and transmission of information. It uses the Cyclic Redundancy Code (32 bits) error-checking technique discussed in Chapter 1 to detect and correct network transmission errors. The adapter also uses the Bus Master technique to efficiently exchange information with other RS/6000 elements over the Micro Channel. Up to four Ethernet High-Performance LAN Adapters can be installed in a single RS/6000 system. Chapter 6 will discuss Ethernet Networks further.

Token-Ring High-Performance Network Adapter

The Token-Ring High-Performance Network Adapter (#2970) allows an RS/6000 system to participate in an IBM Token-Ring (IEEE 802.5) local area network. Token-Ring networks transfer information using the Token-Ring protocol covered earlier in the chapter. Token-Ring networks can be operated at transmission speeds of just over 4 million bits/sec (4 Mb/sec) or just over 16 million bits/sec (16 Mb/sec). However, every node in the network must be using the same transmission speed. The Token-Ring High-Performance Network Adapter supports either transmission speed. The adapter has a single 9-pin D-shell connector. A cable is provided with the adapter for attachment to an IBM Cabling System socket or that of the Multistation Access Unit component of a Token-Ring network wiring system. The Token-Ring High-Performance Network Adapter uses the Bus Master and Streaming Data Procedure functions in the Micro Channel architecture to efficiently exchange information with other RS/6000 elements. Up to four Token-Ring High-Performance Network Adapters can be installed in a single RS/6000 system. Chapter 6 will discuss Token-Ring networks further.

WAN Communications Adapters

All RS/6000 systems can participate in a variety of *Wide Area Networks* (WANs). Unlike LANs, WANs allow computers to communicate with other computers and remote devices over global distances. For more about WANs, see Chapter 6.

4-Port Multiprotocol Communications Controller

The 4-Port Multiprotocol Communications Controller (#2700) allows RS/6000 systems to simultaneously participate in up to four different communications networks. Three components make up this communications link. First is the base 4-Port Multiprotocol Communications Controller itself. This is a standard Micro Channel card that contains surge protection circuitry, cyclic redundancy-checking circuitry, and other communications circuitry. It is the job of this card to prepare any information received or to be transmitted, relieving the RS/6000 Main Processor of many tasks (e.g., address searches and CRC generation). It provides four independently operated communications ports (ports 0, 1, 2, and 3). These ports are programmed to support EIA-232D (ports 0–3), EIA-422A (ports 0 and 2), V.35 (ports 0 and 1), or X.21 (port 0 only) physical interfaces. The 4-Port Multiprotocol Communications Controller uses the Micro Channel's Bus Master capabilities to efficiently exchange information (16 bits at a time) with other RS/6000 elements.

The second component of this communications link is called a **daughter card**. This is a small circuit card that is physically installed on the base 4-Port Multiprotocol Communications Controller. The daughter card contains the circuitry necessary to support four different interfaces: EIA-232D, EIA 422A, CCITT X.21, and CCITT V.35. Since the daughter card resides on the base 4-Port Multiprotocol Communications Controller, it does not require a Micro Channel slot.

The third and final element in this communications link is the 4-Port Multiprotocol Interface Cable (#2705). This cable is attached to the 78-pin connector of the daughter card and provides the different connectors necessary to support the different interface standards: four 25-pin connectors for EIA-232D, two 15-pin connectors for V.35, one 15-pin connector for X.21, and two 25-pin connectors for EIA-422A.

These elements, along with the appropriate programming, can support either async, bisync, or SDLC protocols over the physical interfaces already discussed. While the AIX operating system provides support for transmission speeds of up to 19.2 Kb/sec over EIA-232D, the 4-Port Multiprotocol Communications Controller hardware is designed to support transmission speeds up to 64 Kb/second with user-provided programming. Up to seven 4-Port Multiprotocol Communications Controllers can be installed in any RS/6000 model, provided there are that many available Micro Channel slots.

X.25 Interface Co-Processor/2

The X.25 Interface Co-Processor/2 (#2960) allows RS/6000 systems to participate in X.25 packet-switched communications networks. The X.25 Interface Co-Processor/2 is a standard Micro Channel card that provides a single port that can be configured to support one of three physical interfaces: X.21, EIA-232D, or V.35. The card handles detailed manipulation of the information associated with communications, easing the workload of the RS/6000 Main Processor. Information can be transferred at a rate of up to 64 Kb/sec over the X.21 interface, 19.2 Kb/sec over the EIA-232D interface, and 56 Kb/sec over the V.35 interface. To facilitate efficient operation, the card has 512 KB of memory used to temporarily hold information just received or about to be transmitted. The X.25 Interface Co-Processor/2 uses the Micro Channel's basic "I/O Slave" method of exchanging information (16 bits at a time) with other RS/6000 elements.

A 37-pin D-shell connector is provided on the end of the X.25 Interface Co-Processor/2. One end of the appropriate cable (depending on which of the three physical interfaces is being used) is attached to this connector, and the other end provides the physical interface required by the network. Up to four X.25 Interface Co-Processor/2 adapters can be installed in any System Unit subject to the availability of Macro Channel slots.

Other Communications Options

In this section, we will cover two communications options for RS/6000 systems that don't neatly fit in the other categories:

- ❑ 3270 Connection Adapter
- ❑ Serial Optical Channel Converter

3270 Connection Adapter

The 3270 Connection Adapter (#2990) allows an RS/6000 system to be attached via coaxial cable to a larger System/370 or ES/9000 computer system. Along with the proper software, the 3270 Connection Adapter allows an RS/6000 system to "act like" (**emulate**) IBM 3278 or 3279 terminals commonly used to interact with IBM's larger System/370 or ES/9000 computer systems. Thus, an RS/6000 can double as both a standard RS/6000 workstation and a terminal on a larger computer system.

Serial Optical Channel Converter

The Serial Optical Channel Converter (#2860) makes use of the Serial Links built into the RS/6000 architecture and mentioned in Chapter 1. The Serial Optical Channel Converter is a circuit board that plugs into a specially designed socket on the RS/6000 System Board. Each Serial Optical Channel Converter provides two high-speed, half-duplex (information moves one way at a time) communications based on light pulses carried over fiber optic cable. This link can be used in conjunction with a network **router,** for example, to establish a high-speed communications link with a communications network consisting of many different types of computer systems.

The Serial Optical Channel Converter transfers information to and from the RS/6000 Main Memory via an independent path. That is, communications traffic sent over the Serial Optical Channel Converter does not have to contend with data movement activities occurring over the Micro Channel. Less contention typically means better overall system performance.

RS/6000 Model 5XX and 7XX systems support one Serial Optical Channel Converter while the Models 930 and 950 support up to two Serial Optical Channel Converters. The software driver necessary to operate the Serial Optical Channel Converter is provided with this feature. This option is not supported in RS/6000 Model 2XX or 3XX systems.

Modems

A **modem** is a device that converts computer information into communications signals and transmits them over the telephone lines (i.e., it *mod*ulates the computer information). It is also a modem, at the receiving end, that converts the telephone line signals back into computer information (i.e., it *dem*odulates the telephone line signal). The term "modem" is a combination of the terms "*mod*ulate" and "*dem*odulate."

Why do computers need a modem for telephone line communications? Telephone lines are designed to carry electronically encoded voice messages from one point to another. A device (the telephone) is therefore necessary to convert the speaker's voice into suitable electronic signals for phone line transmission. Although the information in a computer is already electronically encoded, it is not in a form that can be transmitted over the phone lines. For this reason, a device is needed to convert the electronically encoded computer information into suitable electronic signals. A modem can be thought of as a telephone for a computer. Just as both parties need their own telephone to hold a conversation, both computers must have their own modem to transfer information over the phone lines. This section will look at some representative modems used with RS/6000 systems:

- ❑ 5853 Modem
- ❑ 7855 Modem
- ❑ 786X Modems
- ❑ 5822 DSU

5853 Modem

The 5853 Modem, shown in Figure 2.34, is a standalone unit designed to sit on a desktop near the computer system. It is attached to the computer system through an EIA-232D interface and an appropriate cable. The 5853 supports communications speeds up to 2400 bits/sec (bps) over **Public Switched Telephone (PST)** lines. PST lines, also called "switched lines" and "voice-grade lines," are the same type of line as is used for voice communications. They are called "switched" lines because the modem must dial a number just like a telephone user in order to establish the proper connection. The 5853 is compatible with the Bell 103 (0 to 300 bits/sec asynchronous), Bell 212A (300 and 1200 bits/sec asynchronous), and V.22bis (1200 and 2400 bits/sec synchronous) industry standards pertaining to modem operation. For perspective, 1200 bits/sec is about 120 alphanumeric characters per second. The average adult reads at a rate of about 20 or 30 characters a second. The 5853 can transmit information at the same time it is receiving other information. This is called **full duplex** operation.

The 5853 is said to be "intelligent" because a built-in microprocessor interprets high-level commands (from a computer program) to perform various modem functions. For example, the modem can be instructed to automatically place or answer a telephone call. These capabilities are called **auto-originate** and **auto-answer** respectively. This modem uses the IBM and Attention command sets to control these functions, providing compatibility with programs and systems that use these commands. When the 5853 answers an incoming call, it senses the kind of communications being sent (e.g., 212A, 103, or V.22bis; 300 or 1200 bits/sec, etc.) and automatically

Figure 2.34. 5853 Modem.

adapts to the proper operating mode. Pulse or tone dialing is supported, and the built-in speaker allows you to hear the call progress tones as the link is being established. The modem's built-in test programs check the health of the modem every time power is turned on.

7855 Modem

Figure 2.35 shows the 7855 Modem. This modem is designed to operate over either public switched or **leased lines** using either asynchronous or synchronous protocols. Unlike the public switched lines, leased lines maintain a constant communications link. That is, you need not dial a telephone number to establish the connection; leased lines are always connected. They are called "leased" because the user pays for exclusive rights to use the line continuously.

When operating in asynchronous mode, transmission speeds of 9600 bits/sec are supported over voice-grade, public switched telephone lines. (Up to 12,000 bits/sec can be achieved if line quality is good.) Further, transmission speeds of up to 19,200 bits/sec can be achieved if the information being transmitted lends itself to the data-compression techniques used by the 7855 (compatible with class 5 of the Microcom Networking Protocol). This represents transmission speeds up to five times faster than possible with the 5853 Modem. If telephone line quality is poor, the 7855 Modem will automatically reduce its transmission speed as necessary. The 7855 automatically adapts if necessary to accommodate the transmission speed and character formatting being used by the modem on the other end of the communications line. There is a version of the 7855 designed to be mounted in a modem rack (7855-18).

Figure 2.35. 7855 Modem.

The 7855 Modem also supports full duplex communications at speeds of up to 12,000 bits/sec using synchronous protocols (e.g., bisync or SDLC). It provides compatibility with the IBM 5841, 5842, and 5853 Modems except that the 7855 does not support the IBM command set. Instead, the 7855 supports the popular Enhanced Attention (AT) command set to control basic modem operations under program control. A microprocessor chip provides intelligence to the modem, allowing for functions such as auto-dial and auto-answer. The 7855 Modem also supports the Link Problem Determination Aid (LPDA2) "call out" and "disconnect" commands. LPDA2 allows a network operator to remotely issue commands that manipulate network elements such as modems. The 7855 performs a self-test every time it is turned on to help detect any problems.

When the 7855 is used with a leased telephone line and the line goes down for some reason, the 7855 can be programmed to automatically dial a predefined telephone number and establish a public switched telephone line communications link. This feature, called the **Switched Network Backup Utility (SNBU),** allows communications to continue in the event of a leased line failure. The 7855 can be configured either locally or remotely via a communications line. Once the modem is configured, a password security feature can deter others from changing that configuration. Standards supported by the 7855 Modem include the CCITT V.32, V.22 bis, V.22, V.24, V.28, V.54, Bell 212, and Bell 102 standards. The 7855 attaches to an EIA-232D port on the RS/6000. A built-in speaker allows the user to monitor call progress tones.

The ability to communicate at these speeds over switched phone lines is useful in situations where there is an irregular need to transfer large amounts of information to remote computer systems. Some examples of such situations would include the distribution of programs, program modifications, graphics files, image files, and digitized voice messages.

786X Modems

The 786X family of modems provides various models, all designed to work primarily over leased lines. However, 786X modems with the optional SNBU feature can automatically revert to public switched telephone lines to keep communications going (at slower speeds) in the event of a leased line failure. All 786X modems are microprocessor-based and have a 20-key keypad with a 16-character display for operator interaction. Many functions in the modems can also be manipulated remotely through network management programs. The modems have built-in diagnostic and test functions, including detailed measurements of communications line parameters. When the modem is receiving a transmission, it automatically adjusts to the speed of the transmitting modem. These modems can be used to communicate

Figure 2.36. 786X Modem.

from one computer to another (**point to point**) and as the controlling or subordinate modem on a single communications line with multiple modems attached (**multipoint**). This multipoint capability allows multiple devices to share a single communications line.

The 7861 and 7868 modems (each with multiple models) are the two basic types of modems in the 786X family. The 7868 series is simply versions of the 7861 designed to be rack-mounted. Since the 7868 series is functionally identical to the 7861 (Figure 2.36), we will focus on the latter.

The 7861 modems operate at from 4800 to 19,200 bits/sec depending on the model. All models support the enhanced LPDA. LPDA is very helpful when isolating problems in a large communications network consisting of many modems, workstations, and computers. They also provide four interfaces, allowing up to four workstations to be cabled to a single modem. This is called **fan-out.** Alternately, these four ports can be used to attach the modem to two control units for backup purposes. This is called **fan-in.** Through **data multiplexing,** the 7861 Modem allows synchronous and asynchronous devices transmitting at different speeds to share a single communications line.

5822 DSU

The 5822 *Data Service Unit* (DSU) is shown in Figure 2.37. The 5822 can be thought of as a modem used with digital communications networks rather than the telephone-type communications lines discussed so far. Since information inside a computer system is in digital form, digital networks are better suited to transmitting computer information, and they can do so at higher speeds and more reliably. The

Figure 2.37. 5822 DSU.

5822 supports transmission speeds up to 56,000 bits/sec over Digital Data Service networks based on standards published in the *Bell Systems Technical Reference PUB 62310*. The 5822 attaches to an RS/6000 async port (i.e., EIA-232D) or a V.35 interface of a computer on one side and to the digital network on the other side. The attachment configuration can be either point to point or multipoint.

OTHER OPTIONS

Before leaving the chapter, we will cover a few other options for RS/6000 systems:

- 7202 Expansion Rack
- Battery Backup options
- 6094 Dials/Programmable Keyboard
- 6093 Tablets
- 5084 Digitizers
- Mouse
- Keyboard
- Security Cable

7202 Expansion Rack

The 7202 Expansion Rack provides additional expansion capability to RS/6000 Model 9XX systems. It is an industry-standard (EIA RS-310-C) 19-inch rack that provides mounting space, electrical power, and cooling for up to six drawers. These drawers can be things like the 9333 Disk Drive Subsystem, the 9334 Model 10 SCSI Expansion Unit, or the 1/2-Inch 9-Track Tape Drive Drawer (#6140).

Up to six such drawers can be installed in a single 7202 Expansion Unit provided there are enough Micro Channel slots and disk controllers in the RS/6000 Processor Rack.

Battery Backup Options

The Battery Backup option (#6150) is used exclusively with the RS/6000 Model 9XX systems. It provides 1500 watts of standby power to allow the Model 9XX system to continue operations uninterrupted in the event of a short power failure. When installed in the RS/6000 Model 9XX Processor Rack, the Battery Backup option is designed to provide sufficient power to operate up to three drawers (the Processor Drawer and two others) for at least ten minutes. If power is not restored before the battery begins to run low, the RS/6000 system is designed to automatically perform an orderly shutdown, protecting user data and allowing for quick recovery once power is restored.

With the addition of the Battery Backup Extender Cable (#6151), up to six drawers (e.g., 9333 or 9334) can be sustained for at least ten minutes. Both the Battery Backup option and the Battery Backup Extender Cable can also be installed as an option in the 7202 Expansion Rack to sustain up to six drawers in the Expansion Rack for at least ten minutes. The 1/2-Inch 9-Track Tape Drive Drawer is not supported by these Battery Backup options.

6094 Dials/Programmable Keyboard

The 6094 Dials and Lighted Program Function Keys are input devices used with RS/6000 systems as well as other IBM computer systems. They are designed to increase the ease with which users can manipulate computer-generated graphics.

The 6094 Dials (6094 Model 10) is a standalone desktop unit that consists of eight dials (potentiometers). While these dials can be programmed by the application program to perform almost any function, they are commonly used to control pan, zoom, rotation, and so on, of two-dimensional and three-dimensional computer-generated images.

The 6094 Lighted Program Function Keys (6094 Model 20) is also a standalone device providing 32 keys whose functions are programmed by the application program. Each keytop contains an indicator light that is turned on and off by the application program. These indicator lights can be used to assist the user—for example, by showing which keys are active at any given point during application program interaction.

With the addition of the 6094/RISC System/6000 Serial Attachment Feature (#4060), the 6094 Dials and Lighted Program Function Keys can be attached to any async port on the RS/6000. Without this feature, a Graphics Application Input Adapter (#2810) and one Attachment Cable Kit (#4015) are required. In this case, both 6094 models can be attached to a single Graphics Application Input Adapter using a single Attachment Cable Kit. The 6094 Dials and Lighted Program Function Keys are supported by all RS/6000 models except the Model 9XX systems.

6093 Tablets

The 6093 Tablets are input devices designed to ease the manipulation of computer graphics images. A Tablet consists of a flat surface and either a six-button Cursor (#1512), a four-button Cursor (#1511), or a two-button Stylus (#6351).

The cursors are small devices held in the user's hand that are slid across the Tablet's flat surface. The computer senses this motion and responds by moving a special symbol (also often called a cursor) on the computer's display. The four or six buttons on the cursor are pressed to take actions as defined by the application program being used. That is, the meaning of the cursor's buttons is fully programmable and can change based on the needs or preferences of users.

Another application for the 6093 Tablets is to facilitate the entry of a drawing into the RS/6000 system, called **digitizing** a drawing. This is done by placing the drawing on the Tablet between the flat surface and the cursor. A small window in the cursor has a cross-hair sight that allows the user to accurately locate the cursor over specific points of the drawing. When one of the buttons is pressed, that point is entered into the computer system and later can be used to reconstruct the drawing inside the computer system.

The two-button stylus provides another way to interact with and manipulate graphics images. This device looks much like a ballpoint pen and is used in much the same way. A switch in the tip of the stylus is activated by pressing the pen against the Tablet's flat surface. If the user places a drawing in the Tablet's flat surface, locates the stylus tip, and presses the button(s) on the stylus, the drawing can be digitized.

There are two models of the 6093 Tablet, differing only in the size of their flat surfaces. The Model 011 CursorPad Tablet has a surface area of 8.1" x 10.4" (207 mm x 265 mm), while that of the Model 012 Tablet is 14.2" x 16.1" (378 mm x 410 mm). The resolution of the 6093 Tablet can be defined by the application program to a maximum of 1279 lines per inch. The 6093 Tablets attach to the standard Tablet Port provided on all RS/6000 systems except the Model 9XX systems. The 6093 cursor and stylus features cannot be used simultaneously.

5084 Digitizers

The 5084 Digitizer is an input device designed for the entry of large-scale drawings into computer systems (i.e., digitizing drawings). It consists of a large flat surface and a 16-button Cursor that has four indicator lights. The 16-button Cursor is a small device the user holds in the hand and slides across the Digitizer's flat surface. The buttons on the cursor are pressed to digitize points of a drawing placed on the surface. The output from the 5084 Digitizer can be in either binary or ASCII data formats.

There are three models of the 5084 Digitizer, differing only in the size of their flat surfaces. The Model 1 has an active surface 24" × 36" (610 × 915 mm) in size, the Model 2's active surface is 36" × 48" (915 × 1220 mm), and the Model 3's active surface is 44" × 60" (1120 × 1525 mm). The resolution of the 5084 Digitizers can be defined by the application program to a maximum of 1279 lines per inch. The 5084 attaches to any RS/6000 model through an async port (EIA-232D).

3-Button Mouse

The 3-Button Mouse (#6041) is an input device that can be used with all RS/6000 models except the Model 9XX systems. The user slides the Mouse on a desktop to control cursor movement, draw lines, define points, and so on. The three buttons provided on the Mouse are typically used to select a menu item or take some other action after the cursor is positioned on the screen. The Mouse augments the keyboard as a means of interacting with RS/6000 systems. It attaches to the RS/6000 System Unit through the standard Mouse Port.

Keyboards

When an RS/6000 system is used as a workstation, a keyboard is required. The Enhanced Keyboard (#6010) shown in Figure 2.38 has 101 keys and is the same layout as those used by other IBM products (including the IBM PS/2 computers and many different types of terminals). This means that once familiar with this layout, a user will not have to adapt to different keyboard layouts when using other IBM computer equipment. The keytops are engraved with U.S. English characters. Other keyboards used with RS/6000 systems (some with 102 keys) have keyboard engravings to support other languages (U.K. English, French, German, Japanese, etc.).

The keyboard cable plugs into the Keyboard Port provided on all RS/6000

Figure 2.38. The layout of the Enhanced Keyboard is used with many different IBM products, including RS/6000 systems.

models except the Model 9XX systems. Small retractable legs on the bottom of the keyboard can be extended to change the angle of the keyboard if desired.

Security Cable

The RS/6000 Security Cable is used to tie down RS/6000 Model 320 systems to help prevent unauthorized movement of the System Unit. It is made of hardened steel and is designed to be attached to a secure piece of furniture.

OPTION COMPATIBILITY MATRIX

With the many options and peripherals available for RS/6000 computers, users can easily become confused as to what options work with which models. Figure 2.39 summarizes what works with what for planning purposes. Appendix A lists some other devices supported by RS/6000 systems. Due to complexities and various configuration limitations not addressed in this book, the assistance of IBM representatives or authorized dealers should be sought before finalizing any RS/6000 system configurations.

	Model 320	Model 320H	Model 520	Model 530H	Model 550	Model 930	Model 950	Xstation 130
GRAPHICS DISPLAYS								
5081 Color Displays	YES	YES	YES	YES	YES	NO	NO	YES
6091 Color Displays	YES	YES	YES	YES	YES	NO	NO	YES
Monochrome Display 8508	YES	YES	YES	YES	YES	NO	NO	YES
Other PS/2 Displays						NO	NO	YES
GRAPHICS OPTIONS								
POWERgraphics Gt1 (#4208)	NO	NO	NO	NO	NO	NO	NO	NO
Grayscale Display Adapter (#2760)	YES	YES	YES	YES	YES	NO	NO	NO
Color Graphics Display Adapter (#2770)	YES	YES	YES	YES	YES	NO	NO	NO
POWERgraphics Gt3 (#2777)	YES	YES	YES	YES	YES	NO	NO	NO
POWERgraphics Gt4 and Gt4x	YES	YES	YES	YES	YES	NO	NO	NO
7235 POWER GTO	YES	YES	YES	YES	YES	NO	NO	NO
5086/5085 Attachment Adapters	YES	YES	YES	YES	YES	YES	YES	NO
Xstation 130 Video Memory Upgrade	NO	NO	NO	NO	NO	NO	NO	YES
ASCII TERMINALS								
3151 Terminals	YES	YES	YES	YES	YES	YES	YES	NO
3164 Color Terminals	YES	YES	YES	YES	YES	YES	YES	NO
PS/2 ASCII Terminal Emulation	YES	YES	YES	YES	YES	YES	YES	NO
PRINTERS								
Personal Printer Series II	YES	YES	YES	YES	YES	YES	YES	YES
5204 Quickwriter	YES	YES	YES	YES	YES	YES	YES	YES
5202 Quietwriter III	YES	YES	YES	YES	YES	YES	YES	YES
4224 Printer	YES	YES	YES	YES	YES	YES	YES	YES
4234 Printer	YES	YES	YES	YES	YES	YES	YES	YES
6252 Impactwriter	YES	YES	YES	YES	YES	YES	YES	NO
4019 LaserPrinter	YES	YES	YES	YES	YES	YES	YES	YES
3816 Page Printer	YES	YES	YES	YES	YES	YES	YES	YES
6262 Printer	YES	YES	YES	YES	YES	YES	YES	NO
PLOTTERS								
6180 Color Plotter	YES	YES	YES	YES	YES	YES	YES	YES
6182 Auto-Feed Color Plotter	YES	YES	YES	YES	YES	YES	YES	YES
6184 Color Plotter	YES	YES	YES	YES	YES	YES	YES	YES
6187 Color Plotter	YES	YES	YES	YES	YES	YES	YES	YES
MAIN MEMORY EXPANSION								
2 MB SIMM Memory (#4001)	NO	NO	NO	NO	NO	NO	NO	
4 MB SIMM Memory (#4002)	NO	NO	NO	NO	NO	NO	NO	
8 MB SIMM Memory (#4003)	NO	NO	NO	NO	NO	NO	NO	
8 MB SD1 Memory Card (#4008)	YES	YES	YES	NO	NO	YES	NO	NO
16 MB SD1 Memory Card (#4016)	YES	YES	YES	NO	NO	YES	NO	NO

(Continued)

Figure 2.39. Option compatibility matrix. This table indicates which options work with which computer systems.

	Model 320	Model 320H	Model 520	Model 530H	Model 550	Model 930	Model 950	Xstation 130
32 MB HD1 Memory Card (#4032)	YES	YES	YES	NO	NO	YES	NO	NO
32 MB HD2 Memory Card (#4065)	NO	NO	NO	NO	NO	NO	NO	NO
64 MB HD1 Memory Card (#4035)	YES	YES	YES	NO	NO	YES	NO	NO
8 MB HD3 Memory Card (#4063)	NO	NO	NO	YES	YES	NO	YES	NO
16 MB HD3 Memory Card (#4066)	NO	NO	NO	YES	YES	NO	YES	NO
32 MB HD3 Memory Card (#4067)	NO	NO	NO	YES	YES	NO	YES	NO
64 MB HD3 Memory Card (#4069)	NO	NO	NO	YES	YES	NO	YES	NO
PS/2 1 MB Mem Exp Kit (#4005)	NO	NO	NO	NO	NO	NO	NO	YES
PS/2 2 MB Mem Exp Kit (#4006)	NO	NO	NO	NO	NO	NO	NO	YES
PS/2 4 MB Mem Exp Kit (#4204)	NO	NO	NO	NO	NO	NO	NO	YES
DISKETTE STORAGE								
Int. 5.25" Diskette Drive (#2620)	NO	NO	YES	YES	YES	YES	YES	NO
Ext. 5.25" Diskette Drive (#4869)	YES	YES	YES	YES	YES	NO	NO	NO
2.88 MB 3.5" Diskette Drive (#2610)								
DISK DRIVES								
30 MB Dir. Attach Disk Drive (#2110)	NO	NO	NO	NO	NO	NO	NO	YES
160 MB Dir. Attach Disk Drive (#2121)	NO	NO	NO	NO	NO	NO	NO	NO
160 MB Dir. Attach Disk Drive (#2123)	YES	NO	NO	NO	NO	NO	NO	NO
320 MB SCSI Disk Drive (#2540)	YES	YES	NO	NO	NO	NO	NO	NO
355 MB SCSI Disk Drive (#2500)	NO	NO	YES	NO	NO	NO	NO	NO
400 MB SCSI Disk Drive (#2560)	YES	YES	NO	YES	NO	NO	NO	NO
640 MB SCSI Disk Drive Pair (#2542)	NO	NO	YES	NO	NO	NO	NO	NO
670 MB SCSI Disk Drive (#2510)	NO	NO	YES	NO	NO	NO	NO	NO
800 MB SCSI Disk Drive Pair (#2562)	NO	NO	NO	NO	YES	NO	NO	NO
857 MB SCSI Disk Drive (#2530)	NO	NO	YES	YES	YES	YES	YES	NO
SCSI Disk Drawer (#6100)	NO	NO	NO	NO	NO	YES	YES	NO
7204 Ext. Disk Drive Model 320	YES	YES	YES	YES	YES	NO	NO	NO
7203 Ext. Portable Disk Drive	YES	YES	YES	YES	YES	NO	NO	NO
9334 SCSI EXpansion Unit	YES	YES	YES	YES	YES	YES	YES	NO
9333 Disk Drive Subsystem	NO	NO	YES	YES	YES	YES	YES	NO
CD-ROM DRIVES								
Internal CD-ROM Drive (#2600/2601)	NO	NO	YES	YES	YES	YES	YES	NO
7210 External CD-ROM Drive	YES	YES	YES	YES	YES	NO	NO	NO
TAPE DRIVES								
150 MB Int. 1/4" Tape Dr. (#2636/2637)	NO	NO	NO	NO	NO	YES	YES	NO
7207 150 MB Ext. 1/4" Tape Drive	YES	YES	YES	YES	YES	NO	NO	NO
2.3 GB 8mm Internal Tape Drive (#6146)	NO	NO	YES	YES	YES	YES	YES	NO
7208 2.3 GB 8mm Ext. Tape Drive	YES	YES	YES	YES	YES	NO	NO	NO
9348 Magnetic Tape Unit	YES	YES	YES	YES	YES	NO	NO	NO
1/2-Inch 9-Track Tape Drawer (#6140)	NO	NO	NO	NO	NO	YES	YES	NO
I/O CONTROLLERS								
SCSI Int./Ext. I/O Controller (#2828)	YES	YES	NO	NO	NO	NO	NO	NO
SCSI Internal I/O Controller (#2829)	NO	NO	YES	YES	YES	NO	NO	NO

Figure 2.39. *(Continued)*

	Model 320	Model 320H	Model 520	Model 530H	Model 550	Model 930	Model 950	Xstation 130I
SCSI External I/O Controller (#2835)	YES	YES	YES	YES	YES	YES	YES	NO
Disk Drive Subsystem Adapter (#6210)	NO	NO	YES	YES	YES	YES	YES	NO
ASYNC ADAPTERS								
Dual Async Adapter/A (#2925)	NO	NO	NO	NO	NO	NO	NO	YES
8-Port Async Adapters	YES	YES	YES	YES	YES	YES	YES	NO
16-Port Async Adapters	YES	YES	YES	YES	YES	YES	YES	NO
64 Port Async Ctr/Concentrator	YES	YES	YES	YES	YES	YES	YES	NO
Async Expansion Drawer (#6002)	NO	NO	NO	NO	NO	YES	YES	NO
LAN ADAPTERS								
Ethernet LAN Adapter (#2982)	NO	NO	NO	NO	NO	NO	NO	YES
Ethernet LAN Adapter (#2980)	YES	YES	YES	YES	YES	YES	YES	NO
Token-Ring Network Adapter (#4215)	NO	NO	NO	NO	NO	NO	NO	YES
Token-Ring Network Adapter (#2970)	YES	YES	YES	YES	YES	YES	YES	NO
WAN ADAPTERS								
4-Port Multiprotocol Comm. Ctr. (#2700)	YES	YES	YES	YES	YES	YES	YES	NO
X.25 Interface Co-Processor/2 (#2960)	YES	YES	YES	YES	YES	YES	YES	NO
OTHER COMMUNICATIONS OPTIONS								
3270 Connection Adapter (#2990)	YES	YES	YES	YES	YES	YES	YES	NO
Serial Optical Channel Cvtr. (#2860)	NO	NO	YES	YES	YES	YES	YES	NO
MODEMS								
5853 Modem	YES	YES	YES	YES	YES	YES	YES	YES
7855 Modem	YES	YES	YES	YES	YES	YES	YES	NO
786X Modem	YES	YES	YES	YES	YES	YES	YES	NO
5822 DSU	YES	YES	YES	YES	YES	YES	YES	NO
OTHER OPTIONS								
7202 Expansion Rack	NO	NO	NO	NO	NO	YES	YES	NO
SCSI Device Drawer (#6100)	NO	NO	NO	NO	NO	YES	YES	NO
Battery Backup OptionS	NO	NO	NO	NO	NO	YES	YES	NO
6094 Dials/Keyboard	YES	YES	YES	YES	YES	NO	NO	NO
6093 Tablets	YES	YES	YES	YES	YES	NO	NO	NO
5084 Digitizers	YES	YES	YES	YES	YES	NO	NO	NO
3-Button Mouse (#6041)	YES	YES	YES	YES	YES	NO	NO	Standard
Keyboards	YES	YES	YES	YES	YES	NO	NO	Standard
Security Cable	YES	YES	NO		NO	NO	NO	YES

Figure 2.39. *(Continued)*

3

Using Your RS/6000

The previous chapters closely examined the various models of the RS/6000 family and associated optional equipment. This chapter will begin our look at how you put that hardware to work, namely, the all-important **software**. Software is a general term for the many programs that execute in computers. It is software that harnesses the RS/6000 system's computational power and allows you to perform many diverse and useful tasks. The chapter begins by taking you step-by-step through some "hands-on" interaction with an RS/6000 system. This serves as a good introduction to the system and allows you to actually use the computer even if you never have before.

Later in the chapter, you are introduced to the kinds of software used to perform useful work with RS/6000 systems. The three general categories of software along with the job each performs will be discussed. Finally, we will discuss the RS/6000 system's compatibility with other computer systems.

GETTING YOUR FEET WET

One easy way to start learning about an RS/6000 system is to sit down and start using one. The steps in this section and those that follow will help you learn by doing just that. But first, you may want to view the 25-minute videotape titled "IBM RISC System/6000 — An Introduction" that is provided with every RS/6000 system. This tape provides an overview of RS/6000 hardware and software. It also covers keyboard basics and using a mouse, and introduces the on-line education tools we will use in this chapter. If you are nervous about working with computers, start with an open mind and you will likely be surprised at how easy RS/6000 systems are to use.

To perform the exercises in this chapter, you will need a user identification (user ID) and, if security has been activated on your system, a password. The user ID and password are given to you by the person in your organization who is designated as the **systems administrator**. By providing the RS/6000 system with your user ID and password, you are identifying yourself to the system and allowing it to verify that you are an authorized user. If you don't have a user ID and password, now would be a good time to get them. If you can't get them right now or if you don't have immediate access to an RS/6000 system, just read along and you will still see what it's like to work with an RS/6000 system.

You may also find the **RISC System/6000 Quick Start Kit** handy during the activities that follow. This is a set of quick reference cards provided with every RS/6000 system that describes how to perform basic user tasks. They are designed to be taped to your keyboard for easy reference.

If your computer does not respond as described in the procedures that follow, it may be that your system has been updated or somehow customized by a systems administrator or programmer. Check with them or the appropriate RS/6000 manuals to resolve any difficulties.

Before We Begin

Before you can use an RS/6000 system, you must obtain a user identification (user ID) and password (if password security is activated on your system). The user ID is simply a nickname you go by when interacting with the computer system. Associated with each user ID is a set of information called the **user profile**. A user profile is created by the system administrator for each user ID; it contains information such as the tasks you can or cannot do, programs that will automatically run when you **log in**, and so on.

In addition to a user ID, each user can be assigned a unique and secret code (a password) that must be entered every time he or she signs on to the system. The purpose of the password is to prevent someone else from signing on to the system under your user ID. You may or may not be prompted for a password, depending on whether or not the system administrator has activated that level of security.

One caution before we begin our hands-on activities. In order to properly turn off an RS/6000 system, you must be logged in with the authority of a systems administrator so that you can first issue the "Shutdown" command and wait for the "shutdown complete" message. This prevents the RS/6000 system from being interrupted unexpectedly, which can cause information to be lost. For this reason, do not turn the RS/6000 system off unless you are authorized and have first taken the necessary steps.

Armed with this information, you are now ready to use your RS/6000 system. To use the facilities of an RS/6000 system, you must first identify yourself to the system by entering your user ID and password. This is called **logging in** to the RS/6000 System. To log in:

If Your RS/6000 System Is Not Turned On

- ❑ Turn on your display and all peripheral equipment attached to the RS/6000 system.
- ❑ Insert the key into the key-lock mode switch located on the front of the System Unit.
- ❑ Turn the key so that the top edge of the key is pointed toward the "Normal" label above the key-lock mode switch.
- ❑ Turn the RS/6000 System Unit on by flipping the power switch to the "1" or ON position.
- ❑ The computer is now going through its initialization. When you see a screen similar to that shown in Figure 3.1, proceed with the next heading, titled "If Your Computer Is Already Turned On."

Note: This procedure does not apply if you are using a rack-mounted RS/6000 model (Model 930). See your "Operator Guide" for rack-mounted power-up system procedures.

If Your Computer Is Already Turned On

- ❑ If you are using a simple ASCII terminal like those shown in Chapter 2 and the display is dark, check to see if the terminal's power switch is turned on and then press the Enter key.
- ❑ If you are near your RS/6000 System Unit, verify that the key is positioned so that the top edge of the key points toward the "Normal" label above the key-lock mode switch. If you are not near your RS/6000 System Unit (e.g., if you are using a remote ASCII terminal), you must assume that the key is positioned properly.

You should now see a screen similar to that shown in Figure 3.1.

- ❑ Type in your user ID and press "Enter" (⏎).

```
IBM AIX Version 3 for RISC System/6000
© Copyright by IBM and by others 1982, 1990
Login:
```

Figure 3.1. The log-in screen presented by AIX on an RS/6000 system. From this screen, the user enters his or her user ID and password to identify himself or herself to the system.

If security has been activated, you will now be prompted to enter your password.

❑ Type in your password and press "Enter" (↵).

After the RS/6000 system verifies a match between your user ID and your password, you are logged in. The system will then automatically access your user profile and do whatever the system administrator has indicated in that profile. You may be presented with a Welcome message and the "$" command prompt. Alternately, the RS/6000 system may automatically run a program for you (i.e., AIXwindows, AIX Desktop, etc.). In any event, you are now ready to perform useful work.

What Is InfoExplorer?

The AIX operating system for the RS/6000 comes with a program called **InfoExplorer.** InfoExplorer is a tool with which you can access the specially prepared information also provided with every RS/6000 system. This information consists of some articles, a set of user documentation, and course material all specially designed for use with the InfoExplorer program. The articles provide conceptual information and background about RS/6000 systems and the AIX operating system. The user documentation is just what you would find in the many manuals in the AIX operating system user reference library. The course material provides interactive computer education modules on various topics related to RS/6000 hardware or the AIX operating system.

The articles, user documentation, and course materials are stored in the RS/6000 system either on disk or on a CD-ROM. The InfoExplorer program is used to quickly find specific information based on keyword searches or menu prompts and display the needed information on a user's display screen.

Since the user documentation is stored inside the computer, it is called **on-line documentation** or **machine-readable documentation**. Most extensions to the AIX operating system (e.g., AIXwindows Environment/6000) come with on-line documentation about that extension that is simply added to the disk at installation of the extension. Alternately, you can purchase a complete set of the InfoExplorer information that covers the AIX operating system and its extensions on a single CD-ROM. A single CD-ROM can store about 20,000 pages of documentation. The CD-ROM version, called the **IBM RISC System/6000 CD-ROM Hypertext Information Base Library**, simply replaces the disk version of all InfoExplorer information, thus freeing valuable disk space. In order to read the CD-ROM version, the RS/6000 must be equipped with one of the CD-ROM drives described in Chapter 2. However, a single CD-ROM drive can be shared by multiple RS/6000 systems in a local area network.

The on-line user documentation provided with the InfoExplorer information means that the user need not dig through thousands of pages of books in order to find help in a specific area. IBM testing indicated that researching information with on-line documentation was about three times faster than digging through the many books provided with the AIX operating system (and that is after you find the book). On-line documentation is also more convenient than keeping the rather large set of the AIX operating system documentation on a shelf. (**Note:** The documentation for the earlier IBM RT system came in a library of manuals containing over 15,000 pages and taking up over 15 feet of shelf space.) InfoExplorer functions such as **bookmarks** and user **notes** provide familiar convenience tools, allowing users to keep their place in the on-line documentation and make electronic notations specific to their needs. A **Hypertext** function allows for quick access to additional or background information relevant to the topic at hand. With Hypertext, key words and

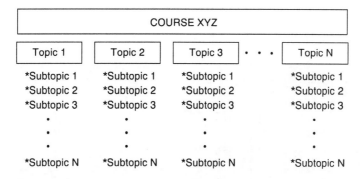

Figure 3.2. InfoTrainer on-line education is organized into courses, topics, and subtopics as shown.

phrases throughout all of the InfoExplorer information are highlighted. When a highlighted term or phrase is selected, more information about that term or phrase is presented. When the user is done with that Hypertext information, the screen returns to where he or she left off.

As mentioned earlier, the InfoExplorer information also contains some on-line courses that provide **On-line Education**. Using a function within the InfoExplorer program called the **InfoTrainer**, the user can select from a series of courses that subsequently will be presented on the user's display, thus providing an interactive learning session. The student is presented with visual information, asked to provide simple responses, and informally quizzed on the topics presented. (The quiz results aren't scored or recorded.)

The educational information is organized as **courses**, **topics**, and **subtopics** as illustrated in Figure 3.2. Depending on the topic selected, it will take between 10 and 45 minutes to complete one topic.

One of the courses provided is called "**Using InfoTrainer**." This course introduces the concept of computer-based education and teaches users how to find their way around the courses, topics, and subtopics.

It is recommended that the user take the "Using InfoTrainer" course before taking any other InfoTrainer courses. Let's take it now.

Taking the First Course with InfoTrainer

The only thing you need to use InfoTrainer is your user ID (and a password if security is activated on your system). Once you have these, you can take the "Using Info-Trainer" course using any RS/6000 workstation or ASCII terminal. However, there

Figure 3.3. If you are an AIX Desktop user, your screen will look like this after logging in.

are three different procedures for taking this course, depending on your RS/6000 hardware and software configuration:

1. AIX Desktop user
2. AIXwindows user
3. Nongraphics user

You must follow the procedure that applies to you. If you are not sure which type of user you are, there is an easy way to tell. First log in to the system, and then return here.

After you have logged in to the system, look at the screen. If you are an AIX Desktop user, you will see a group of graphics images or icons similar to that shown in Figure 3.3. If you are an AIXwindows user, you will see a window like that

AIX command prompt

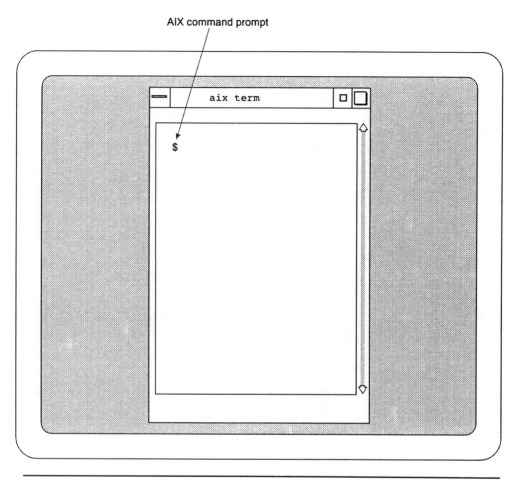

Figure 3.4. If you are an AIXwindows user, your screen will look like this after logging in.

shown in Figure 3.4. If you are a non-graphics-capable user (e.g., an ASCII terminal user), you will see the "$" command prompt and a blinking cursor as shown in Figure 3.5. After you have determined which type of user you are, skip to the correct procedure below. If your system doesn't behave like any of these examples, it means that your RS/6000 system has been customized in some other way. You will have to get assistance from your systems administrator.

Accessing InfoTrainer as an AIX Desktop User

□ Position the RS/6000 system's mouse (see Chapter 2) on a flat surface with some clearance for movement.

AIX command prompt

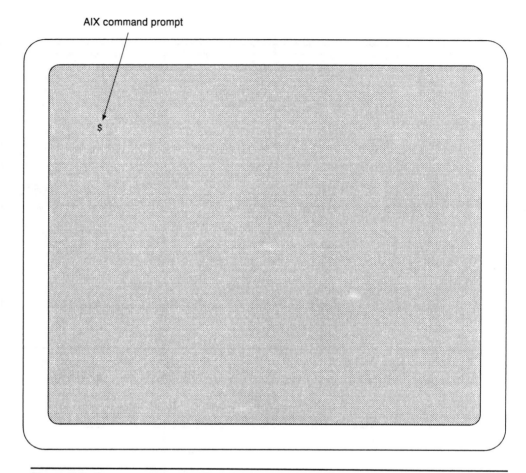

Figure 3.5. If you are a nongraphics user, your screen will look something like this. The AIX command prompt "$" indicates that the system is ready to accept a command.

◻ Rest your hand on the mouse and slide it along the desk surface until you see the hand-shaped cursor moving in conjunction with your sliding the mouse. Slide the mouse so the cursor is positioned directly on top of the InfoExplorer icon shown in Figure 3.6.

Figure 3.6. Graphical image or icon representing the InfoExplorer.

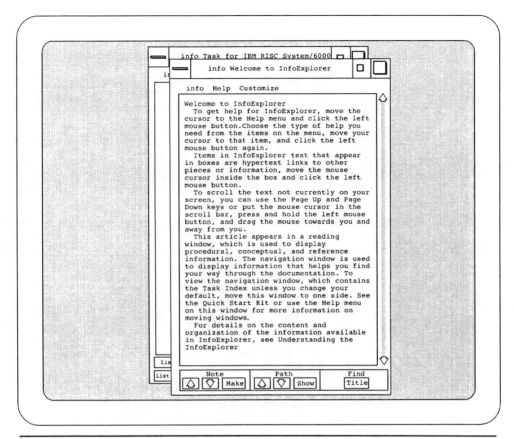

Figure 3.7. Screen presented when you first enter the InfoExplorer function.

- ▢ Click the leftmost mouse button two times in rapid succession.

Two new windows will appear, one overlapping the other as shown in Figure 3.7. The top window is the "Welcome to InfoExplorer" message providing some information basic to using InfoExplorer.

- ▢ Read the "Welcome to InfoExplorer" information.

After you have read the information, it is time to "close" the "Welcome to InfoExplorer" window and proceed.

- ▢ Slide the mouse so the cursor is positioned over the "**close button**" in the upper right-hand portion of the window as shown in Figure 3.8.
- ▢ Press the left mouse button once.

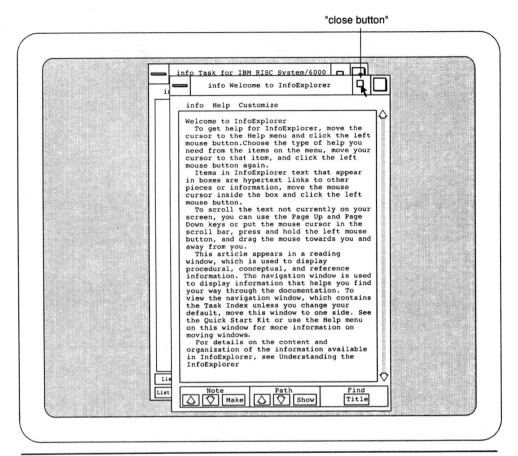

"close button"

Figure 3.8. To remove or "close" the "Welcome to InfoExplorer" window, position the cursor over the "close button" as shown and press the left mouse button.

The "Welcome to InfoExplorer" window disappears, revealing the InfoExplorer "Task Index" shown in Figure 3.9. This is the main menu of information available through InfoExplorer, grouped by tasks you may wish to perform. To get to the Info-Trainer function within the InfoExplorer:

▫ Position the cursor over the block in the lower right-hand corner of the window labeled "Education" as shown in Figure 3.10.

▫ Press the left mouse button once.

You are now presented with the InfoExplorer's "Education menu," shown in Figure 3.11. From here, you can get an overview of the AIX operating system education

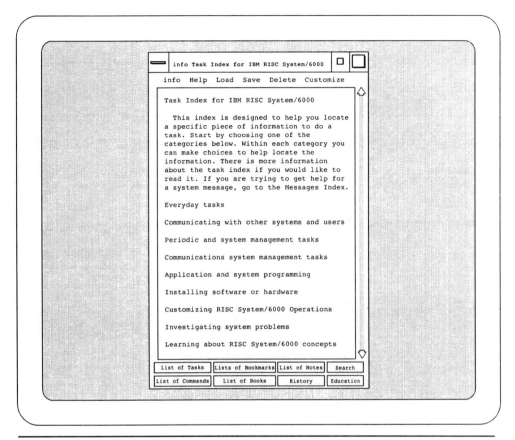

Figure 3.9. The "Task Index" is used to help locate information associated with performing specific RS/6000 system tasks.

tools available for RS/6000, access InfoExplorer articles, or take InfoTrainer interactive courses. You will notice that there are two versions of the "Using InfoTrainer" course: one for users of graphics-capable workstations (as assumed in this procedure) and one for workstations or terminals that are not graphics capable. Now let's take this course:

▢ Position the cursor over the "Using InfoTrainer (Graphical Interface)"
  line of the Education menu.

▢ Press the left mouse button once.

You are now presented with the first screen of the "Using InfoTrainer" interactive course, shown in Figure 3.12.

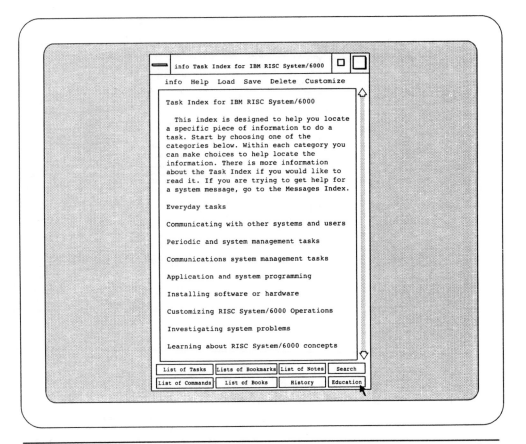

Figure 3.10. Position the cursor over the "Education" block to get to the InfoExplorer "Education menu."

▫ Read the information shown on the screen.

▫ If you are not completely familiar with how to work with windows on the RS/6000 system, position the cursor over the "Scrolling/Resizing Windows" Hypertext and press the left mouse button once. Your screen will look like Figure 3.13. Read all screens of Hypertext information about scrolling and resizing windows. To return back to the "Using InfoTrainer" course, position the cursor over the "Return to InfoTrainer Course" highlighted text presented at the bottom of the last Hypertext screen and press the left mouse button.

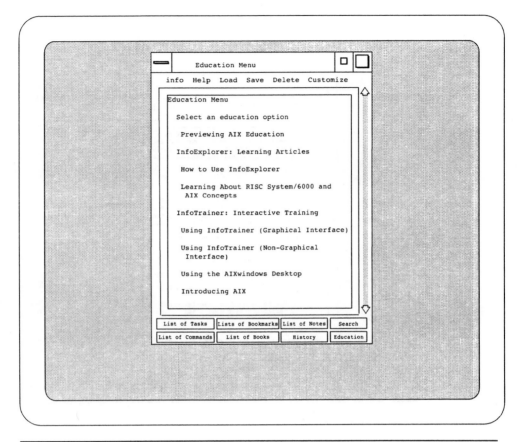

Figure 3.11. From InfoExplorer's "Education menu," you can choose from various articles and training courses.

☐ Follow the directions that appear on the screens in the "Using Info-Trainer" course and you will have no trouble completing the course.

After you complete this course, you are ready to learn more about RS/6000 by taking the other InfoTrainer courses provided with the AIX operating system. You will also be familiar enough with InfoExplorer to read the articles and access the on-line documentation provided with the system. Time spent experimenting with InfoExplorer and InfoTrainer is time well spent.

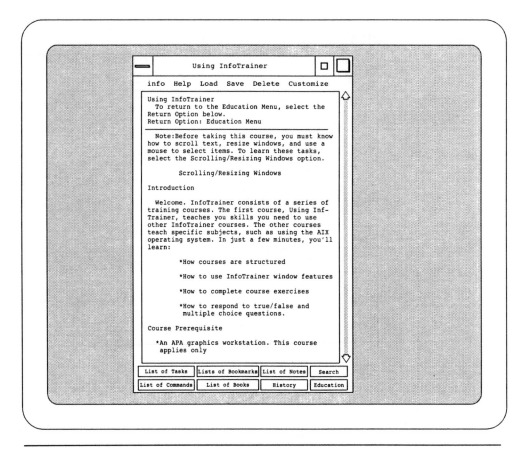

Figure 3.12. First screen shown in the "Using InfoTrainer" course.

Accessing InfoTrainer as an AIXwindows User

- ☐ Position the RS/6000 system's mouse (see Chapter 2) on a flat surface with some clearance for movement.
- ☐ Rest your hand on the mouse and slide it along the desk surface until you see the arrow-shaped cursor moving in conjunction with your sliding the mouse.
- ☐ Slide the mouse so the cursor is positioned anywhere within an "aix term" window as shown in Figure 3.14.
- ☐ Now type "info" (in lowercase letters) at the AIX "$" prompt and press Enter.

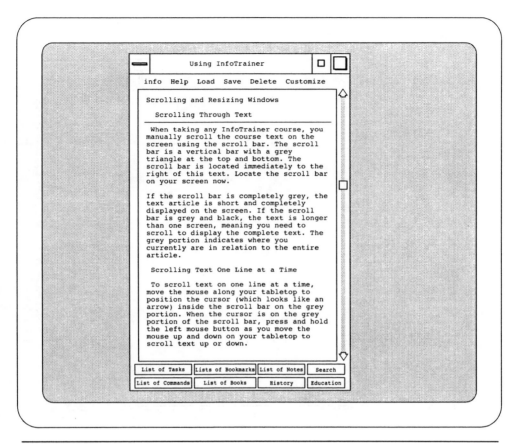

Figure 3.13. After following the Hypertext link, you are presented with text to help you work with windows.

Two new windows will appear, one overlapping the other as shown in Figure 3.15. The top window is the "Welcome to InfoExplorer" message, providing some information basic to using InfoExplorer.

❑ Read the "Welcome to InfoExplorer" information.

After you have read the information, it is time to "close" the "Welcome to InfoExplorer" window and proceed.

❑ Slide the mouse so the cursor is positioned over the **close button** in the upper right-hand portion of the window as shown in Figure 3.16.

AIX command prompt   cursor arrow

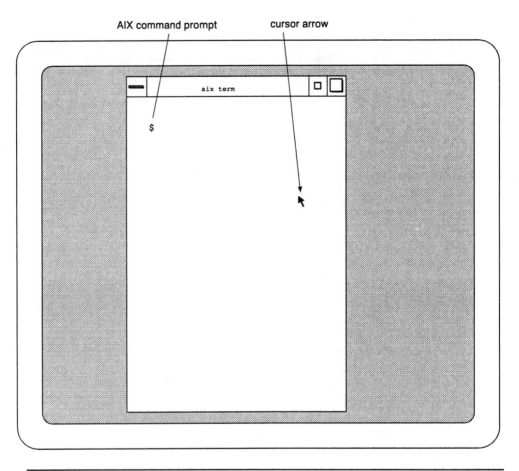

Figure 3.14. You must position the cursor somewhere in the "aix term" window in order to enter a command at the AIX "$" command prompt.

□ Press the left mouse button once.

The "Welcome to InfoExplorer" window disappears, revealing the InfoExplorer "Task Index" window shown in Figure 3.17. This is the main menu of information available through InfoExplorer, grouped by tasks you may wish to perform. To get to the InfoTrainer function within the InfoExplorer:

□ Position the cursor over the block in the lower right-hand corner of the window labeled "Education" as shown in Figure 3.18.

□ Press the left mouse button once.

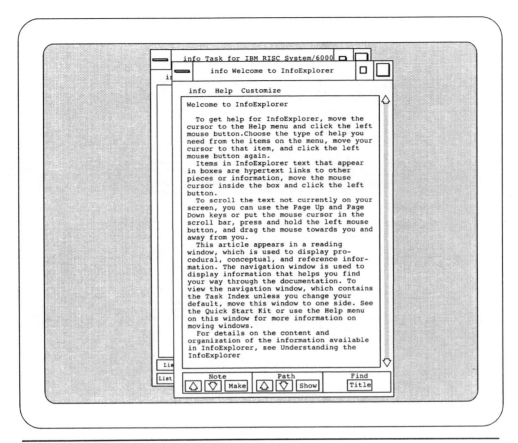

Figure 3.15. Screen presented when a user first enters the InfoExplorer function.

You are now presented with InfoExplorer's "Education Menu" window, shown in Figure 3.19. From here, you can get an overview of education tools available for RS/6000, access InfoExplorer articles, or take InfoTrainer interactive courses. You will notice that there are two versions of this course: one for users of graphics-capable workstations (as assumed in this procedure) and one for workstations or terminals that are not graphics capable. Now let's take this course:

- ▫ Position the cursor over the "Using InfoTrainer (Graphical Interface)" line of the Education menu.
- ▫ Press the left mouse button twice in rapid succession.

You are now presented with the first screen of the "Using InfoTrainer" interactive course, shown in Figure 3.20.

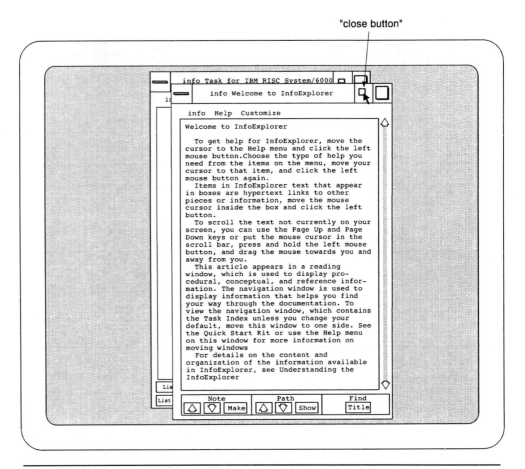

"close button"

Figure 3.16. To remove or "close" the "Welcome to InfoExplorer" window, position the cursor over the "close button" and press the left mouse button.

▫ Read the information shown on the screen.

▫ If you are not completely familiar with how to work with windows on the RS/6000 system, position the cursor over the "Scrolling/Resizing Windows" Hypertext and press the left mouse button once. Your screen will now look like Figure 3.21. Read all screens of Hypertext information about scrolling and resizing windows. To return back to the "Using InfoTrainer" course, position the cursor over the "Return to InfoTrainer Course" highlighted text presented at the bottom of the last Hypertext screen and press the left mouse button.

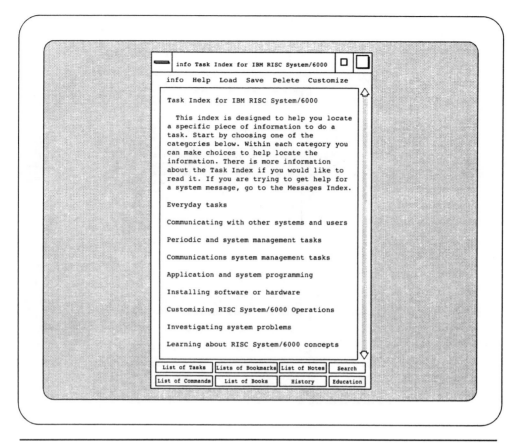

Figure 3.17. The "Task Index" screen is used to help locate information associated with performing specific RS/6000 system tasks.

◻ Follow the directions that appear on the screens in the "Using Info-Trainer" course and you will have no trouble completing the course.

After you complete this course, you are ready to learn more about RS/6000 by taking the other InfoTrainer courses provided with the AIX operating system. You will also be familiar enough with InfoExplorer to read the articles and access the on-line documentation provided with the system. Time spent experimenting with InfoExplorer and InfoTrainer is time well spent.

Accessing InfoTrainer as a Nongraphics User

◻ Type "info" (in lowercase) at the "$" prompt and press Enter.

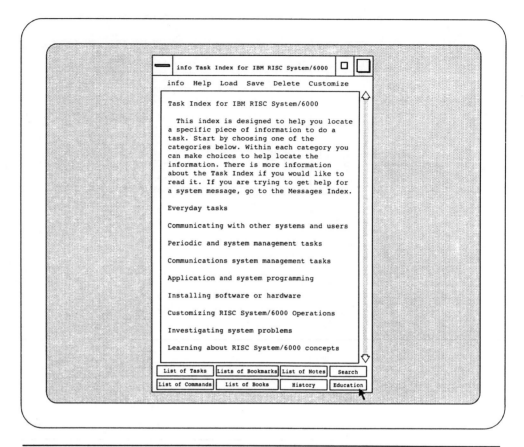

Figure 3.18. Position the cursor over the "Education" block to get to the InfoExplorer "Education menu."

You are now presented with the "Welcome to InfoExplorer" screen shown in Figure 3.22. Read this introductory information.

- Press and hold down the Cntrl key and while holding it down, press the "o" key—then release both. This moves the cursor to the menu items shown along the top of the display.
- Press the Right Arrow key "→" twice to position the cursor over the "Display" menu item.
- Now press the Enter "↵" key.

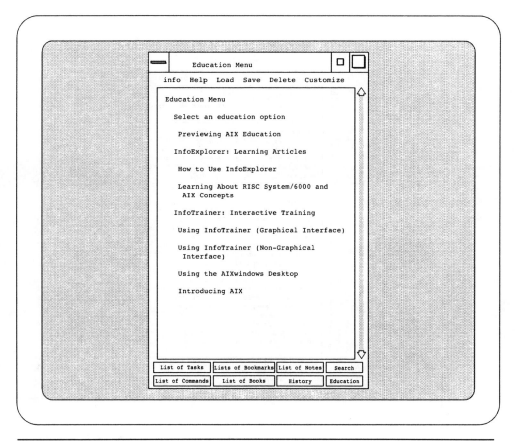

Figure 3.19. From InfoExplorer's "Education menu," the user can choose from various articles and training courses.

You will see some additional menu items appear in a small window, as shown in Figure 3.23.

□ Press the Down Arrow "↓" key three times to position the cursor over the "Education" menu item.

□ Press the Enter "↵" key.

You are now presented with the InfoExplorer "Education menu" screen shown in Figure 3.24.

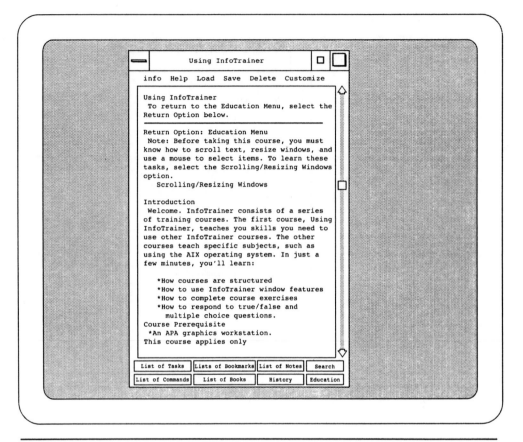

Figure 3.20. First screen shown in the "Using InfoTrainer" course.

❑ Press the Tab key "→" four times to move to the "Using InfoTrainer (Non-Graphical Interface)" item.

❑ Press the Enter "⏎" key.

You now see the first screen in the "Using InfoTrainer" course as shown in Figure 3.25. Now let's learn how to use the keyboard to navigate through this and any other InfoTrainer course:

❑ Press the Tab "→" key one time to position the cursor over the "Scrolling Through Text" Hypertext.

❑ Press the Enter "⏎" key.

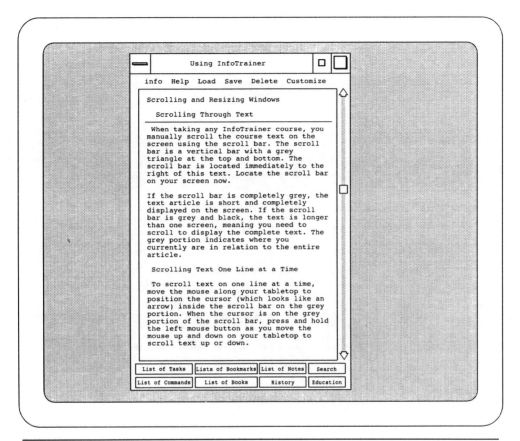

Figure 3.21. After following the Hypertext link, the user is presented with text to help work with windows.

The Hypertext information, shown in Figure 3.26, is now presented on the screen. Follow the directions presented on the screen and you should be able to read the two screens of Hypertext information, return back to the "Using InfoTrainer" course, and then complete the course.

After you complete this course, you are ready to learn more about RS/6000 by taking the other InfoTrainer courses provided with the AIX operating system. You will also be familiar enough with InfoExplorer to read the articles and access the on-line documentation provided with the system. Time spent experimenting with Info-Explorer and InfoTrainer is time well spent.

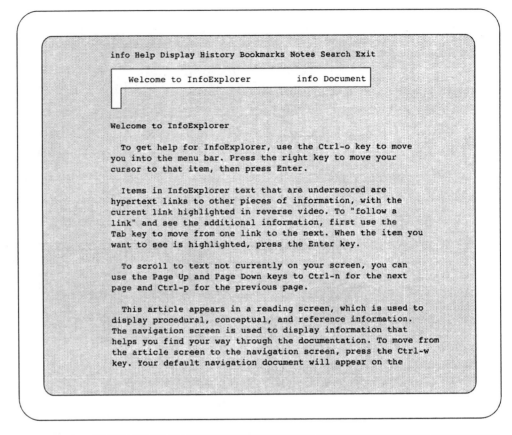

```
    info Help Display History Bookmarks Notes Search Exit

    ┌─────────────────────────────────────────────────────────┐
    │  Welcome to InfoExplorer            info Document        │
    └─┐                                                        
      │
    
    Welcome to InfoExplorer

      To get help for InfoExplorer, use the Ctrl-o key to move
    you into the menu bar. Press the right key to move your
    cursor to that item, then press Enter.

      Items in InfoExplorer text that are underscored are
    hypertext links to other pieces of information, with the
    current link highlighted in reverse video. To "follow a
    link" and see the additional information, first use the
    Tab key to move from one link to the next. When the item you
    want to see is highlighted, press the Enter key.

      To scroll to text not currently on your screen, you can
    use the Page Up and Page Down keys to Ctrl-n for the next
    page and Ctrl-p for the previous page.

      This article appears in a reading screen, which is used to
    display procedural, conceptual, and reference information.
    The navigation screen is used to display information that
    helps you find your way through the documentation. To move from
    the article screen to the navigation screen, press the Ctrl-w
    key. Your default navigation document will appear on the
```

Figure 3.22. "Welcome to InfoExplorer" screen seen by nongraphics users.

THE REAL SOFTWARE—A MODEL

The term "software" is analogous to the term "publication." Newspapers are a category of publication. Annual reports, novels, and Who's Who directories are some other categories of publications. These different categories fill very different needs. The same situation exists with software. There are different categories of software, diverse in function and purpose. We have just explored some special-purpose programs provided with all RS/6000 computers. These programs, however, do not allow you to perform useful work, which is why you bought a computer in the first place. The "real software" that allows the user to perform useful work is purchased separately.

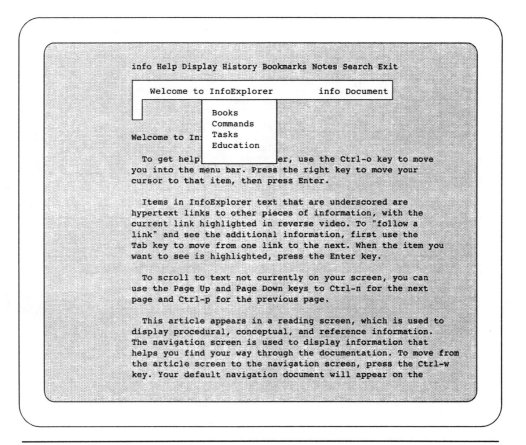

Figure 3.23. The submenu items under the "Display" menu item appear in a window.

The basic categories of "real software" used in RS/6000 systems can be understood through the simple software model shown in Figure 3.27. There are three basic categories or software layers used in RS/6000 systems: the **application program** layer, the **operating system** layer, and the **device driver** layer. Each software layer performs a completely different job, but all three work closely together to perform useful work for the user. While there are some special-purpose programs that do not fit neatly into any of these three categories, the majority of software does. Later chapters will focus on the application and operating system layers of RS/6000 systems. For now, let's briefly look at each of the three layers in our software model.

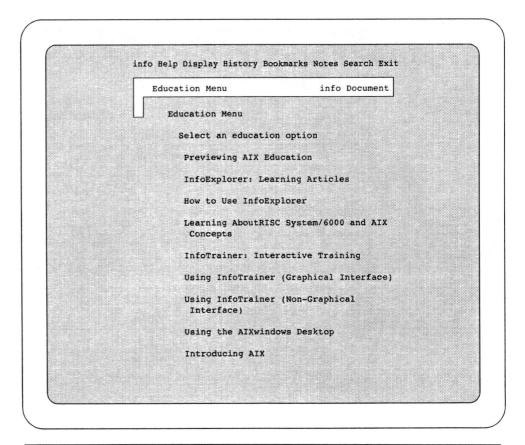

Figure 3.24. "Education menu" presented by InfoExplorer.

Application Programs

The top software layer in the software model is the "application program" layer (highlighted in Figure 3.28). The programs in this layer "apply" RS/6000 systems to a specific task (i.e., computer-aided design, word processing, accounting, etc.) and thus are called "application" programs. They actually perform the task the user purchased the computer for, while the other two layers play important support roles.

The "user's view" arrows in the figure indicate that the user usually interacts with the application program layer and less frequently with the operating system. By working closely with the other software layers, the application program processes

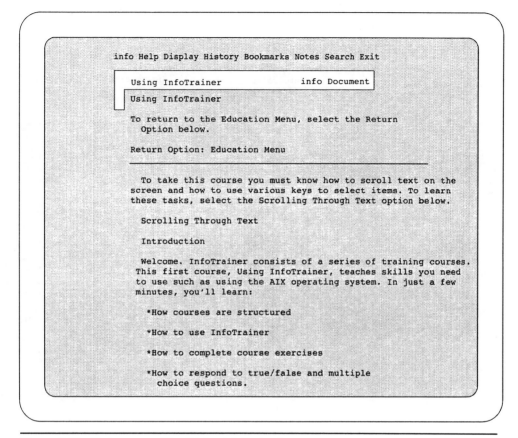

Figure 3.25. First screen of the "Using InfoTrainer" course.

the various keystrokes made by the user and responds by displaying information on the computer's display or some other output device.

As we will see later in the chapter, many programs written for other computers that run the UNIX operating system (i.e., open systems) can be migrated to the RS/6000 and the AIX operating system by the software developer. This allows RS/6000 users to capitalize on many application programs originally developed for other open systems. There is an application program that can help users with just about anything they wish to do. Want a program that computes the number of eggs needed to completely fill a swimming pool? Look around. It may be hard to find, but it probably exists. Some examples of more common functions that application programs provide include accounting, computer-aided design, statistical analysis, finan-

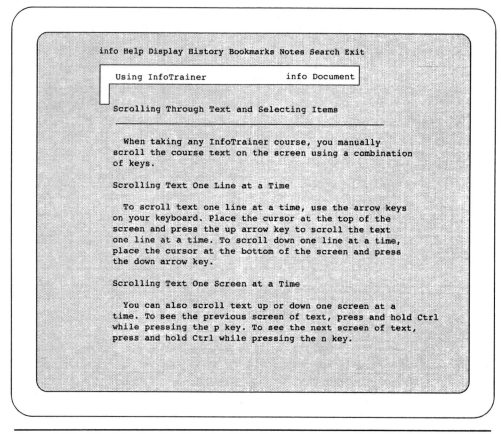

Figure 3.26. After following the Hypertext link, the user is presented with text to help navigate inside InfoTrainer courses.

cial modeling, word processing, desktop publishing, database management, electronic mail, animated computer graphics, and so on. Chapter 4 is devoted to discussing various application programs.

Operating Systems

The next layer in our software model is called the "operating system" (highlighted in Figure 3.29). The operating system must manage the hardware resources of the computer system and perform tasks under the control of application programs and keyboard commands typed by the user. The application program can rely on the operat-

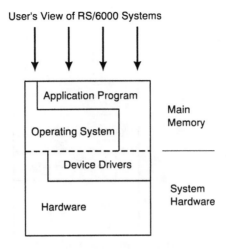

Figure 3.27. Conceptual software model of RS/6000 system's basic software structure. The three layers of the software model work together to perform useful work for the user.

ing system to perform many of the detailed "housekeeping" tasks associated with the internal workings of the computer. Thus, the operating system is said to provide the "environment" in which application programs execute. Operating systems also accept commands directly from the user copy files, change a user's password, and so on.

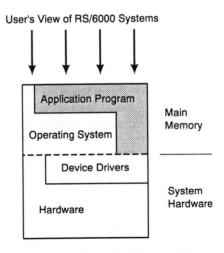

Figure 3.28. The application program software layer of the software model. It is the application program that defines the particular task the computer is performing for the user.

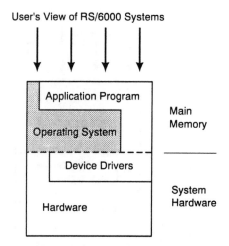

Figure 3.29. The operating system software layer of the software model. The operating system provides the "environment" in which the application program(s) run.

The base operating system used by RS/6000 systems is AIX Version 3. There are also many extensions to the AIX operating system (AIXwindows Environment/6000, AIX Xstation Manager/6000, AIX Personal Computer Simulator/6000, etc.) that allow the user to customize the operating system environment. Chapter 5 will cover the AIX operating system and its extensions.

Device Drivers

The third and final layer of software in our software model is called the "device driver" layer (highlighted in Figure 3.30.). "Device driver" is a fancy term for a set of highly specialized programs, usually written by the manufacturer of computer hardware. These specialized programs reside in RS/6000 Main Memory or often in memory provided right on the adapters they control.

Unlike application programs or operating systems, device drivers are only used by other programs. That is, device drivers never interact directly with the users, and they exist only to help application programs and the operating system perform their tasks. They interact directly with computer hardware elements under the control of the operating system or application program layers. Device drivers also help shield application programs from the hardware specifics of computers, allowing for evolutionary product improvements without sacrificing application program compatibility.

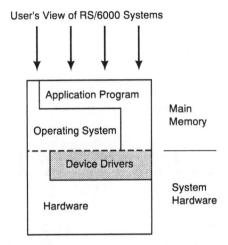

Figure 3.30. The device drivers software layer of the software model. Device drivers directly control the hardware elements of RS/6000 systems and shield application programs and operating systems from hardware details.

How the Layers Work Together

In order to get a feel for how these three software layers work together to perform tasks for the user, let's quickly trace a typical series of events that might occur when you strike keys during a computer session.

In our example depicted in Figure 3.31, a salesperson is using a word-processing application program from an ASCII terminal to type a memo to a prospective customer. Let's set the stage and then see what the various software layers do.

The word-processing application program has just finished processing the latest set of keystrokes and has instructed the operating system to provide the next set of keystrokes when they are available. Since the ASCII terminal used by the salesperson is attached to an async port on the RS/6000, the operating system then asked the async port device driver to provide the next keystroke when available.

Now that the stage is set, let's see what happens as the salesperson continues to type the letter. When the "t" key on the keyboard is pressed to start the next word, the terminal sends the ASCII code corresponding to the "t" character over the EIA-232D cable to the async port on the RS/6000. The async port then interrupts the Main Processor and notifies it that new information is ready for use. Here is where the software layers of our model come into play. First, the device driver verifies that all went well with receiving the information, and then it notifies the operat-

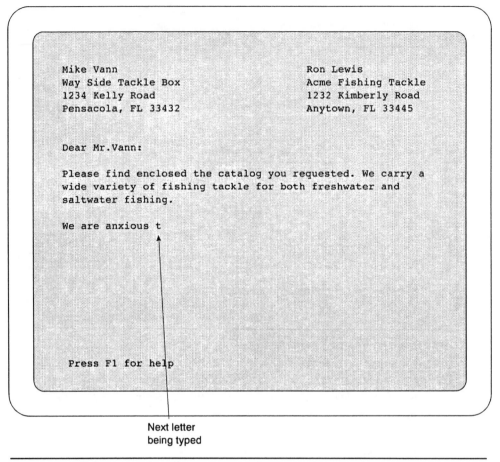

Mike Vann   Ron Lewis
Way Side Tackle Box   Acme Fishing Tackle
1234 Kelly Road   1232 Kimberly Road
Pensacola, FL 33432   Anytown, FL 33445

Dear Mr.Vann:

Please find enclosed the catalog you requested. We carry a
wide variety of fishing tackle for both freshwater and
saltwater fishing.

We are anxious t

Press F1 for help

Next letter
being typed

Figure 3.31. Salesperson is typing a memo using a word-processing application program on an RS/6000 system. The salesperson is typing the letter "t" in the word "to."

ing system that the information is correct, ready, and waiting for use. The operating system then makes the information available to the application program and then reactivates the application program, which was dormant waiting for the next keystrokes. The application program processes the information as necessary, instructs the operating system to wait for the next keystrokes, and the whole thing starts all over again.

For simplicity, I have glossed over many of the detailed steps that the computer must perform simply to process keystrokes. For example, the async port accepts many keystrokes until a batch of keystrokes are ready and only then interrupts the RS/6000 Main Processor. However, our overview of the keystroke process serves to give a basic picture. As complicated as the keystroke process may be, computers easily perform these processor steps in small fractions of a second.

Similar but still more complicated cooperation among the three software layers occurs for most functions performed by the computer, such as reading or writing a file on a disk, creating complex graphics, and so on.

RS/6000 SOFTWARE COMPATIBILITY—WHY IT IS IMPORTANT

Computer systems that run the UNIX operating system have been in existence for many years. As a result, a wide variety of application programs have been developed for the UNIX operating system. The flexibility afforded by virtue of this large and diverse software base allowed computers running the UNIX operating system to fill many different needs. Of course, this sea of available application programs did not exist when the original UNIX operating system was first announced. It took the independent efforts of a great many people over many years' time to develop the large application software base that exists today. In order to capitalize on that software base, application software compatibility was a primary objective in the design of the AIX operating system. That is, most application programs written for UNIX operating systems can easily be migrated to the RS/6000 system and the AIX operating system by the software developer.

It is important to understand that of the three software layers in our software model, compatibility with programs in the application programs layer is the important thing. Why? First of all, application programs typically represent the lion's share of a user's software investment. Further, being forced to abandon an application program due to incompatibilities may also make the user throw away whatever data and training/experience have accumulated with the application program—both of which can be substantial. Some users have developed custom application programs at considerable cost in development time and money. Incompatibility at the application program level would render these programs virtually useless. Finally, and perhaps most importantly, application layer compatibility allows RS/6000 system users to choose from the thousands of application programs that have been developed for the UNIX operating system.

What about the operating system and device driver layers? The ability to run earlier UNIX operating system software is not important for several reasons. Operating systems typically represent only a small fraction of the user's software investment. Further, a new operating system is usually necessary to allow the users to have access to new features of the computer system not considered by the programmers of the old operating system. Of course, one of the primary purposes of the device driver layer is to allow the computer hardware to change without affecting compatibility with the operating system and application programs. This is done by changing the way a device driver interacts with the hardware without changing the way the device driver interacts with the operating system or application programs. The user is supplied with new device drivers to support RS/6000 hardware.

INSIDE RS/6000 COMPATIBILITY

To understand RS/6000 compatibility you must understand a little about the way application programs are written. First, a programmer writes an application program's instructions or **code** using a **programming language** (e.g., C, FORTRAN, COBOL, etc.). A programming language is basically a library of computer instructions (easily understood by programmers) from which a programmer may choose to write programs. The list of programming language instructions that make up an application program is called the program's **source code**. In order to run the application program on a computer, the source code instructions must be converted into instructions a computer can understand. This conversion process is called **compiling** the program. When the source code is compiled, the result is called **object code** and can be directly executed by the computer hardware.

In addition to programming languages, the programmer can use predefined lists of operating system commands to do things like start programs, present menus, and so on. These predefined lists are called **shell scripts**. With this background, let's look at the way RS/6000 systems and the AIX operating system provide compatibility with programs written for the UNIX operating system.

The first thing to understand about RS/6000 compatibility is that any model of the RS/6000 family is **object code compatible** with all other RS/6000 models. That is, you can take the object code for an application program written for, say, an RS/6000 Model 320H, load it on a properly configured RS/6000 Model 550, and run the program with no changes.

Most application programs written for UNIX operating systems — and other AIX operating systems on the RT system, PS/2, or S/390 computers — will be highly **source code compatible** with RS/6000 systems. This means that a programmer must make some (usually minor) changes in the application program source code, load the source code written for the UNIX operating system on an RS/6000 system, and then recompile the source code using the appropriate RS/6000 compilers. The new object code generated can then be executed on the RS/6000 system.

The **syntax** or grammar of source code for various languages is defined by independent standards bodies. This compliance to industry standards is what makes an "open system" open and is the essence behind RS/6000 software compatibility.

Application Programs

In the last chapter we learned that three basic software layers in RS/6000 systems cooperate to perform useful work for the user. This chapter concentrates on the top layer of our software model — application programs (highlighted in Figure 4.1). It is the application program that actually "applies" the RS/6000 system's computational power to a particular task. Some RS/6000 users choose from available application programs designed, written, and sold by other companies. These are called **prewritten** application programs. Other users choose to design and write their own **custom application** programs or use a combination of prewritten and custom application programs. This chapter will look at both application program alternatives. While some basic types of prewritten application programs commonly used with

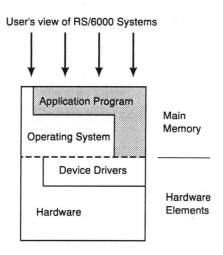

Figure 4.1. RS/6000 system's software model with the application program layer highlighted. Application programs "apply" the RS/6000 system's computational strength to users' tasks.

RS/6000 systems will be discussed, this chapter is by no means a consumers' guide to application programs. Comprehensive coverage of the many application program products available today for RS/6000 systems would fill many books and would quickly become obsolete. This chapter will help the reader make more informed decisions when building an application programs library.

CAN PREWRITTEN PROGRAMS FIT THE BILL?

Today's prewritten application programs range from simple programs that concentrate on a very specific task, to powerful and very complex groups of programs designed to work together. They perform myriad functions as diverse as the environments in which you find computers today. There are many prewritten application programs that are useful in almost any environment (e.g, word processors, spreadsheets, etc.). These are known as **cross-industry** application programs because they are not specific to any particular industry segment. Other prewritten applications address the specialized needs of a particular industry (e.g., manufacturing, utilities, etc.). These are called **industry-specific** application programs. Let's examine some examples of each.

Cross-Industry Application Programs

Just as a pencil and paper can be useful in almost any environment, there are application programs that provide basic tools useful in almost any environment. Despite the diversity of such cross-industry application programs, most of them are an implementation or combination of five basic functions, which I will call the **"Big Five"**:

1. Word processing
2. Spreadsheets
3. Database management
4. Graphics and presentation
5. Communications

There are many cross-industry application programs that are direct and general implementations of these Big Five functions, resulting in tools more flexible than a pencil and paper. Other cross-industry application programs combine specialized implementations of the Big Five functions, resulting in programs more tailored to more specific yet still commonly needed functions such as accounting (database), project scheduling (database and graphics), and so on.

Let's quickly examine the Big Five:

Word Processing

Word-processing application programs allow RS/6000 systems to generate virtually any kind of document. The user types documents in on the keyboard in much the same way as with a typewriter. Since the document is temporarily stored in memory, it can easily be modified.

Basic capabilities found in even the simplest word-processing program include changing, inserting, moving, and deleting text. Today's word-processing programs offer other important features such as spell checking, grammar checking, automatic generation of table of contents, page numbers, indexes, and so on. A more advanced form of word processing, called **desktop publishing**, allows you to lay out text and graphics on a page and print the results on a high-quality printer. The advantages of word processing over manual methods plus the common need to create documents has made word processing one of the most popular applications of computers today.

An RS/6000 system equipped with a good-word processing application program will quickly spoil anyone used to a typewriter and rival the conventional dedicated word-processing systems. In ASCII terminal environments, the performance of RS/6000 systems allows even the smallest model to support many heavy word-processing users. As a workstation, the graphics resolution of RS/6000 systems and the Display PostScript support in the AIX operating system lend themselves to the generation of high-quality text and graphics used in desktop publishing.

After you finish the document, you can store it on the disk or a diskette. The 1.44 MB diskettes used by RS/6000 systems can hold over 700 pages of text and can fit in a shirt pocket or small purse, providing easy transportability of documents. Letter-quality printers like those discussed in Chapter 2 generate very clear and crisp documents.

Spreadsheets

Computers originally were developed to do numerical calculations. A popular way of working with numbers on RS/6000 systems is through "spreadsheet" application programs. These are programs that allow you to enter numbers and equations in a free-form manner. Virtually any calculations you can do on a sheet of paper can be done automatically through the use of a spreadsheet program. Common applications of spreadsheet models include financial analysis, sales monitoring, forecasting, and simple statistics. Through these mathematical models, "What if" questions are quickly answered by changing the parameters (cells) in the model and watching the effects of the change ripple through the entire spreadsheet. Spreadsheets were quick to catch on because the "blackboard" format employed by these programs is very familiar and immediately useful to even novice users.

The large memory systems available in RS/6000 computers and the AIX operating system allow for the construction of extremely complex and powerful spreadsheet models. The performance of RS/6000 computers will allow them to do many calculations ("recalcs") associated with large spreadsheet models quickly. Some spreadsheet application programs can take advantage of the high-resolution graphics capabilities of RS/6000 workstations to generate high-quality graphs.

Database Management

In order to deal with large amounts of information efficiently, it is necessary to organize the information in a uniform manner. For example, the information in a telephone book is organized into an alphabetical list of names, addresses, and telephone numbers. If you have ever lifted a Manhattan telephone book, you know that phone books can contain a fair amount of information.

Computers also require information to be organized in some fashion. **Database management** application programs are the major tool for organizing large amounts of information through computers. Database managers typically organize information into **files, records,** and **fields**. Don't be intimidated by the words. This is exactly how the information in a phone book is structured. Figure 4.2 shows an example telephone book listing and the corresponding computer database structure. The phone book itself is analogous to a "file" or set of information, also called a

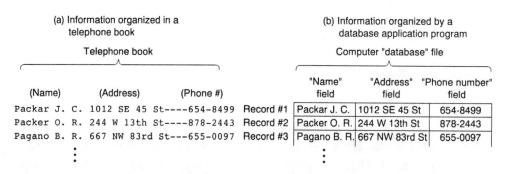

Figure 4.2. (a) The information structure used in a telephone book. (b) The same information organized into a database structure. In order to efficiently manipulate large amounts of information, it is necessary to first organize the information into a consistent format. The organization used by database application programs is not unlike that used in a telephone book.

database. The information about one person in the phone book would be analogous to a record. The records contain the information for a given entry, and each record contains the same information about its respective entry. In this case, a record would contain the name, address, and phone number of the person. Each of these three items would be analogous to a field within a record. For example, the address part of a phone book entry would be called the "address field."

Manually looking up information in a phone book quickly becomes fatiguing. The same is true for manually manipulating any large body of information. Once the information is entered into a database application program, however, it can be retrieved quickly and easily. Databases can contain information about a store's inventory, a library's books, personnel records, medical records, or virtually any other type of information. Organizations such as banks, airlines, and insurance companies commonly use extremely large databases shared by many users. Office workers and executives may use database application programs to maintain personal telephone books and appointment calendars, for example. Many database application programs also provide a complete programming language, which allows users to customize their database environments.

The fixed disks available with RS/6000 systems provide enough storage for the construction of extremely large databases. The high levels of performance available through RS/6000 systems help speed up queries and other database activities.

Graphics and Presentation

Since Neanderthal times, we have drawn images to present and interpret information. Images are native to humans and thus are both enjoyable and powerful communication devices. The greater the amount of information to be conveyed, the greater the need for graphic representations. It is no surprise, then, that many environments (business, academic, scientific, etc.) rely heavily on images to convey information to customers, peers, employees, management, and so on. With the increased use of computers, it is also no surprise that computer-generated images (called "computer graphics") are common today.

Business graphics application programs provide the user with a tool to construct a computer image. These programs vary widely in price and function. Some products accept numerical information from the user and create representative line graphs, bar charts, and pie charts. Others provide the user with a free-form drawing tool, with the limitations being only those of the user's imagination. They may have predefined libraries of images such as animals, airplanes, ships, symbols, state and country outlines, and so on.

Once an image is defined, it can be merged into documents through desktop publishing, saved on disk, printed, or photographed to make full-color slide presentations. Some programs can sequence through a series of images and provide auto-mated presentations right on the computer screen.

The graphics subsystems of RS/6000 and associated high-function displays provide high-quality graphics capability including real-time animation. A 1280×1024 PEL image with literally millions of different colors can be created. This allows for the creation of extremely lifelike images. The performance available in the larger RS/6000 workstations can support full motion or animation of these images. The high-quality laser printers and plotters that work with RS/6000 systems can be used to make hard copies of the graphics images.

In more advanced applications, computer-generated graphics are becoming more important to research scientists who must analyze ever-increasing amounts of data. These large sets of data may be the result of simulations performed on super-computers, for example. Through the use of advanced computer graphics techniques, large amounts of information can be displayed in ways more meaningful to scientists analyzing the information. Graphically displaying large amounts of information, called **visualization**, is becoming increasingly important to fields such as environ-mental research, astronomy, computational chemistry, and medical imaging. Offer-ings like the AIX Visualization Data Explorer/6000 (5765-057) and the more power-ful IBM POWER Visualization System (built around RS/6000 systems) provide a foundation on which applications can be built to handle and graphically display extremely large sets of data.

Communications

Simply stated, it is the job of the communications application program to move information from one computer to another. You can think of communications as the thing that ties the other four of the "Big Five" together. For example, communica-tions allows documents generated by word-processing application programs or images created by graphics application programs to be electronically sent anywhere in the world in just minutes. Since communications application programs often work so closely with the other types of application programs, they often are combined with the others into a single product. For example, a spreadsheet or database applica-tion program may be capable of directly communicating with a larger host computer in order to access the large computer's database. The user need not be bothered with the details of communication and may not even know it is occurring.

The AIX operating system for RS/6000 systems itself has significant commu-nications support built in, as we will see in the next chapter. RS/6000 systems have many communications options that allow them to participate in many industry-stan-dard communications networks. Chapter 6 is devoted to discussing example RS/6000 communications configurations.

Another area of communications that is emerging in importance to the business community is called **telephony**. Telephony is the marriage of computer automation and telephone communications systems. There are many examples of telephony in use today, from computer-based answering or "phone mail" systems to automated telemarketing applications. The RS/6000 family, along with IBM Callpath DirectTalk/6000 Voice Processing System, provides a platform on which telephony applications can be developed. The DirectTalk/6000 family of products includes software (i.e., Callpath DirectTalk/6000) and hardware (i.e., 9291 Single Voice Server and 9295 Multiple Voice Server) that allows a programmer to more easily construct many different types of telephony applications. IBM has announced its intention to add **voice recognition** technology in Callpath DirectTalk/6000 in the future, which will allow telephone users to use verbal commands to interact with the telephony applications.

Variations on the Big Five

Many cross-industry application programs have been developed by employing combinations or variations of the Big Five functions above to perform various tasks. The first and simplest variation of the Big Five application programs is combining several of the Big Five functions into a single, all-in-one application program product. Just like all-in-one food processors and all-in-one pocket knives, all-in-one application programs enjoy widespread popularity. All-in-one products, also called **integrated** application programs, can be very useful in almost any environment. There are application programs that combine, for example, the spreadsheet, database, and graphics programs into a single product. Another approach is to provide a group of application program **modules** designed to work together. The modular approach maintains many of the advantages of integrated programs while allowing the user to purchase only the functions he or she needs.

Integrated and modular application programs have some advantages over an equivalent collection of independent application programs. First, since all the functions (e.g., word processing, graphics, database) are designed by the same person/firm, the user sees a consistent user interface across the different functions. The user doesn't have to remember the different conventions presented by two independent application programs. Another advantage of series and integrated application programs is that they allow the user to easily move information between the different functions within the package. For example, data generated by the spreadsheet part of the integrated program can be transferred to the graphics part to produce graphs of the information. This data transfer may not be so simple between independent application programs. A disadvantage of integrated applications, however, is that you don't select the individual applications (e.g., word processing, database, graphics); they are chosen for you by the developer of the integrated application program. For example, if you don't like the word-processing part of the integrated package, you can't replace it.

Aside from integrated application programs that are direct combinations of the Big Five, programmers have developed other types of application programs by combining more specialized versions of the Big Five. These combinations of the Big Five applications are designed to perform more specific tasks, such as appointment calendaring (database), telephone management (database and communications), and so on.

Industry-Specific Application Programs

The cross-industry application programs discussed to this point are of a highly general nature, able to fill the common needs found in even the most diverse environments. They were designed to be as general as possible to cover the largest market possible — sort of the "all things to all people" approach.

In most cases, users will also have some needs that are more specialized to their particular industry or environment. Therefore, another type of prewritten application program (called an **industry-specific** application program) may be desirable. As the term "industry-specific" implies, this type of prewritten application program is specially designed to address the needs of a well-defined environment. A research lab office has different application program needs than a dental practice. Each would benefit by an appropriate prewritten, yet highly specialized industry-specific application program. Many software companies have put a great deal of effort into developing industry-specific programs for the UNIX operating system. Since RS/6000 systems and the AIX operating system were designed to accommodate application programs originally written for the UNIX operating system, many of these programs have been migrated to the RS/6000 by the software publisher. This allows RS/6000 systems to be useful in highly specialized business/professional/scientific environments.

There are industry-specific applications designed for engineers, manufacturing companies, insurance companies, real estate offices, medical practices, construction companies, law practices, churches, and so on. As with cross-industry application programs, industry-specific programs are modular — meaning that they are really several different programs designed to work closely together. Each program or "module" can be used individually or share information with the others. Modular programs allow you to pick and choose only the modules you need, which reduces costs for those not needing "the works."

An example of a modular, industry-specific application program is IBM's **Computer-Aided Three Dimensional Interactive Application (CATIA).** CATIA

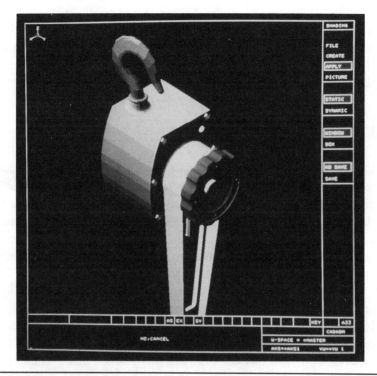

Figure 4.3. CATIA is used by engineers to model three-dimensional objects inside the RS/6000 system.

is a tool used by engineers to design and manufacture mechanical components and mechanisms. With CATIA, an engineer working on an RS/6000 equipped with a high-function display can design a mechanical component in three-dimensional space as a solid object. This is called **Computer-*A*ided *D*esign** (CAD). Once the object is modeled in the CATIA, it can be easily rotated to view it from any angle (Figure 4.3). It can also be passed to other programs that can apply stresses to the component and check for problems. The component can be matched to other components modeled in CATIA to make sure they will fit together without interference.

After the engineer is satisfied with the design, the **Computer-*A*ided *M*anufacturing (CAM)** modules of CATIA can automatically generate the highly specialized **numerical control program** used by computerized manufacturing equipment (e.g., mills and lathes) to manufacture the part. Other industry-specific computer-aided design packages for the RS/6000 help electrical engineers design electrical circuitry, seismologists analyze earthquakes, scientists statistically analyze experimentation results, and so on.

And these are just a few examples of industry-specific application programs.

Many software companies have written industry-specific application programs for use on RS/6000 systems, and new application programs are appearing almost daily. Before considering custom software (discussed next), industry-specific software should be carefully considered.

CUSTOM APPLICATION PROGRAMS

Cross-industry and industry-specific application programs fit many needs like a mitten fits a hand. They are readily available, flexible, and convenient tools. In some cases, however, users may find that the fit of their application program needs to be that of a tight glove. This is especially true in environments where RS/6000 systems are needed to perform highly unusual and specific tasks or where there is a need to conform to existing procedures. In these cases, it is often better to develop **custom** application programs written to exact specifications.

Custom applications are tailored to specific needs. Custom application programs are usually written by a programmer within the company or by an outside consulting firm. In either case, the basic development steps are to first define a software specification that describes what the program(s) will do. Then a preliminary version of the program is written that demonstrates the function that eventually will be in the final program. This preliminary version is evaluated by the user and the specification is altered to reflect any needed changes. Last, the final program is written and then installed at the user's location. Typically, training will be provided by the developer, and any problems are ironed out. Once the user accepts the program, the software then has to be supported. That is, users will need a place to go when they have questions not addressed by the manuals. Support also includes making necessary changes to the application program as the user's needs change over time. This kind of ongoing support is critical to the success of any computer automation project.

Most of the time, custom application program development is initially more expensive and time-consuming than the prewritten application program approach. In many environments, however, this additional expense and time can be recovered by the increased productivity that can result from custom applications that precisely fit the needs of the environment. An additional benefit of custom application programs is their ability to change as your needs change. Getting major modifications to prewritten application programs may be difficult or impossible in some cases. The RS/6000 functions and programming tools provide a very productive software development environment. Chapter 5 will discuss some of the programmer productivity and migration tools used with RS/6000 systems.

5

AIX for the RS/6000

Few areas in information processing create more confusion and apprehension than the operating system layer of our software model shown in Figure 5.1. This chapter will help remove some of the mystery associated with the *Advanced Interactive eXecutive* (AIX) operating system used with all RS/6000 systems. The reader will become familiar with basic operating system terms such as "interactive processing" and "multiuser" and then move in for a closer look at the AIX operating system on the RS/6000 computers.

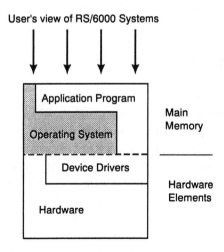

Figure 5.1. The Operating System layer of our software model plays a housekeeping role in the RS/6000 system.

INTRODUCTION TO OPERATING SYSTEM CONCEPTS

The operating system provides the necessary interface that allows the user and application programs to interact with RS/6000 computers. The user can interact directly with the operating system's user interface to manage files on a disk, start application programs, print files, and so on. The operating system also performs tasks directly under the control of application programs without any user assistance. The application program initiates tasks by directly interacting with the operating system through the *Application Program Interface* (API). This is simply a set of operating system commands that can be issued directly by the application program. The API simplifies the job of the application programmer, who need not get involved with the details of hardware interaction. Further, when an application program uses the API, it is shielded from changes in the computer hardware as new computers are developed. That is, the operating system (and device drivers) can be changed to support new computer hardware while preserving the API unchanged, allowing application programs to run unchanged on the new computer.

In order to understand the job of the operating system, it is necessary to understand a few basic concepts:

- Batch versus interactive processing
- Multiuser
- Multitasking

Batch versus Interactive Processing

There are two basic types of work a computer can perform: **batch processing** and **interactive processing**. To understand the difference between these two concepts, let's use an analogy and examine the difference between communications through the postal service and those through the telephone.

If you wish to ask a distant friend some questions, you can either write a letter or phone. With the first option you gather all of your thoughts, put them on paper, and then submit the letter to a mailbox. A few days later (assuming your friend is responsive) you go to your mailbox and you get the responses to your questions in the form of a document. This is analogous to batch processing with a computer in that you submit a request for the computer to answer some question(s) or perform some task(s). Some time later (from minutes to days) you can go to the printer and get the computer's responses in the form of a report. In the early days of computing, batch processing was the only alternative for computer interaction. You would sub-

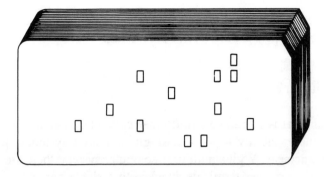

Figure 5.2. Earlier computer systems used paper cards to input programs and data. The information was encoded on the cards by punching hole patterns.

mit your request (called a **batch job**) to the computer by placing a stack of computer punch cards (see Figure 5.2) in an electromechanical device called a card reader. The computer would read the cards, perform the requested task(s), and respond by generating a computer printout. Today, batch processing still has its place, but the batch jobs are usually submitted by typing commands into a computer terminal rather than by using punched cards. However, some card readers are still in use today.

Moving back to our analogy, sometimes you can't simply write down your list of questions in a letter because some of the questions you have will depend on the answer to one or more initial questions. In this case, you either have to send several letters back and forth between you and your friend or call your friend and have a dialogue over the phone. You also might want to call your friend rather than write if you need an answer to your question in a hurry. Having a dialogue with your friend over the phone would be analogous to interactive processing on a computer. With interactive processing, you have a dialogue with the computer system from a terminal. That is, you type in questions or requests for activity and the computer immediately responds. The primary advantage of interactive processing is that the user gets an immediate response, which is required in many applications (e.g., computer-aided design, airline reservations, or a retail checkout line). Interactive processing was developed after batch processing and is now widely used in most computer applications.

Many applications of computers use a combination of batch and interactive processing. For example, a payroll clerk might type information from time cards into a computer terminal in a dialogue style (interactive processing). Once all time cards are entered and verified to be correct, the clerk could issue a command to the terminal that tells the computer to print all checks (a batch job). The clerk would later get the checks from the printer. The AIX operating system on the RS/6000 system supports both batch and interactive processing.

What Is Multiuser?

A computer is said to be a **multiuser** computer system if the hardware and software have the capability to share a single computer system among two or more users simultaneously. With a multiuser computer system, there are from two to many hundreds of computer terminals attached to a single computer. Each terminal provides its user with a "window" into the computer system and allows the user to perform tasks independently of all other users. While the single computer system is being used simultaneously by many users, each user is unaware of the activities of the other users and seems to have his own computer system. However, a user may see the computer "slow down" (increase response time) as more and more users sign on to the computer and start doing work.

There are several advantages of a multiuser computer system over single-user systems. Since the computer system hardware and programs can be simultaneously shared by many users, no one has to stand in line waiting for a turn on the computer. Everyone (assuming there are enough terminals attached) has access to the computer whenever it is needed to do a job. Other advantages offered by a multiuser system are in the areas of security, accounting, backup/recovery, and so on.

The AIX operating system and the RS/6000 can act as either a single-user technical workstation or a multiuser computer system.

What Is Multitasking?

Many people confuse multitasking with the term "multiuser" just discussed. The latter refers to the capability to share a single computer system among two or more users simultaneously. **Multitasking**, also called **multiapplication**, is the ability to simultaneously run two or more independent application programs for a single user. The opposite of multitasking is **single tasking**, which means that the computer user must finish using one application program before another can be started. The AIX operating system used with RS/6000 systems supports a full multitasking environment.

There are many environments in which multitasking is helpful. The office environment, for example, is one in which workers are often interrupted in the middle of one task to perform another. The multitasking capability of operating systems fits naturally into this interrupt-driven environment by allowing the user to easily switch back and forth between several simultaneously active application programs as the interruptions occur. Another advantage afforded by multitasking is the ability to have the computer system perform batch processing tasks while you are simultaneously working with some other application program. This type of batch processing is called **background processing.** With background processing, a programmer could start a compile (batch processing) and then immediately go to work on some other program. An engineer could start a finite element analysis of a mechanical design (batch processing) and then immediately begin working on another design project. Without the background-processing capability provided through multitasking, the user would have to wait for the batch processing to complete before going on to any other tasks.

AIX—An Executive Overview

The UNIX operating system was originally developed by AT&T's Bell Labs in 1969. Over the years, it has continually been enhanced by various independent organizations (both academic and business), often in a nonstructured way. These independent efforts collectively resulted in a very powerful, somewhat cryptic, often awkward, and usually flexible operating system. The UNIX operating system became popular for several reasons. First, AT&T licensed the operating system to many different computer manufacturers, which offered the UNIX operating system for their computers rather than choosing to write their own operating systems. Second, the UNIX operating system is prevalent in colleges and universities. As students learned the UNIX operating system in these academic environments, it was only natural that they would seek out systems after entering the nonacademic world. Finally, the C programming language fostered by the UNIX operating system is a highly popular one, offering very flexible and powerful programming structures.

The UNIX operating system has evolved to be the basis for the **open systems** marketplace, where compatibility with industry standards is the hallmark. Compatibility means that programs written for one brand of "open system" can easily be migrated to another brand. The open system concept is also good for application program developers since they can easily offer their products on many different brands of computers. This is also good for users because they have a multitude of software from which to choose no matter which brand of open system they buy. On the down side, open systems discourage vendors from offering programming features unique to their systems, in that compatibility problems can arise as they diverge from industry standards. This tends to hold back some innovative ideas in the name of compatibility and makes product differentiation more difficult.

IBM took the basic UNIX operating system and incorporated many enhancements developed by other organizations (e.g., UC Berkeley), added many enhancements of their own, and came out with their version called the **Advanced *I*nteractive e*X*ecutive (AIX)**. An entire family of AIX operating system products was developed, comprised of AIX operating system versions for the smaller Personal System/2 computers, RS/6000 computers, and the larger System/370 and System/390 family of mainframe computers. This open system approach was a departure from IBM's proprietary systems like that of the AS/400 minicomputer or the MVS operating system for IBM's S/370 and S/390 mainframes. The RS/6000 and the associated version of the AIX operating system represents IBM's second-generation operating system workstation/server. (The IBM RT System was the first.)

The AIX operating system for the RS/6000 is a multitasking, multiuser operating system adhering to industry standards. The base AIX operating system product itself provides all of the essential functions necessary to make up a complete computer system. There are, however, several separately purchased extensions to the AIX operating system that, when installed, become a part of the operating system, as shown in Figure 5.3. These extensions each add new functions to the AIX operating system. This building-block approach allows each user to select only the functions needed, minimizing software costs and required hardware resources.

The AIX operating system and its extensions perform all housekeeping tasks for the RS/6000 and interact with users to do things like start application programs, change passwords, erase files, and so on. The base AIX operating system comes with command-driven user interfaces that require the user to type in somewhat cryptic commands. AIXwindows Environment/6000 is an extension to the AIX operating system that provides an easier-to-use graphical user interface. These graphical user interfaces, along with the *System Management Interface Tool* (SMIT) and on-line documentation (InfoExplorer), provided as standard, make the RS/6000 version of the AIX operating system easier to use than any of its previous versions. The AIX operating system maintains a high level of compatibility with earlier UNIX operating system versions and industry standards to provide compatibility with many application programs written for other open systems. IBM has also added improvements such as a more flexible disk management approach, improved security, and better data availability. Traditional UNIX operating system application development tools are addressed (e.g., the Source Code Control System, subroutine libraries, and the "Make" command) as well as some newer tools (e.g., object-oriented programming and computer-aided software engineering products). The AIX operating system communications functions address traditional UNIX operating system communications (e.g., asynchronous ASCII protocol), current industry standards (e.g., TCP/IP and the Network File System), and the IBM System Network architecture (e.g., 3270 emulation and LU 6.2 protocols). Finally, Personal System/2 computers

User's view of RS/6000 System

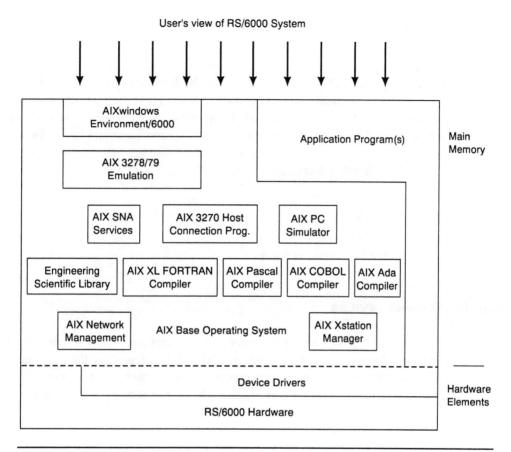

Figure 5.3. The basic functions necessary to provide a complete computer system are provided as standard with AIX. Optional extension products can be added in a building block fashion as necessary to add function to AIX.

(or Personal Computers) can be attached to RS/6000 systems in order to share disk, printers, data, and so forth. Through the AIX Personal Computer Simulator/6000, you can even execute many Personal System/2 application programs on the RS/6000.

Basically, IBM has started with the UNIX operating system base, incorporated enhancements made by many organizations, and added some of their own ideas, all without losing compatibility with industry standards (POSIX, SVID2, or X/open). The AIX operating system with the RS/6000 is an "open system," and IBM has stated the intention of evolving the AIX operating system to conform to new industry standards as they emerge.

A CLOSER LOOK AT AIX

The previous section provided an overview of the AIX operating system (5756-030). Even though the AIX operating system for the RS/6000 systems is easier to use than the earlier AIX operating system versions, it has many complex features and functions. A complete description of these features would warrant a separate book. However, the remainder of this chapter will look at some of the most important topics, including:

- User interface/services
- Systems management
- Disk management
- Application development
- Communications support

User Interfaces/Services

The manner in which a user interacts with a computer system is determined by the **user interface** provided by the program(s) being executed by the computer system. Like other things concerning computers, the style, ease of use, and productivity of user interfaces have evolved over time. The AIX operating system on the RS/6000 offers several different user interfaces selectable by the user. These user interfaces can be broken down into two types:

1. Command shells
2. Graphical user interfaces

An example of a command shell is shown in Figure 5.4. This is a very simple user interface in which the user must type in AIX operating system commands at a command prompt in order to accomplish operating system tasks such as starting application programs or examining the contents of a disk. For example, the user would type in "ls" (list command) at the command prompt, as shown in Figure 5.5, in order to see a list of the files contained on disk.

There are three different command shells provided with the AIX operating system, differing in the command syntax and prompt:

- Korn shell
- Bourne shell
- C shell

AIX command prompt

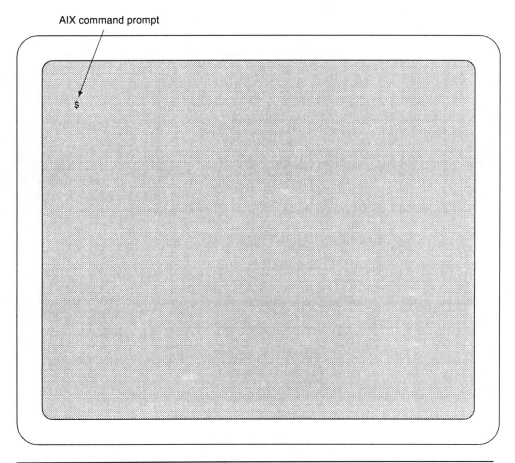

Figure 5.4. AIX command prompt presented by a command shell provided with AIX.

With any of these command shells, the user traditionally must remember (or look up) somewhat cryptic commands and type them in using the keyboard. For this reason, command shells are more useful to experienced users. However, the Systems Management Interface Tool of AIX is available through the command shells and provides menus that can be used to perform basic operating system functions.

Since ASCII terminals attached to an RS/6000 cannot display graphics, graphical interfaces are not supported — thus command shells (and SMIT) are the only option. However, JSB Multiview for AIX RS/6000 (5601-279) is an extension to the AIX operating system that provides **windowing** on up to 32 ASCII terminals. With windowing, the display screen of an ASCII terminal is subdivided into multiple rectangular sections called "windows" — each dedicated to a different task. A single user can then interact and quickly switch between up to six different windows — each run-

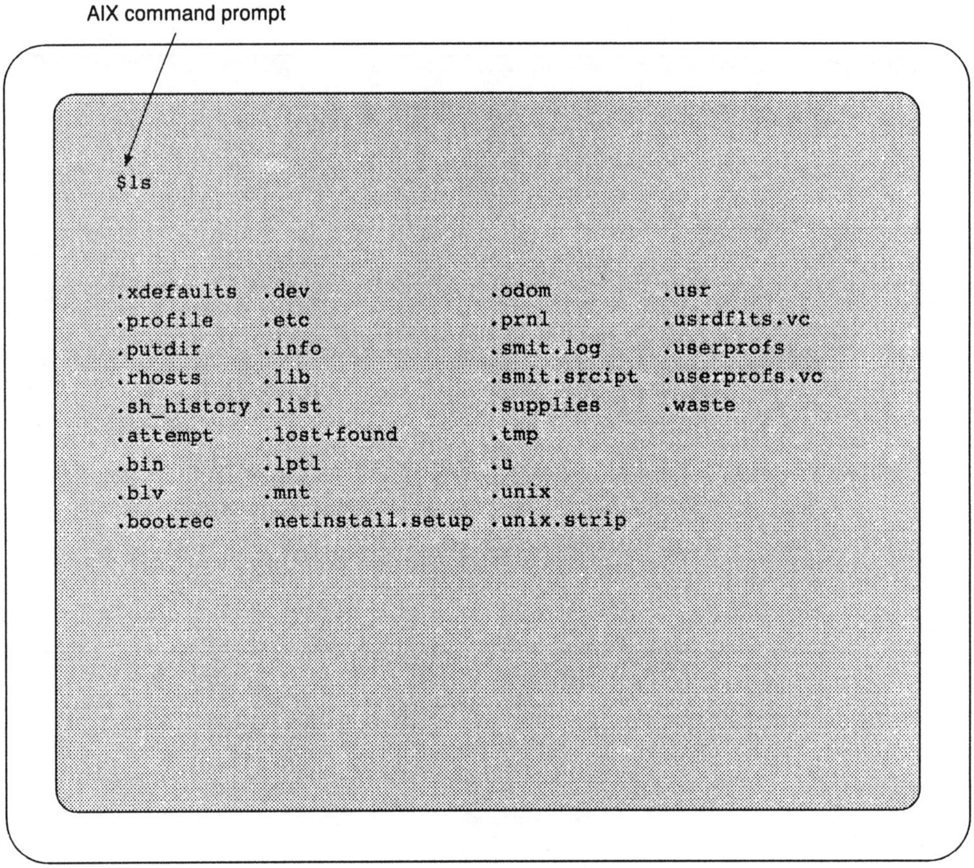

AIX command prompt

```
$ls


.xdefaults  .dev              .odom        .usr
.profile    .etc              .prnl        .usrdflts.vc
.putdir     .info             .smit.log    .userprofs
.rhosts     .lib              .smit.srcipt .userprofs.vc
.sh_history .list             .supplies    .waste
.attempt    .lost+found       .tmp
.bin        .lptl             .u
.blv        .mnt              .unix
.bootrec    .netinstall.setup .unix.strip
```

Figure 5.5. The "ls" command is used to list the files contained on a disk, as shown.

ning a different program. Windowing allows you to simultaneously interact with several application programs, which supports the frequent interruptions found in typical office environments. When you start a new application program, you automatically create a new window. All interaction between the user and that application program occurs in that application's window. By having multiple windows visible at once on a computer screen, the user can easily interact with multiple application programs (i.e., windows facilitate multitasking). Many application programs designed to run on standard ASCII terminals can also run under JSB Multiview without modification. Even with JSB Multiview, however, graphical interfaces and graphical application programs are not supported on ASCII terminals.

For users interacting with RS/6000 systems through a graphics display or an

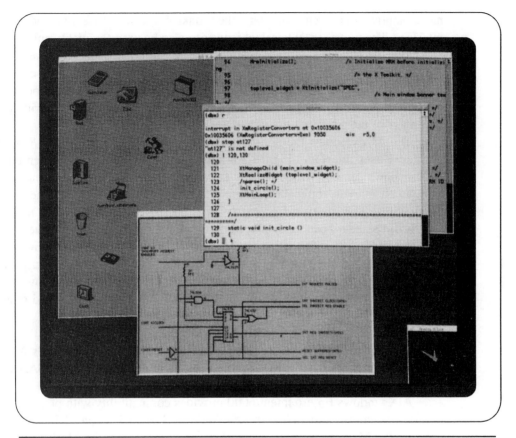

Figure 5.6. Graphical user interface provided by AIXwindows Environment/6000.

Xstation, graphical user interfaces like that shown in Figure 5.6 are an attractive alternative to command shells. Graphical user interfaces and application programs written to take advantage of them provide a more sophisticated user interface that is often more productive and easier to use. As with ASCII terminals and JSB Multiview for AIX RS/6000, graphical user interface environments divide the display screen into multiple windows, each dedicated to a different task. However, graphical user interfaces provide support for graphics, allowing for a more natural and productive user interface. For example, graphical user interfaces allow a user to interact with the computer system through **icons**. Icons are basically menu items that are displayed as small graphical images rather than text. With icons, rather than typing a command or selecting a menu item "erase file," you would have a small image of a trash can that, when selected, would allow you to erase a file. Since icons often are more natural to nontechnical users, they make for a more effective and easier user interface. The mouse used to select icons can also be used to quickly enlarge, shrink, and move the windows around, much as you would move sheets of paper around on a desk. When you start a new application program, you automatically create a new window. All interaction between the user and that application program occurs in that application's window. However, the application program must be written to take advantage of the particular graphical user interface being used.

The AIXwindows Environment/6000 (5601-257) extension to AIX provides a graphical user interface. Figure 5.6 shows a typical image as presented by the AIXwindows Environment/6000. By selecting various icons with a mouse, the user can quickly start an application program, browse existing files, create new files, and delete files. The many different styles and sizes of text available through the **PostScript** standard can be displayed on the screen, making for effective and attractive presentation of information to the user. This feature of AIXwindows Environment/6000, called **Display PostScript,** allows the user to view PostScript text and images on the screen. The **Desktop** function provided with AIXwindows Environment/6000 provides an icon-based interface for working with files and other basic tasks.

The look of the screen and methods of interaction employed by the AIXwindows Environment/6000 are based on the Open Software Foundation's **Motif** user interface, guidelines from IBM's *Systems Application Architecture* (SAA), and the Operating System/2 **Presentation Manager**.

AIXwindows Environment/6000 provides compatibility with programs written to industry standards including the X-Windows System Version 11 Release 3 developed by the Massachusetts Institute of Technology (MIT), the Motif user interface defined by the *Open Software Foundation* (OSF), and Silicon Graphic Inc.'s *Graphics Library* (GL). That is, programs specially written to these standards can usually be migrated to the RS/6000 and AIXwindows Environment/6000 with minimal programming efforts. Finally, when used with the IBM AIX Xstation Manager/6000 (5601-457) program product, AIXwindows Environment/6000 lets users work with graphical applications with local area networks attached to an IBM Xstation. In fact, users can view multiple applications running on different RS/6000 systems and other brands of open systems in the LAN. More on this in Chapter 6.

In addition to programming needed to perform traditional operating system tasks, AIX includes some commonly needed programs that provide various services of interest to AIX users. Most notable of these user services is the **InfoExplorer.** This feature of the AIX operating system allows a user to electronically look up information in the AIX manuals, which can reside either on CD-ROM disks or on normal disks. The InfoExplorer makes sifting through the substantial documentation much quicker and easier. InfoExplorer also provides on-line training courses through the InfoTrainer function within InfoExplorer. Chapter 3 covered the InfoTrainer in more detail.

Another user service provided is the **mail facilities.** The user can choose from two different mail programs. The more basic mail program commonly found in today's UNIX operating systems allows users to create and send simple documents or messages to one another. For more advanced mail functions, the user can choose to install the **message handling** program, which offers additional capabilities like message sequencing, message annotation, mail folders, date sorting, and so forth.

The AIX operating system comes with other programming that allows a user to pass through the local RS/6000 system and sign on to a remote RS/6000 system over communications lines. This is called **asynchronous terminal emulation** and will be covered further in Chapter 7.

There is an extension to the AIX operating system that provides a user with service not part of more traditional UNIX operating systems — namely, the AIX Personal Computer Simulator/6000 (5601-263). This simulator allows an RS/6000 user to run many application programs originally designed to run under the IBM *Disk Operating System* (DOS) on IBM Personal Computers or IBM Personal System/2 computers. It basically makes the application program think it is running in a personal computer, when in actuality it is running on an RS/6000 system under the AIX operating system. The simulator by itself allows the RS/6000 system to run multiple DOS applications programs on multiple terminals for multiple users. When you have both the AIX Personal Computer Simulator/6000 and the AIXwindows/6000 installed on an RS/6000 system, you can take advantage of the multitasking/multiuser environment to run multiple, concurrent DOS applications in multiple windows for a single user. The JSB Multiview extension to the AIX operating system would also allow a nongraphics-capable user to run multiple (nongraphics) PC programs under the AIX Personal Computer Simulator/6000. In either case, however, some DOS applications may not function properly under the AIX Personal Computer Simulator/6000 (if they directly manipulate hardware elements rather than using provided software interfaces). You can usually find out if a DOS application program will work under the AIX Personal Computer Simulator/6000 by contacting the software publisher.

Systems Management

With any computer system, there are various tasks that must be performed in support of the computer system itself by someone trained to be a systems administrator. These are called systems management tasks and involve things such as authorizing new users and making backup copies of the disk information. These tasks can be done by stepping through menus or, for more experienced administrators, by issuing AIX operating system commands.

RS/6000 systems are installed by IBM personnel and can come with AIX installed on the disks. There are computer-based courses (i.e., InfoExplorer) provided with the AIX operating system that allow a user to sit at a terminal and learn about various subjects. Some courses are for the users and others are for the systems administrator and any programmers who may use the system. In addition, RS/6000 systems provide access to the IBMLink network. IBMLink allows the users and the systems administrator to electronically research technical issues, ask questions through electronic mail, resolve technical problems, place service calls, and so on. The services provided by IBMLink are available seven days a week around the clock.

One of the first jobs to be done by a systems administrator is to tell the system who is authorized to use it. This is done by creating a **user profile** for each system user. The user profile contains information such as the user's nickname (called a user identification), password, security level, and accounting information for departmental billing for computer services. The AIX operating system's built-in security, if enabled, will then require the user to enter the correct password before being allowed access to the system. If desired, security can be defined so the user is restricted to specific functions. In fact, security enhancements were made to the AIX operating system based on the stringent security requirements of the National Computer Security Center Trusted Computer System Evaluation Criteria Class C2. (**Note:** RS/6000 systems have not been certified B1 compliant as of publication date.)

Now that the users can begin to use the RS/6000 system, the disks will begin to accumulate information often vital to the day-to-day operations of the organization. This information becomes an asset to the organization and should be protected as such. The AIX operating system provides several functions that allow the systems administrator to protect against the loss of this information, be it from user errors, hardware failures, intentional corruptions, or whatever. Through AIX operating system facilities, the systems administrator can make backup copies of the information on disks to magnetic tape. These backups are done on a regular basis (e.g., daily) and the backup tapes are stored in a safe place at another physical location. If the information on the RS/6000 disks is somehow lost, the backup tape can be used to **restore** the RS/6000 disks to the state when the last backup was made. In environments where quick recovery from disk failures is even more important, a function of the AIX operating system (called "mirroring") allows for duplicate copies of information to be kept current on two or three different disk drives. This function allows for immediate recovery from disk failures. We will cover mirroring further in the next section.

Since RS/6000 systems are often used in environments where operating system experience is limited, the AIX operating system provides assistance in this area. The *Systems Management Interface Tool* (SMIT) provides menus to guide the systems administrator through administrative functions such as creating a user profile, adding a new printer, managing disk storage, or changing a password. Rather than having to remember and type in the somewhat cryptic commands, the user can select menu items and will be prompted for needed information. Then the AIX operating system automatically builds, issues, and logs the command(s) needed to accomplish the task. While interacting with SMIT, on-line help text is available to help resolve any confusion. More experienced systems administrators can still choose to directly issue traditional commands to accomplish these same tasks.

Disk Management

One of the jobs performed by the systems administrator of a computer system is to subdivide and allocate (manage) the available disk storage in order to meet the needs of the users. The systems administrator utilizes functions of the operating system to manage the disks. Many UNIX operating systems conceptually subdivide a computer's disk storage into multiple smaller disks called **file systems**. These file systems can then be used to hold programs, data files, and so on. The systems administrator must decide how large each file system need be during the initial installation of the application program. However, it is often difficult to judge how large a given file system needs to be until the system has been in productive use for a while. Since it is difficult to increase the size of a file system after the system is in productive use, herein lies a problem with the disk management approach taken by most traditional UNIX operating systems. Another limitation commonly found in UNIX operating systems is that a single file system cannot span more than one physical disk drive. That is, the file system size is limited to the size of each individual disk drive installed in the computer system rather than by the total amount of disk storage in the computer system. As application programs grow more sophisticated, file systems larger than a single physical drive are desirable.

To address these limitations, the AIX operating system for the RS/6000 has expanded on the file system concept of the UNIX operating systems (and earlier AIX versions) with the *Logical Volume Manager* (LVM). The LVM conceptually partitions a group of physical disk drives (up to 32) into equal-sized sections called **physical partitions.** A **logical volume** is a collection of these physical partitions, conceptually equivalent to a file system. One key difference in this approach is that a single logical volume can consist of physical partitions from multiple disk units in the computer system. This means that a logical volume can be larger than any individual disk unit in the system if necessary. Another is that physical partitions can easily be added to a logical volume in order to increase its size without disrupting normal operation or moving any other partition.

One other function of the LVM is **mirroring.** This feature allows for multiple or "mirror" copies of a logical volume to be automatically maintained in disk storage. Each physical partition of a mirrored logical volume has one or two other physical partitions allocated on different physical disks to hold identical copies of the data. If a permanent disk error occurs while reading a mirrored logical volume, the LVM will automatically read the data from one of the mirror physical partitions and write any new data to a new area of disk. Thus the mirroring function of the LVM often allows an RS/6000 system to recover from permanent disk errors without disrupting normal system operation. Systems providing redundancy for automatic error-recovery purposes are said to be designed for **high availability.** However, since you are keeping multiple copies of information in the disk system, more disk space will be required when using the mirroring function.

Application Development

Many organizations find that writing their own custom application programs is the best method of solving problems through computers. The AIX operating system comes standard with two full-screen editors (vi and INed) and tools to support the development and maintenance of custom application programs. These include traditional UNIX commands and utilities such as the **Make** command used to easily rebuild complex systems of programs after changes have been made. Another traditional UNIX operating system function supported by the AIX operating system is the **Source Code Control System,** which provides a mechanism to record and control when, why, and by whom changes are made to the source code of a program under development. The Source Code Control System is especially important in larger projects, where multiple programmers may be working on a single project. Subroutine libraries provided include **libc.a,** the **enhanced floating point math library,** and the **4.3 BSD compatibility library**.

The AIX XL C Compiler provided with the AIX operating system supports the development of programs written in the popular C programming language. A programming language can be thought of as a library of instructions from which a programmer constructs a program. The instructions of C (and other programming languages) are designed to be easily understood by the programmer, facilitating productivity while writing programs. However, the resulting list of instructions (the program) cannot be directly understood by the RS/6000 hardware circuits. The XL C Compiler takes the list of C instructions written by the programmer and automatically converts them to a series of instructions that are executable by the RS/6000 processor circuitry.

The programmer can select one of three C language versions at compile time:

- ❑ ANSI mode (ANSI C Standard)
- ❑ SAA mode (IBM's SAA C language definition)
- ❑ Extended mode

Also provided with the AIX operating system is the **AIX Assembler,** which allows the programmer to write programs using the RS/6000 system's instruction set. Tools used to help in debugging programs are provided, such as the **absolute debugger** and the **symbolic debugger**.

In addition to C and assembler programming languages, provided as standard with the AIX operating system, there are extensions to the AIX available that provide additional programming languages. Such extensions ("compilers") include XL FORTRAN Compiler/6000 (5601-248), XL Pascal Compiler/6000 (5601-254), Ada/6000 (5706-291), VS COBOL Compiler/6000 (5601-258), and APL2/6000 (5765-02). These compilers are designed to meet existing industry standards that specifically define the elements of each language. The language you select depends on the requirements of the application program and the skills of your programmer(s). Any of these languages supports the architectural features of RS/6000 hardware. All of these compilers (including XL C) offer a fast, nonoptimizing mode to facilitate early stages of program development.

In addition to these traditional programming languages, the AIX operating system provides another type of programming structure for automating a series of operating system commands, called **shell scripts**. Shell scripts can be used to issue a single operating system command or to define a complex series of operating system commands that present the user with menus and initiate other application programs. No matter how many operating system commands are contained in a shell script, all commands in the shell script can be executed by simply typing in the name of the shell script. Shell scripts are a shorthand for users or systems administrators, allowing them to automatically execute long lists of operating system commands.

The AIXwindows Environment/6000 extension to AIX (discussed earlier in the chapter) through the X development environment provides a multiwindow programming environment. This allows an application programmer to do things like examine source code in one window and monitor the executing program in another. Alternately, the programmer may be accessing AIX on-line documentation in one window while writing a program in another, allowing him or her to see both simultaneously. AIXwindows Environment/6000 also provides tools to ease the development of effective graphical user interfaces for programs—namely, the **XWindows Graphics Support Library** and **Enhanced X-Windows Display PostScript**. Support for a **graphics library** compatible with the popular Graphics Library developed by Silicon

Graphics, Inc., is also a part of AIXwindows. This graphics library provides support for the development of programs that generate complex graphic images.

Still another set of tools for the programmer developing programs that rely heavily on computer generated images is the **AIX Personal graPHIGS Programming Interface/6000** (5601-230). This extension provides a set of subroutines for generating and manipulating graphics images through the ANSI and ISO standard known as the *Programmer Hierarchical Interactive Graphics System* (PHIGS).

Many of today's larger program development projects have become extremely complex — involving tens, hundreds, or even thousands of people who may be geographically dispersed around the world. Managing such projects and ensuring a quality result has become a discipline in and of itself, with computer-based tools emerging to help with this task. The discipline is known as *Computer-Aided Software Engineering* (CASE). While CASE methods were developed to address the needs of large application development projects, CASE concepts and tools can be employed no matter what the size of the project is.

The AIX operating system programming tools discussed so far (AIX and AIXwindows) provide the foundation for CASE. In addition to these, IBM offers some packages of selected CASE products (both IBM and non-IBM) designed to provide complete CASE tools for various environments, including:

- CASE FORTRAN Solution
- CASE C Solution
- CASE C++ Solution
- CASE Embedded C Solution
- CASE Integrated C Solution
- CASE Integrated Ada Solution

Some specialized application programs directly monitor and control machines. This is commonly done in manufacturing and process companies where computers are used to monitor and control various processes. For example, a computer may be involved in adjusting furnace controls to keep a vat of chemicals within a tight temperature range. The computer must be able to respond very quickly, or in **real time**, to signals from sensors that measure temperature changes. Because of improvements such as priority control, scheduling, interrupt priority, and timer control, the AIX operating system used with RS/6000 systems is better suited to real-time environments than were earlier AIX versions.

The built-in features of the AIX operating system along with additional tools (i.e., AIXwindows, optional compilers, CASE solutions) make for productive application program development and maintenance.

Communications Support

Communications facilities included in the AIX operating system allow a properly equipped RS/6000 computer to communicate with a variety of different computing equipment in a variety of ways. Traditional open systems utilized terminals and printers that communicated with the computer system over asynchronous communications links using the *American Standard Code for Information Interchange* (ASCII) protocol. With this communications method, one character at a time (letter, number, period, comma, etc.) was sent from the computer's communications port through a simple cable to the communications port of the attached device. This is how all ASCII terminals and printers communicated with the UNIX operating system. This simple ASCII method was also used to send information from one computer system to another over a similar type of cable. RS/6000 systems and the AIX operating system still utilize the same ASCII method to communicate with ASCII terminals and printers. AIX also supports communications with other computer systems via the ASCII method.

As more and more vendors offered computer systems and the need for inter-computer communications evolved, the more effective *Transmission Control Protocol/Internet Protocol* (TCP/IP) was developed. This is a more efficient way of encoding and sending information than via the more traditional asynchronous ASCII links. Since TCP/IP was an industry standard, it also allowed computer systems from many different vendors to communicate with each other in a single network. The AIX operating system supports TCP/IP over **Ethernet/802.3 networks** and **Token-Ring Networks** if the computer systems are near each other (i.e., on the same campus). The AIX operating system also supports the TCP/IP protocol between distant computer systems over **X.25 packet-switching** and asynchronous communications networks.

In addition to TCP/IP, other communications protocols have also emerged to meet the needs of more sophisticated communications environments. These include the *Network File System* (NFS) and the *Network Computing System* (NCS), both of which are supported in the AIX operating system. The NFS protocol and application programs written to utilize it allow one computer system in either an Ethernet or Token-Ring LAN to access information located on another computer system in the same network. This allows information to be distributed in a network in such a way as to make that information most available to those who need it and so that it can best be managed. The NCS protocol support in the AIX operating system, along with application programs designed to take advantage of it, provides a way to distribute a computer's workload across the various computer systems in a network. For example, a computer currently experiencing a heavy workload can dispatch some of its work to another, less-busy computer in the network. This load balancing makes for more efficient use of all computing power in the network.

To further support distributed computing environments, the AIXwindows/6000 extension to the AIX operating system supports the industry-standard **X-Windows** protocol. This protocol allows graphics created on one computer system to be displayed on another. Also, the AIX Xstation Manager/6000 is an extension that allows an Xstation 120 or 130 (covered in Chapter 1) to participate in a local area network of RS/6000 systems. The Xstation Manager/6000 extension provides the necessary programming to start up and manage an Xstation, giving it access to any X Windows compatible computer in the network. IBM has announced its intentions to follow prevailing industry standards in the area of communications as they emerge (e.g., OSI communications standards).

Other communications methods supported by the AIX operating system allow RS/6000 systems to communicate with IBM's larger S/390 (or S/370) computer systems by imitating (**emulating**) terminals typically used with these IBM systems. There are three extension products that work with the AIX operating system to provide support for this terminal emulation: AIX 3278/79 Emulation/6000 (5601-256), AIX X-Windows 3270 Emulator/6000 (5765-011), and AIX 3270 Host Connection Program/6000 (5601-260).

The AIX 3278/79 Emulation/6000 extension allows an RS/6000 workstation user to interact with a larger IBM S/390 computer over a coax cable to a 3/74 control unit or similar attachment. In this configuration, the RS/6000 appears to be a 3278 or 3279 terminal or printer. That is, the RS/6000 user can interact with programs running on the S/390. Further, the RS/6000 user can exchange files between the RS/6000 and the S/390.

The AIX X-Windows 3270 Emulator/6000 also makes an RS/6000 appear to the larger S/390 computer to be a 3278/79 terminal or printer. However, the X-Window 3270 Emulator is designed to work over local area networks (Token-Ring or Ethernet) using the TCP/IP protocol. The X-Window 3270 Emulator supports host-generated graphics (i.e., GDDM) and runs under the AIXwindows Environment/6000 graphical user interface. A single user can interact with multiple host computers (i.e., multiple sessions).

The AIX 3270 Host Connection Program/6000 extends these same functions to RS/6000 ASCII terminal and Xstation users. Further, the AIX 3270 Host Connection Program/6000 allows RS/6000 systems to be attached to the System/390 host computer remotely over a *Systems Network Architecture* (SNA) network. SNA is IBM's own blueprint or architecture for computer communications. It is designed to provide for effective and flexible communications today and to protect investments in IBM hardware and software as communications evolve over time. With AIX 3270 Host Connection Program/6000, a single user can also interact with multiple host computers at the same time (i.e., multiple session support).

The AS/400 Connections Program/6000 (5621-051) extension allows an

RS/6000 system to communicate with an IBM Application System/400 (AS/400). In this environment, the RS/6000 system appears to the AS/400 to be a 5250 terminal, allowing the RS/6000 user to sign on to an AS/400 system and interact with AS/400 application programs. Files can be transferred between the RS/6000 and the AS/400, and RS/6000 programs can interact (through the provided application programming interface) with AS/400 application programs. The connection can be over a local area network or over an SNA or TCP/IP network.

Both the AIX 3270 Connection Program/6000 and the AS/400 Connection Program/6000 use the services provided by AIX System Network Architecture Services/6000 (5601-287) extension to AIX. This extension supports various standards defined in SNA, including the **Logical Unit 6.2** peer-to-peer protocol in which all computers in the network have equal ability to initiate or receive communications. The communications services provided by AIX System Network Architecture Services/6000 are available to an application programmer.

The AIX Network Management/6000 (5601-253) and AIX NetView Service Point (5621-107) extensions to AIX allow RS/6000 systems to participate in the monitoring and troubleshooting of an SNA communications network via IBM's **NetView** network management product running on an IBM host computer. For example, let's say an RS/6000 in Pittsburgh is part of a network managed from a central System/390 computer located in San Francisco. The network operator in San Francisco uses NetView running on the System/390 to manage the entire network. Now let's say a problem develops in the communications link between the RS/6000 in Pittsburgh and the System/390 in San Francisco. AIX Network Management/6000 will automatically notify the network operator in San Francisco that a network problem has been detected. This is done through an **Alert** message, which is automatically sent by AIX Network Management/6000 to the computer in San Francisco. Once an Alert notifies the network operator of the problem, there are tools available in NetView that help identify and correct the problem. Thus the San Francisco–based network operator can use his or her expertise to analyze and fix the communications problem without having to travel to Pittsburgh.

While our example was an SNA network, non-SNA networks using the TCP/IP protocol can also be managed in a similar way by AIX Network Management/6000 (but not AIX NetView Service Point) through the use of special messages similar to Alerts called "SNMP Traps." In either case, these extensions to AIX make for more speedy problem determination and correction, resulting in less network down time.

The RS/6000 computers and the AIX operating system are also designed to cooperate with the **AIX Access for DOS Users** product for Personal System/2 computers. This product works with the DOS Server support provided as standard with the AIX operating system to allow Personal System/2 computers (PS/2s) and Personal Computers (PCs) to work in harmony with RS/6000 systems. First, the PS/2 computers can act like an ASCII terminal, allowing the user to interact with the RS/6000 system as with any other terminal. With AIX Access for DOS Users, any properly equipped PS/2 computer can be used as a terminal for an RS/6000 system. That is, the AIX Access program allows a PS/2 computer to emulate an ASCII terminal. While the PS/2 computer is emulating an ASCII terminal, it still keeps its ability to run PS/2 programs. After the PS/2 computer is initialized, AIX provides the user with a list of servers available (RS/6000 systems or other vendors' equipment). Upon selection of a server, the user is prompted for a user ID and password. The user is then presented with the familiar DOS prompt from which he or she can access programs residing on either the RS/6000 system or the PS/2 computer.

AIX Access for DOS Users also provides for the free exchange of information between the PS/2 computer and the RS/6000 system. Since the PS/2 computer has some computing power of its own, it is called an **intelligent workstation** and can do things that a normal ("dumb") workstation can't. For example, information in RS/6000 files can be brought down to the PS/2 computer and manipulated using a spreadsheet program. Further, a file created on the PS/2 computer (using the vi editor provided in AIX Access for DOS Users, for example) can be transferred up to the RS/6000 system and accessed by the AIX operating system like any other file. Finally, the RS/6000 disks can be used as an extension to the PC's disk space through the use of **shared volumes**. Shared volumes are areas of the disk that can be accessed by either DOS or AIX. Through these shared volumes, the RS/6000 system can be the central storage element in a network of PS/2 computers and RS/6000 system users, allowing any authorized user access to the information. In the same way that information can be shared, printers and communications links can also be shared. For example, through the AIX Access for DOS Users **virtual printer** function, a PS/2 user can automatically send documents to RS/6000 printers. AIX Access for DOS Users can be used with PS/2 computers attached to RS/6000 systems via Ethernet, Token-Ring Networks, or traditional asynchronous ASCII connections.

AIX Access for DOS Users allows the PS/2 computer and RS/6000 systems to cooperate in such a way that the user can take advantage of the best of both. The PS/2 computer can be used for things like spreadsheet programs, graphics, and word processing, where it provides functions and response times tuned to these applications. At the same time, the RS/6000 system contributes things like information security, centralized systems management, large disks, extensive communications, high-speed printers, and so forth. AIX Access for DOS Users allows the user to perform the needed functions on the system best suited for the job.

RS/6000 Communications

The RS/6000 system's standard features and options along with the AIX operating system and its extensions provide users with flexibility when configuring RS/6000 systems for various communications environments. This flexibility, however, can also cause confusion when trying to determine which options and programs are needed for a particular environment. This chapter will help guide you through the jungle of communications available through RS/6000 systems.

Chapter 2 examined some communications hardware options used with RS/6000 systems and provided a brief tutorial on communications interfaces and protocols. Chapter 5 looked at the communications software support in the AIX operating system. In this chapter, we will examine some of the most popular communications environments and provide example configurations for each.

COMPUTER COMMUNICATIONS—AN INTRODUCTION

Just as a woodworker cherishes a solid block of mahogany, people cherish accurate, timely, and manageable information. If one activity is most crucial to any size organization, it is the act of communicating this information to the proper decision maker. Based on the information available to the decision maker, important choices are made that can have far-reaching effects on how successful the organization is. Improve communications in an organization and you are likely to improve productivity and effectiveness. Ironically, as an organization grows, it becomes more important and more difficult to maintain efficient and accurate communications—the very thing that facilitated growth in the first place. Communications difficulties grow geometrically with the size of the organization.

Today's businesses, universities, research facilities, and so on, are quickly finding in computers a communications tool unequaled in significance since Bell invented the telephone. Computers are already commonplace in these environments, and now there is an increasing emphasis on computer communications. This communication can occur exclusively between two computers or among a group of computers in a communications network. It allows information to move at electronic speeds; and further, it allows users at remote locations access to vital information on a distant computer. RS/6000 hardware and the AIX operating system together represent a powerful communications tool.

ASCII TERMINAL NETWORKS

We have seen that a single RS/6000 system can be shared among a group of users, each equipped with an ASCII terminal used to enter and view RS/6000 information. The RS/6000 and the pool of ASCII terminals (and printers) constitute an **ASCII terminal network**. Figure 6.1 shows a small ASCII terminal network consisting of eight terminals (i.e., eight users) and two printers. This type of configuration might be used in a business environment for applications such as basic accounting or inventory control. In our example network, there are four locations accessing a single RS/6000 system. The RS/6000 system, three terminals, and a printer are at the first location. Since these terminals and the printer are conveniently located in the same place (e.g., the same building) as the RS/6000 System Unit, they are **local** devices. Local terminals and printers are attached via industry-standard EIA-232 async communications ports (one port per terminal or printer). RS/6000 systems come standard with two such ports. The 8-Port Async Adapter EIA-232 will provide the additional ports needed in our example configuration making for a total of ten EIA-232 ports. The AIX operating system comes with the necessary support for the EIA-232 ports and the async communications protocol they use.

Location #2 is distant (e.g., across town or around the world) from location #1 and thus **remote** from the RS/6000 System Unit. For this reason, a long-distance communications line must be used to attach the terminal used by personnel at Location #2. Distant terminals and printers are called remote devices. Since only one terminal is needed at location #2, a simple modem link can be used. At location #1, the 5853 Modem attaches to an EIA-232 async port in the same way a local terminal or printer would be attached to the RS/6000. The built-in asynchronous communications functions of the AIX operating system provide the necessary software support for the modem link. At location #2, a second 5853 Modem is attached to the remote terminal. The modems at each end of the telephone line handle the electronic details associated with sending and receiving information over the telephone line. The communication takes place over a **switched** telephone line like those used to carry normal residential or business telephone calls. The line is called "switched" because it can make a connection between any two locations by dialing the proper phone num-

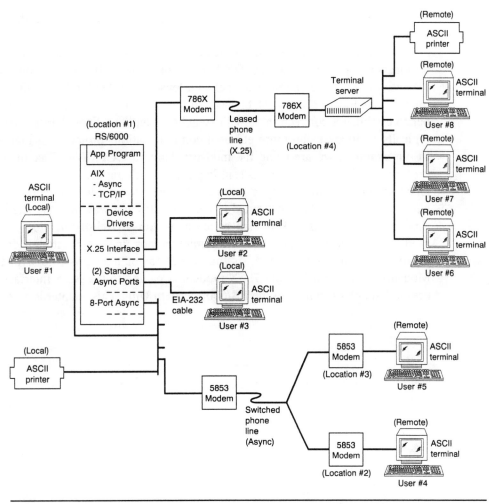

Figure 6.1. Example ASCII terminal network used to share a single RS/6000 system among a pool of users both local and remote.

ber, just as when you make a normal telephone call. Since this switched line can connect any two locations, location #3 can share the same communications link, as indicated in the figure. This is the least expensive way (in terms of computer hardware and telephone line charges) to connect a remote terminal to an RS/6000 system. However, since both locations #2 and #3 are sharing a single communications link, only one of the two terminals (either that at location #2 or that at location #3) can be connected to the RS/6000 at a time. Further, it can be bothersome to have to dial a phone number every time you wish to utilize the RS/6000. Finally, the switched-line communications link shown typically operates using the relatively slow asynchronous communications protocol.

The communications link to location #4 shows another way to attach remote terminals and printers to the RS/6000. This link uses a different (and typically more expensive) type of telephone line, called a **leased** line. With a leased line, the communications link is always established, so there is no need to dial a telephone number to establish a connection as with switched telephone lines. Further, leased lines typically facilitate using more efficient communications protocols at higher speeds. In our example, we are using the industry-standard **CCITT X.25** communications protocol in which information is sent in packets of characters rather than one character at a time as with the async protocol. Because these packets of information are automatically "switched" or routed in the most efficient way over the X.25 network, this communications link is also called a **packet-switching** network. The 786X modems used on both sides of the communications line are capable of operating at up to 19,200 bits per second, or four times faster than possible with the 5853 Modems. At location #1, the 786X modem is cabled to the X.25 Interface Co-Processor/2 adapter installed in the RS/6000 System Unit. This adapter is a processor in

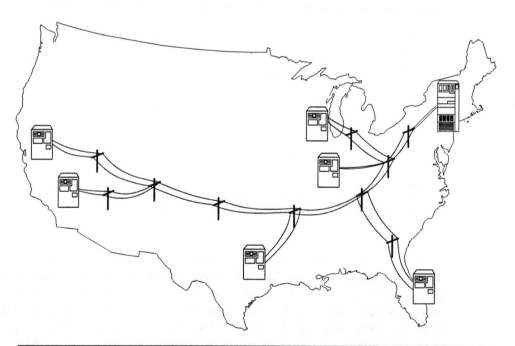

Figure 6.2. Example of a distributed computer network for a retail chain headquartered in New York City.

its own right which handles the high-speed information flow associated with X.25 communications links. The AIX operating system provides support for the industry-standard *Transmission Control Protocol/Internet Protocol* (**TCP/ IP**) over the X.25 network. At location #4, the 786X modem is attached to the X.25 network and a **terminal server.** It is the job of the terminal server to collect the information from the attached terminals and printer at location #2 and send it over a single X.25 communications line. The terminal server must also intercept all information sent from the RS/6000 and route it to the proper terminal or printer at location #2. In this way, the terminal server allows multiple terminals and printers at a single location to be attached to a distant RS/6000 system over a single communications line. This significantly reduces the amount of communications hardware needed at both ends of the communications link and allows a single communications line to be simultaneously shared by multiple devices.

DISTRIBUTED COMPUTER COMMUNICATIONS

In some cases, the computing needs of an organization can be met with a single computer system and an ASCII terminal network like that just described. This is especially true for smaller organizations or those where most computer users are at a single location. In many cases, however, the needs of an organization may be best satisfied by using multiple computer systems. That is, instead of providing remote users with remote workstations as discussed in the previous section, you provide remote users with their own small computer systems. For example, a retail chain may want a computer system at each retail location as well as a computer system at headquarters (Figure 6.2). As shown, all computer systems are joined through a communications network that allows them to easily move information (e.g., daily cash register receipts) from place to place as necessary. This is called a **distributed computer network.**

When you place (or **distribute**) the computer systems at the sites where they are needed, several nice things happen. First, since all users are locally attached to their respective computer systems, they enjoy improved system performance (reduced response time) compared with remotely attached workstations, which are often slowed down by communications-line limitations. Further, the distributed computer system can act to consolidate communications. This is especially true at larger remote locations, where it may be necessary to have a large number of communications lines to support all of the remote workstations. With a distributed computing approach, the remote users would be locally attached to their distributed system, which could then communicate summary information to the central computer through a single communications line.

In some cases, it may be an advantage to provide the remote locations with some control over their distributed system. For example, they may have unique requirements that can be met by an available prewritten application program. They could then acquire the program and get the support of a local software firm in meeting their unique needs — all without becoming computer experts or blindly relying on the headquarters computer staff. This might make the remote location more productive while reducing the workload at headquarters.

On the disadvantage side, a large distributed computer network is often more difficult to manage than a single computer system. However, since RS/6000 systems were designed for a distributed environment, there are network management tools that help ease this task. The AIX Network Management/6000 and AIX NetView Service Point extensions to the AIX operating system provide tools that help manage distributed networks, as was discussed in Chapter 5. When a distributed network is to be managed by a central System/390 computer system, for example, IBM's NetView program product provides many needed functions. Now let's look at the two example distributed networks in which RS/6000 systems can participate: RS/6000 distributed networks and RS/6000 and S/390 distributed networks.

RS/6000 Distributed Network

Multiple RS/6000 systems can be attached together through communications lines to create a distributed computer network. Our example distributed network consists of three small RS/6000 systems (e.g., Model 520s), each distributed to a remote location, and a larger RS/6000 (e.g., Model 930) at the organization's headquarters. Figure 6.3 shows example RS/6000 hardware and software configurations for the headquarters location and one of the remote locations. The remote location configuration (Model 520) would be duplicated for every remote location. Further, the RS/6000 at each end would be equipped with the appropriate local workstations to support the users at the respective locations. These are also not shown so as not to be confused with options needed to support the communications link.

The Model 520 used at the remote location is equipped with an X.25 Interface Co-Processor/2. This adapter, along with the 7861 Modem, allows the RS/6000 system to communicate over an X.25 network at speeds up to 19,200 bits per second. Since the remote RS/6000 system need only communicate with the central RS/6000 system, this is the only adapter needed. The TCP/IP functions provided with the AIX operating system provides the necessary programming to support the TCP/IP protocol.

At the central location, the larger RS/6000 is in constant communication with all remote locations. It collects the summary information needed by headquarters to consolidate all remote location activity. In our example, one communications line is

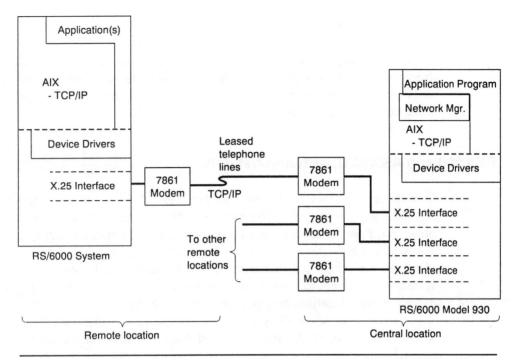

Figure 6.3. Example configuration used to communicate between distant RS/6000 systems.

used for each remote location. This means the central RS/6000 must have at least three X.25 Interface Co-Processor/2 adapters. At the central site there is one 7861 Modem for each communications line, making for a total of three.

With this communications configuration, there are many different ways in which the distributed RS/6000 systems can work together. First of all, the AIX mail facilities are fully available, allowing any user to, for example, send a document to any other user attached to any system in the distributed network. Further, the basic networking utilities included with the AIX operating system allow users attached to the central RS/6000 Model 930 to sign on to remote RS/6000 Model 520s just as if they were physically attached to that system. This can be especially useful if a user of the central system provides technical support to the other network nodes, since he or she can now directly sign on to any RS/6000 system in the network from his local terminal. These utilities also allow users to execute commands and run programs on any RS/6000 in the network or freely exchange files between systems. However, unlike the case with ASCII terminal networks, the application programs used in a distributed environment must be designed up front to cooperate over the communications link.

When at least one of the RS/6000 systems in the network has the Network

Management/6000 extension, more tools are provided to manage the network. Special messages called SNMP Traps can be sent by any RS/6000 (or any other open system supporting the popular SNMP protocol) to report problems to Network Management/6000. Once a problem is detected, Network Management/6000 provides tools with which to diagnose and fix the problem. Further discussion of these AIX communications functions can be found in Chapter 5.

RS/6000 and AS/400 Distributed Network

In some cases, it may be desirable to distribute RS/6000 systems while having an AS/400 computer system at the central or headquarters location. There are many prewritten business applications available for AS/400 systems today, and AS/400 systems have strengths in the areas of database management and communications. However, the central location may wish to capitalize on the strengths of RS/6000 systems (i.e., standards compliance, workstation performance, etc.) to meet the needs of remote locations or departments within the business.

In any case, RS/6000 systems can participate in a distributed computer network consisting of RS/6000 systems and AS/400 computers. Figure 6.4 shows an

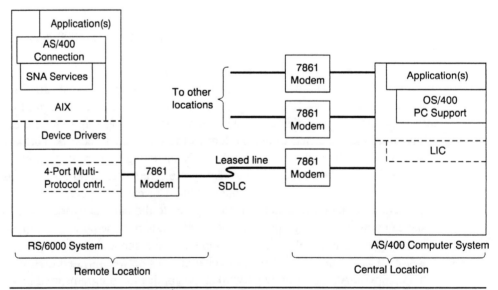

Figure 6.4. Example configuration used to attach RS/6000 systems to AS/400 computers.

example of a RS/6000 configuration that can be used to communicate with an AS/400 computer.

The 4-Port Multiprotocol Adapter in the RS/6000 provides the electrical interface and circuitry necessary to communicate with the AS/400 using the SDLC protocol. The 7861 Modem can allow the computers to communicate at 19,200 bits/sec over a leased telephone line.

The AS/400 Connection Program/6000 allows the RS/6000 to act like (**emulate**) a 5250 terminal — the type most often used with AS/400 systems. This allows a RS/6000 user (i.e., a workstation user or an ASCII terminal user) to log in to the AS/400 system and interact with any AS/400 applications for which he or she has authorization. The AS/400 Connection Program/6000 also interacts with the PC Support Program running the AS/400 to effect file transfers between the RS/6000 and the AS/400. An application programming interface is provided in the AS/400 Connection Program/6000 that allows for the development of application programs that perform direct interaction between application programs running on the RS/6000 and application programs running on the AS/400. SNA Services/6000 is a prerequisite for the AS/400 Connection Program/6000.

RS/6000 and System/390 Distributed Network

In some cases, it is desirable to distribute RS/6000 systems while having a System/390 (or a System/370) computer system at the central or headquarters location. The larger System/390 computers can provide more computational resource than even the largest RS/6000 system in the areas of performance, capacity, peripherals, and so on. The central location may need the kind of muscle provided by a System/390 computer. In other cases, the central location may already have a System/390 computer system and wish to distribute a mid-sized computer system to remote locations or departments within the business to better meet user needs. In any case, RS/6000 systems can exist in a distributed computer network consisting of RS/6000 systems and System/390 computers.

Figure 6.5 shows an example RS/6000 configuration that can be used to communicate with a System/390 computer. The 4-Port Multiprotocol Communications Controller will communicate utilizing the SDLC protocol used by the central IBM System/390 computer system. Again, the 7861 Modem allows the computers to communicate at 19,200 bits per second over leased telephone lines.

The 3270 Host Connection Program/6000 provides the programming necessary for an RS/6000 to act like (**emulate**) the 327X terminals and printers commonly used with System/390 computers. This allows a RS/6000 user (i.e., a workstation

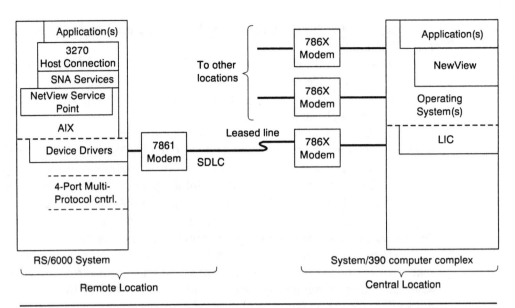

Figure 6.5. Example of a communications configuration used to attach an RS/6000 to a System/370 or System/390 computer.

user or an ASCII terminal user) to log in to the System/390 and interact with any System/390 application(s) for which he or she has authorization. The 3270 Host Connection Program/6000 also interacts with System/390 to effect file transfers between the RS/6000 and the System/390 computer. An application programming interface is provided in the 3270 Host Connection Program/6000 that allows for the development of application programs that perform direct interaction between application programs running on the RS/6000 and application programs running on the System/390.

With the addition of the NetView Service Point/6000 extension to AIX, the remote RS/6000 systems can be centrally managed by the System/390's operating systems and the NetView network management program at the central site. Together, NetView Service Point/6000 and NetView on the System/390 provide network management support for Alert messages (similar to SNMP Traps) that notify the network manager of hardware problems. Once a problem is detected, NetView Service Point/6000 and NetView on the System/390 provide tools to diagnose and resolve network problems.

In addition to the SNA environment shown in our example, there are many other environments in which RS/6000 systems and the System/390 can effectively interact, including non-SNA and TCP/IP environments. Chapter 5 covered other extensions to AIX that support these other distributed computing environments.

RS/6000 AND LOCAL AREA NETWORKS

We have seen how a single RS/6000 computer can be shared by many users through a network in which multiple ASCII terminals communicate with a single RS/6000. In other environments, however, a single RS/6000 system (or some other brand of computer) may act as a workstation serving the needs of a single user. This is often the case in highly demanding environments such as computer-aided design, technical publishing, computer simulation, and so on. When a group of such users are working together, they often have a need to share common information, application programs, and computer hardware.

A *Local Area Network* (**LAN**) provides one way for a local group of computers (e.g., located in the same building or on a single campus) to communicate very efficiently. LANs typically move information much faster than any other communications link covered in this book. This is important because the speed of a communications link can directly affect the overall productivity of the users participating in it. Slow communications can translate to slow response time, leading to frustration and reduced concentration. High-performance communications links are especially important in more technical environments where large amounts of information (CAD design geometry, digitized images and voice, etc.) are frequently moved around the network.

The price one pays for the high-speed communications available with LANs is limited distance, as the term "local" in LAN indicates. Due to electrical limitations, LANs can't be used as a direct communications link between distant computers (e.g., computers across town from one another). However, multiple LANs can be linked together over more traditional communications links.

Each computer that participates in a LAN is called a **node** in the network. An RS/6000 system can act as either a **client node** or a **server node.** A client node can operate as any normal standalone RS/6000 system and can also participate in LAN communications. Any shared resources on the network are accessible by a client node, but the client node itself offers no resource for other nodes to use. A server node can do everything a client node can do and can also offer resources, such as disk storage or a printer, for use by the other nodes in the network.

RS/6000 users participating in a LAN have four basic advantages over similar users not connected by a LAN:

- Data sharing
- Program sharing
- Equipment sharing
- Electronic mail

Data sharing is often the biggest reason to connect computers via a LAN. It is typical for multiple users to need access to the same body of information (e.g., design standards, image libraries, telephone directories, inventory information, etc.). With a LAN and the proper application programs, multiple users can simultaneously share access to a single body of information. Further, that information can be located on any (or even multiple) computers in the LAN.

Since programs are stored in files, just like data, application programs available on one RS/6000 can be loaded and executed by another RS/6000 in the network subject to the applicable software licensing terms.

Equipment sharing is another reason to connect computers via a LAN. Equipment sharing allows server nodes participating in a LAN to share their disk space, printers, communications equipment, and so forth, with other nodes in the LAN. This equipment-sharing function allows for more efficient utilization of the computing equipment participating in the LAN.

Finally, users participating in a network can freely exchange files with one another via electronic mail functions provided in the AIX operating system. Electronic mail allows a user or an application program to send simple text messages or complete documents to any other users in the LAN. This feature facilitates communications within the organization.

With this understanding of the LANs, we will now examine two example LANs commonly used with RS/6000 systems: Ethernet LANs and Token-Ring Networks. It should be understood that many variations and combinations of the simple examples that follow are also possible.

RS/6000 and the Ethernet LAN

Ethernet is a type of local area network commonly used in the open systems arena. The Ethernet LAN is widely supported by many different computer manufacturers, which is why it is commonly found in open systems environments. Ethernet LANs often consist of a mixture of different types and brands of computers.

Figure 6.6 shows the basic architecture of an Ethernet LAN. Each computer is attached as a tap-off of a common cable or information **bus.** For this reason, Ethernet is called a **bus-wired** network. Information is transferred over the PC network at a rate of 10 million bits/second (10 Mbps).

An Ethernet LAN is basically a party line on which all nodes can transmit messages for all nodes to hear. Every node has equal access to the cable and can send a message at any time without warning. When one node transmits a message, it is received by all nodes. Each node then examines the address contained in the message to see if the message is intended for that node. If not, the message is discarded.

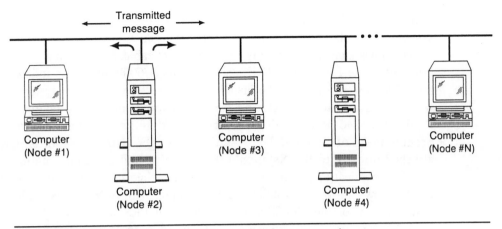

Figure 6.6. Basic architecture of an Ethernet local area network.

To ensure that information is sent around the Ethernet network in an orderly and reliable way, there is a protocol that each node follows when transmitting messages. This protocol is called *Carrier Sense Multiple Access/Collision Detect* (CSMA/CD). Its name is a mouthful, but really it's a quite simple protocol. In fact, we follow this protocol in our everyday telephone conversations. Here, too, only one person can speak at a time or neither is clearly understood. One party waits for the other to finish before beginning to speak. Thus the phone line only carries one party's voice at a time and the message is clear. This is the "CSMA" part of CSMA/CD. The "CD" part of the protocol handles the times when two nodes start transmissions simultaneously. To understand this part of the protocol, think of what you do during a telephone conversation when you begin talking at the same time as the other party. Typically, you both stop talking and begin again a second or two later, hoping that this time one of you begins sooner than the other. This is exactly analogous to the situation with CSMA/CD. If two (or more) nodes begin transmitting a message at the same time, the messages "collide" on the network. The nodes monitor for such a collision, and when one is detected, all nodes stop transmitting and begin again after a pause of random length. Usually, one node will begin its retransmission before the other, thus gaining control of the network.

Figure 6.7 shows an example of a small Ethernet LAN consisting of different computer systems including one RS/6000 system, an Xstation 130, one PS/2 (IBM Personal System/2) running the AIX operating system, one PS/2 computer running DOS (*D*isk *O*perating *S*ystem), and another open system computer—which could be any brand as long as TCP/IP communications is supported over an Ethernet LAN. The Ethernet High-Performance LAN Adapter allows the RS/6000 to physically connect to the Ethernet cable. In this example, the RS/6000 system is utilizing the

TCP/IP protocols, which are supported by functions included in the AIX operating system. The Xstation 130 comes standard with an Ethernet LAN adapter built in, which allows attachment directly to the Ethernet cable. In order to support the Xstation 130 in the LAN, the AIX Xstation Manager/6000 and AIXwindows Environment/6000 extensions must be installed on at least one RS/6000 system in the network accessible to the Xstation. The Xstation Manager extension allows the RS/6000 to send programming over the network to the Xstation 130, which has no programming of its own. The Xstation Manager also allows an ASCII printer attached directly to the Xstation 130 to receive and print information from the RS/6000 application program as if it were attached directly to the RS/6000. The AIXwindows allows an Xstation 130 to interact with X Windows application programs running on the RS/6000. As with distributed RS/6000 networks, the AIX Network Management/6000 extension to AIX provides tools for detecting and resolving network problems. Special messages called SNMP Traps can be sent by any RS/6000 (or any other open system supporting the emerging SNMP industry standard) to report problems to Network Management/6000. Once a problem is detected, Network Management/6000 provides tools with which to diagnose and fix the problem. Network management becomes increasingly difficult as the size of the network is increased.

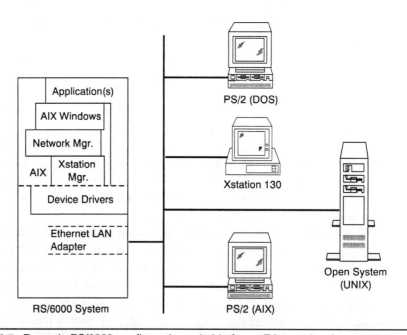

Figure 6.7. Example RS/6000 configuration suitable for an Ethernet local area network.

The PS/2 running its version of AIX, called the AIX operating system PS/2, can participate in the network with the help of the AIX PS/2 TCP/IP and the AIX PS/2 X Windows extensions to AIX PS/2. The other PS/2s running DOS can also participate in our example Ethernet LAN through the AIX Access for DOS Users extension to DOS. This DOS extension allows the PS/2 to double as an ASCII terminal, providing access to AIX application programs on the RS/6000 while still providing all normal PS/2 functions. AIX Access for DOS Users also takes advantage of the PS/2's computing power to support file transfer between the RS/6000 and the PS/2 systems. Finally, AIX Access for DOS Users allows the RS/6000 to share its printers and disk space with the PS/2. That is, the PS/2 can print DOS files on RS/6000 printers and store DOS programs and data on the RS/6000 disks. While the RS/6000 can't understand these files, it will store them for the PS/2 and provide them upon request.

The final computer in our example network could be any open system capable of supporting TCP/IP communications over Ethernet. This ability to have different brands of computers exchanging information over a common LAN is the payoff for the "open systems" approach. While our example LAN has only one such computer, it could easily have had many more.

RS/6000 and the Token-Ring Network

Figure 6.8 shows the basic architecture of the Token-Ring Network. The nodes of the network are arranged in a "ring" pattern, thus giving the network its name. The twisted-pair (two-wire) cable commonly used in the network is connected to the computer's Token-Ring Adapter at one end and to the **8228** *Multistation Access Unit* (MAU) at the other. The MAU is the device, typically located in a wiring closet, that actually makes the electrical connections between the cables to each node in the network. One MAU supports up to eight nodes. A modular jack is used to attach each network node to the MAU, which lets nodes be quickly added to or removed from the network. The MAU can automatically bypass any failing nodes by detecting their inactivity. Multiple MAUs can be cabled together using the same twisted-pair cable to allow more nodes in the network. With the proper cable components, a single Token-Ring Network can contain up to 260 nodes over several kilometers. Multiple Token-Ring Networks can be linked together by a bridge, allowing still more network nodes to communicate with each other. Information is transferred over the network at either 4 or 16 million bits per second using the **token-passing** protocol. With this protocol, a single packet of information called a message frame is passed around the ring from node to node in a continuous circle. The token is the "mailbag" of the network. It carries the network messages (one at a time) from the

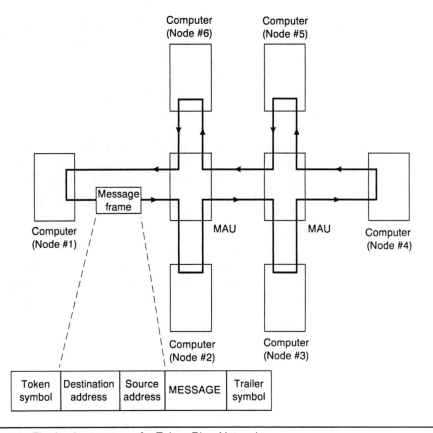

Figure 6.8. The basic structure of a Token-Ring Network.

transmitting node to all other nodes in the network until the recipient is reached and the message is delivered (see Figure 6.8). When a node receives a frame, it looks to see if it is a message or a token frame. If it is a token frame, it means that the network is idle and that node can send a message. If it is a message frame, the node will examine the address contained in the token message to see if the message is intended for that node. If not, the frame will be passed unchanged to the next node in the ring.

Figure 6.9 provides an example of a small Token-Ring Network of different IBM computer systems including two RS/6000 systems, one PS/2 running the DOS operating system, one PS/2 running OS/2 Extended Edition, and one larger IBM computer, which could be either an AS/400 or an S/390 computer system. The Token-Ring High-Performance Network Adapter allows the RS/6000 to physically connect to the Token-Ring Network cable leading to the 8228 Multistation Access Unit. The 8228 is needed as part of the cabling system for any Token-Ring Network. In this example, the RS/6000 system is communicating with other IBM systems using proto-

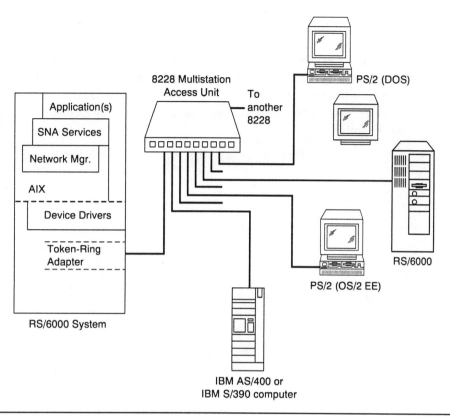

Figure 6.9. RS/6000 configuration capable of participating in a Token-Ring Network with AS/400 and/or S/390.

cols from IBM's System Network Architecture (LU 6.2) — their native tongue rather than the TCP/IP protocols used in the previous example. It should be noted, however, that the TCP/IP protocols can be used over the Token-Ring Network also.

To communicate in this environment, the RS/6000 systems must have the IBM AIX System Network Architecture Services/6000 extension. The PS/2 running DOS can communicate using SNA protocols with the IBM PC SNA Support extension to DOS. The PS/2 running OS/2 EE (Operating System/2 Extended Edition) can also support SNA communications through the SNA support in the Communications Manager included with OS/2 EE. Likewise, the SNA support provided in Operating System/400 (OS/400) used with the IBM AS/400 family of computers allows these systems to participate in our example. The IBM S/390 family of computers (or the S/370 computer systems) can run one of several different operating systems all providing support for SNA communications.

With the addition of the AIX NetView Service Point/6000 extension, the RS/6000 systems can work even more closely with the System/390's operating systems and NetView network management program. Together, these programs provide network management support for Alert messages that notify the network manager of hardware and software problems. Once a problem is detected, AIX NetView Service Point/6000 and NetView provide tools to help diagnose and resolve network problems.

7

RS/6000 and Your Environment

An important first step in bringing an RS/6000 system or any computer into your environment is planning. Largely depending on how well you plan, introducing new computer resource(s) can be like pouring water or gasoline on a fire. Many readers will already have access to a significant number of computers and will add RS/6000 systems to their computer arsenal, while others will be bringing RS/6000 systems in as their first computer. In either case, the information in this chapter should help you understand how to introduce RS/6000 systems into your particular environment.

The chapter starts by discussing the introspection process critical to any automation project and then covers software selection. A general discussion of differences between RS/6000, AS/400, PS/2, and S/390 computers follows. Then some specific RS/6000 hardware configurations appropriate for some example environments are offered.

The latter part of the chapter includes discussions on the following topics:

- Financial decisions
- User education
- Physical planning
- Education
- Technical support
- Ergonomics
- Security
- Service

This chapter is by no means a complete guide to introducing RS/6000 systems into any environment, but it will give you a starting point for developing your plan and will discuss some important issues.

WHAT ARE MY COMPUTING NEEDS?

Many people today use some type of computer system(s) to do their job. These users must constantly ask themselves if their current system is good enough. Those organizations that are still operated using manual methods must ask themselves how automating their organizations might help. This book certainly can't answer the question for you, but it can give you things to consider. Whether your organization has millions of dollars' worth of computer systems or none at all, the way to begin answering these questions is to forget about computer hardware and software and look very closely at your organization. Too often, organizations buy computer systems and then look for problems to solve. A properly managed computer project should start by careful introspection into the collective needs of all functional areas within the organization. Independently attacking specific problems can often result in a "dead-end" computer solution that provides no coherent growth strategy for the future. From the very start, key people from all areas of the organization should be collected into a project team. Since all areas will likely be involved, the top management of the organization must consistently demonstrate a commitment to the project. Without top management involvement, disagreements among the peer business areas are slow to be resolved and the sense of priority is diminished. Lack of consistent top management commitment either at the investigation or the implementation phase of a computer project is a common cause of unsuccessful projects. The cost of a computer project failure is much higher than the cost of doing it right in the first place.

The project team should start by reviewing the overall goals of the organization (or segment of a larger organization) over the next few years. In some cases, these goals will be well known, but in others, a great deal of soul-searching will be necessary. These goals should be as specific as possible and should include any organizational strategies in place to achieve the goals.

After the organization's goals are clearly defined, the project team should look closely at the current day-to-day operations of the organization as it is. Consider the movement of information through the entire organization. Only after the information flow is understood can the team candidly discuss what is good and what is bad about the current way of doing things. Work to identify the sources of problems rather than focusing on symptoms. Understand the interaction between the various areas of the organization. Consider the flow of information from one group to another as you trace the activities. Chances are, not every problem that you will uncover will have a computer solution. For example, an inventory management application program will not solve inventory problems in a business if everyone is free to walk casually into the storeroom unauthorized and get what they need. Computers and application programs are only tools you can use to effectively manage your organization. They will not manage your organization for you.

After you have examined your current operation with a critical eye, you can begin to see if a computer solution makes sense for your business. In a small organization, this type of analysis can be done in a matter of weeks or even days. With larger organizations, it can span months or even years and typically is done on an ongoing basis. Some organizations choose to do the analysis on their own. If you want assistance in solving problems with computers, there are plenty of places to turn — including consultants, software companies, and computer manufacturers.

CHOOSING THE SOFTWARE

Computer systems become a useful tool only when they are executing the appropriate application programs. While there are many ways of generating a strategy for introducing computers, considering software needs before selecting detailed hardware configurations usually makes sense. The hardware requirements, such as memory size, disk space, and so on, will in part be based on the needs of the application program(s) selected.

The application programs you select must perform the tasks needed by your end users both today and in the foreseeable future. Chapter 4 already discussed some basic types of application programs commonly used today. Selecting the basic type of application program is often fairly simple. For example, an accounting department needs an accounting application program, a secretary needs a word-processing application program, an engineer needs a computer-aided design application program. What is more difficult is identifying the specific application program that best fits your particular needs. Is a custom application program preferred, or will a prewritten application program be acceptable? If a prewritten application program is desired, exactly which one is best for your needs? If a custom application program is desired, who should write it and what should it include? The answers to these questions depend largely on specifics of a given environment and are thus beyond the scope of this book. There are, however, a few basics that remain the same whether selecting a program for a multinational corporation or for a corner fish market. First of all, you must precisely understand the task you are trying to put on a computer before pursuing any application program alternatives. A thorough knowledge of the task helps you to identify specific requirements your application program must meet. After a detailed understanding of the task is obtained, a search can begin through the sea of prewritten or "off-the-shelf" application programs. If you can find an appropriate prewritten application program that fits your needs, you can avoid the expense, delay, and effort associated with custom application program development. Good prewritten application programs can be quite flexible. However, since everyone typically has slightly different needs and methods, even within a given business function, you can bet that any prewritten application will have features you don't need and won't have some features you will wish it did.

There are many sources of information about the many prewritten application programs on the market. Of course, software companies and consultants can help you select particular application programs to fit your needs. Many popular computer magazines consistently conduct extensive reviews of prewritten application programs. These can be excellent and timely sources of information.

For specific or highly specialized needs, prewritten application programs may not be adequate. In this case, custom-developed software may be desirable. While the development and maintenance of custom software is a long-term commitment that typically is expensive, it may be less costly in the long run to pay for the development of custom software than to settle for a prewritten application program that doesn't do the job. If you do select the custom software route, an important step is to select the proper developer. Organizations that have their own programming staff can do their own custom application program development. If you don't have your own programmers, it will be necessary to seek outside help, that is, an outside software developer. In either case, it is the developer who will have the largest effect on the ultimate success or failure of the custom development activity. The developer's job is not an easy one. Besides programming expertise, developers must become experts in all aspects of the organizations' activities right down to every step performed. They must be good communicators to understand and discuss users' requirements. They must understand human psychology when defining the user interface for the program. They must be proficient teachers to train the end users on the new program. Finally, they must be dependable and reliable so you know they will be there for technical support and to provide software maintenance and any needed modifications.

WHEN SHOULD I CONSIDER AN RS/6000 SYSTEM?

When looking for ways to meet computing needs, one is faced with a seemingly endless series of questions. Before we get into how to select RS/6000 system hardware to meet your needs, let's pause and glance at some other hardware alternatives.

What about Personal System/2?

While this book is about RS/6000 systems, it is important to understand how they differ from IBM's Personal System/2 (PS/2) family in order to make good buying decisions. In fact, since PS/2 systems can run their own version of the AIX operating system, called PS/2 AIX, many of the same application programs available for RS/6000 systems are also available in PS/2 AIX versions.

The first difference between RS/6000 systems and PS/2 computers lies in performance. The performance offered in the RS/6000 workstation is much higher than that available in the PS/2 workstation. This is especially true in environments where floating-point math must be calculated. RS/6000 systems have been optimized to improve performance in the floating-point calculations commonly found in engineering and scientific applications. This fact, along with the much more powerful graphics capabilities of the RS/6000 systems, allows them to provide, for example, computer-aided design, computer-aided manufacturing, and technical publishing capabilities far beyond those available on a PS/2.

Another point to consider about PS/2 workstations is that they can use other operating systems besides PS/2 AIX, including Disk Operating System (DOS) and Operating System/2 (OS/2). DOS is a widely used operating system with many available applications. OS/2 is a participant in IBM's Systems Application architecture, which is a set of rules designed to allow IBM PS/2, AS/400, and S/390 computers to work closely together. While the AIX operating system (for the PS/2 or the RS/6000) can participate in Systems Application architecture environments, the AIX operating system is not central to IBM's overall Systems Application architecture strategy.

In multiuser environments, a PS/2 running the AIX operating system can support multiple users each accessing the system via an ASCII display. However, the higher performance of the RS/6000 family allows a single RS/6000 system to be shared by many more users than can share any PS/2.

As an alternative to sharing a single RS/6000 or PS/2 (with AIX), either computer system type can be attached together to form a local area network. Local area network configurations allow much of the same data, program, and equipment sharing afforded by multiuser configurations. So which is best? The LAN-versus-multiuser system debate still rages, and it is clear both approaches have merit. Here are some things to consider to help make the decision. Multiuser systems are more mature than LANs simply by virtue of the fact that they have been around longer. This means that there are more "tried and true" business applications for multiuser configurations than for LAN configurations. However, either approach will require some level of technical skill, at least during initial installation. Things like the number of workstations, technical support level, systems management activity, and so on, will determine which approach yields the lowest cost. Again, the most important thing to consider is the application programs that are under consideration for each approach. The approach with the best-fitting application program will normally provide the best results.

What about AS/400 Computers?

AS/400 systems are IBM's mid-range computer system that replaced the popular System/36 and System/38 business computer families. AS/400 computers are multiuser systems designed to meet the needs of business computing. The RS/6000 family has a split personality in that it can be used as a high-function workstation for a single user or as a general-purpose multiuser computer system in typical business environments. Since the AS/400 has no capability to be used as a high-function workstation for things like computer aided design and technical publishing, the RS/6000 family is clearly the pick for those applications.

In the general-purpose multiuser computer system arena, however, there is certainly room for confusion when deciding between the RS/6000 and the AS/400 families of computers. To resolve this confusion, let's look at some of the design points of each family. The AS/400 systems architecture includes a built-in relational database. In other words, the AS/400 hardware and operating system have been designed specifically to provide the database function commonly needed in business environments. Most other computer systems (including the RS/6000) require separately purchased database programs that sit on top of the operating system to provide users with a relational database. Since the AS/400 system's database is implemented in the hardware and operating system, the performance and elegance of the database implementation is improved. Further, the programmer productivity afforded by the built-in AS/400 database makes it a good system for those writing and maintaining their own business application programs. Finally, AS/400 systems are leading the way in the implementation of IBM's Systems Application Architecture (SAA). All things being equal, if you need to coexist with a network of other IBM systems following SAA, an AS/400 may be indicated. It should be noted, however, that AS/400 computers can also participate in non-SAA "open" environments through their support TCP/IP.

The RS/6000 has no built-in database, but relational database programs are available that add this capability to the system. While this added database will add an additional workload to the RS/6000 system, this is only a problem if not considered when selecting which RS/6000 model is needed. For those migrating from a multiuser computer system running the UNIX operating system, the migration to an

RS/6000 system will be much more natural than migrating to an AS/400 system. If you need to coexist with computer systems of many different brands, the "open system" approach taken by the RS/6000 system will be a plus. By supporting many pervasive industry standards, RS/6000 systems and the AIX operating system are designed to participate with other types of computing equipment.

What about System/390 Computers?

The IBM System/390 computer family, along with their predecessors the S/370 family, are also widely used to fill users' needs. Like RS/6000 systems, System/390 computers are multiuser computer systems that allow many users to share the system. Through high-function displays and graphics processors, System/390 computers can also provide a workstation solution to meet the needs of technical professionals performing engineering design, technical publishing, and so on. Either S/390 or RS/6000 systems might provide a user with better performance, depending on the specific applications, the number of users involved, and other variables. Since S/390 computers can also run their own version of the AIX operating system, many RS/6000 applications are available for System/390 AIX and vice versa. For these reasons, the choice between RS/6000 systems and S/390 systems is not always clear and will depend heavily on the details of your situation. However, here are some general things to consider.

The S/390 family spans the computational power range that starts by overlapping with the RS/6000 and includes the largest of all IBM computers. In order to maintain an S/390 computer system, a highly trained programmer called a **systems programmer** is needed. This is because the operating systems used by S/390 computers are both powerful and complex. Experienced personnel are needed to install and manage these operating systems. While remote S/390 computers can easily be managed by systems programming personnel at a central S/390 site, the expertise must be available at some level. While RS/6000 systems and the AIX operating system require a systems operator and a programming staff if custom application software is being developed, no systems programmer is needed.

Another way of comparing a single System/390 computer with a group of RS/6000 systems connected via a local area network brings us to the discussion of centralized computing versus decentralized computing. A single S/390 being shared by a community of high-function display users is considered a centralized computer environment since the significant processing and all auxiliary storage are resident in a single computer. The advantages of the centralized approach include easier system management since the computer operators, system programmers, and programming staff have complete control over the computer system. Important practices such as nightly tape backup of disk storage are easier to monitor and enforce. The decentralized approach is represented by multiple RS/6000 systems located throughout a building or campus and connected via a local area network. The advantage of this approach is that each user gains control over his or her own computer system and is not affected by the activities of the other users or those of the programming staff. Decentralization gives users (especially more-technical users) more independence. There are good and bad to both the centralized and the decentralized approaches.

Many times, the decision between RS/6000 systems and S/390 will be based on your current situation. For instance, if you currently have an S/390 (or S/370) computer, it may be natural to expand with additional S/390 computers. However, it should be noted that RS/6000 systems coexist very well with S/390 computers. If you are using the UNIX operating system today, it may make sense to migrate to the RS/6000 system due to its ability to coexist with other brands of computers. Again we get to the Systems Application Architecture versus the "open system" direction. It becomes a matter of philosophy.

CHOOSING RS/6000 CONFIGURATIONS

Even after you have settled on the application software to be used, selecting the proper RS/6000 hardware and system software components to meet your needs can still be confusing. You must select the RS/6000 system model, disk configuration, feature cards, peripherals, AIX extensions, and so forth. To aid in this activity, let's examine some example environments and outfit them with the appropriate RS/6000 configurations. We will examine a small, a medium, and a large business. With the insight provided by outfitting these hypothetical business environments with technical workstations and general-purpose business systems, you will be better prepared to properly select the RS/6000 system components useful in your environment.

Small-Business Environment—Bob's Gearbox Co.

Our hypothetical small business is a gearbox manufacturer named Bob's Gearbox Company. Bob's has a standard line of gearboxes and also accepts orders for custom gearboxes. It is a private corporation (owned by Bob, of course) with 32 employees. Bob has been in business for five years and has experienced moderate growth. He currently conducts business by noncomputer methods but finds himself needing to streamline his operation as the business grows. Bob is especially concerned that his profits seem to be shrinking as his sales increase. A study of Bob's business shows that he has two basic causes for this. First, his salespeople often commit to discounted pricing on a gearbox order to capture the business. The trouble is that Bob never really knows what it actually costs him to produce a given gearbox. He uses standard cost estimates to price a customer's order and hopes that his actual costs to build the gearbox are somewhere close.

The second basic problem uncovered in the study is that Bob's inventory is not well managed. The production department is often hampered by not having the right parts and raw materials in inventory. This often causes slips in the delivery of customer orders, hurting customer satisfaction and fueling heated arguments between the marketing manager, the production manager, and the materials manager. Finger-pointing is commonplace. The study also showed that 25% of the inventory items in stock are obsolete and will never be used.

In this scenario, it is clear that Bob has outgrown his manual methods of doing business. Bob needs a better way to track the actual costs associated with manufacturing his products. This may uncover the fact that his salespeople often sell gearboxes at or below cost. Bob also needs help tracking his inventory. He needs to know when critical parts are getting low and what parts are slow moving. The deficiencies in Bob's business can be addressed with the proper computer solution.

After looking through manufacturing trade journals and having informal discussions with others in the industry, Bob finds several prewritten industry-specific application programs that seem to fit his needs. After seeing demonstrations and having detailed conversations with others using the application programs, Bob selects one of the packages. The selected package will allow Bob to track manufacturing costs more closely by more accurately letting him know the costs of labor, outside purchases, and inventory that is used in making his products. Bob will also gain better control over his inventory through improved procedures and the inventory-management function of this new application program. Bob also chooses to take advantage of the computer system to automate the general accounting functions of his business, such as payroll, accounts receivable, accounts payable, and general ledger. The order entry and invoicing functions of the application program will allow Bob to better track orders and more quickly bill customers. Of course, Bob will need the RS/6000 system's operating system AIX.

Based on the requirements of the chosen application program and his small number of users, Bob will get the RS/6000 Model 320 shown in Figure 7.1. The Model 320 was selected for its low cost and more than ample computing power. Since the standard 160 MB disk drive will not quite be sufficient to hold the system software, application programs, and associated data, the optional 160 to 400 MB SCSI Disk Select feature will be specified. This will instruct the factory to install a 400 MB SCSI disk drive in place of the 160 MB disk drive normally provided in the standard configuration. The Model 320's ability to expand to 800 MB of disk storage will allow for some expansion as Bob's business grows. If in the future (say five

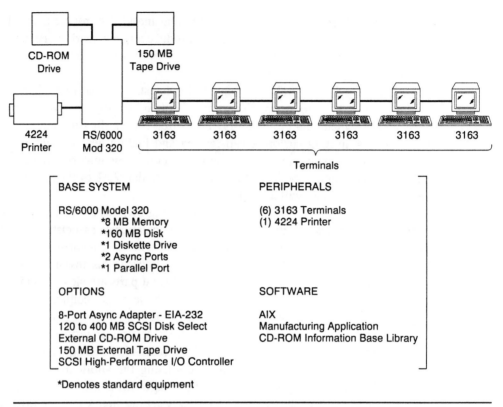

CD-ROM
Drive

150 MB
Tape Drive

4224
Printer

RS/6000
Mod 320

3163 3163 3163 3163 3163 3163

Terminals

BASE SYSTEM

RS/6000 Model 320
     *8 MB Memory
     *160 MB Disk
     *1 Diskette Drive
     *2 Async Ports
     *1 Parallel Port

PERIPHERALS

(6) 3163 Terminals
(1) 4224 Printer

OPTIONS

8-Port Async Adapter - EIA-232
120 to 400 MB SCSI Disk Select
External CD-ROM Drive
150 MB External Tape Drive
SCSI High-Performance I/O Controller

SOFTWARE

AIX
Manufacturing Application
CD-ROM Information Base Library

*Denotes standard equipment

Figure 7.1. An RS/6000 Model 320 configured to suit the needs of Bob's Gearbox Co.

years) Bob needs more processing power, he can easily upgrade to a Model 320H. If he needs more disk space or more Micro Channel slots, he can replace his Model 320 with a still-larger RS/6000 model (e.g., a Model 530H) to get more disk space without giving up his software investment and experience with the selected application program. In an effort to keep expenses to a minimum, Bob selects six 3163 ASCII terminals. One display is for the inventory clerk, one is for the purchasing agent, two are for the accounting department, one is for the production department, and one is for Bob so he can get the management information he needs to make intelligent decisions. Since the Model 320 only comes standard with two async ports, the optional 8-Port Async Adapter EIA-232 is needed. This will provide four extra ports for future expansion. The 4224 Model 3E3 printer will be used to produce the various reports provided by the manufacturing application program at a rate of 600 characters per second. It will be attached to the parallel port provided as standard with the Model 320. Bob decides to choose the 16 MB Memory Select feature.

This will instruct the factory to replace the standard 8 MB Memory Card with a 16 MB Memory Card, conserving slots and ensuring that Bob will have some room for growth. The 150 MB External Tape Drive option will provide a way to back up data on the disk, ensuring that important business information will not be accidentally lost. This tape drive attaches directly to the diskette controller circuitry provided as standard equipment. Finally, Bob will get the 7210 External CD-ROM Drive and the Information Base Library for AIX so that he and the other users can have access to AIX operating system documentation on line without consuming valuable disk space. While Bob could simply purchase the manuals available for the system, the improved productivity afforded by on-line documentation will soon outweigh the added cost of the CD-ROM drive and the Information Base Library. The CD-ROM drive and the 400 MB disk require the SCSI High-Performance I/O Controller. This Model 320 configuration leaves one free Micro Channel slot and one free Memory Expansion slot for future expansion.

Medium-Business Environment—Johnson & Thornbush

Our hypothetical medium-sized business is an advertising agency named Johnson & Thornbush. This company has been in business for 12 years. Their business started with one major account, and today they have 17 large clients. Steve Johnson and Perry Thornbush are both still actively involved in managing the business. There are 74 employees, and almost all of them currently have PS/2s which provide tools for things like market analysis, trend analysis, word processing, financial modeling, and so on.

Steve Johnson recently sponsored a company-wide study to find a way to address the business goals of increasing their marketing effectiveness and reducing their operating costs. This study quickly uncovered the fact that the campaign creation staff relies heavily on the overloaded art department to generate the complex proposals associated with marketing campaigns. The art department generates needed artwork on large drawing boards and has started relying more and more on costly outside subcontractors. They find themselves inundated with urgent requests for new artwork and changes to existing artwork. Even though the art department personnel constantly work overtime, they are unable to keep up with the workload.

Another situation confirmed by the study is that the market analysis being done by one PS/2 user seldom correlates with the market analysis done by another PS/2 user. The cause of the disagreeing information turns out to be that different versions of the area demographic information reside on the various PS/2 fixed disks used in the market analysis. Even though one person has responsibility for periodically updating the demographic information and distributing the updates, it seems that eventually different versions of the information emerge, making the market analysis inaccurate. Further, as market coverage grows, the demographic information is growing in size and is becoming impractical to distribute via diskettes. It is apparent that more-sophisticated data management and analysis techniques will become necessary as the company grows.

The project team decided to find a solution that would increase the output of the art department and centralize the area demographic information. They concluded that the most effective way to increase the output of the art department was to provide them with computer-based graphics tools and desktop publishing capabilities. The graphics tools would allow them to more quickly create the artwork and build a library of graphic images that could be modified and used in many different campaigns. When there was a need to change an image, it could be recalled on the computer display and quickly modified. The desktop publishing capability would allow the art department to combine graphics images and text to create comprehensive and professional-quality proposals in-house. A laser printer and plotter would be used to provide high-quality black-and-white or multicolor hard copy of the graphics as needed. Simple photography equipment will allow the art department to take color photographs of complex graphic images generated on the computer's display. This photography equipment will be used to generate full-color transparencies for slide presentations.

Compared with current methods, these tools help to increase quality, decrease the turnaround time, and reduce costs associated with artwork. A later phase of the project will examine projecting animated computer images directly onto large screens along with digitized high-fidelity sound to provide very effective multimedia presentations.

The team also concluded that the simplest way to centralize the demographic information was to place the information on a single computer system and use a local area network to provide all PS/2 users with access to the information. All PS/2 users would simultaneously share this single copy of the information, ensuring that all were using the same current data for their marketing analysis. This would result in a more accurate market analysis and thus more effective marketing efforts for clients.

After examining several different prewritten graphics and desktop publishing application programs, they select application programs that can run on several different brands of open system workstations. After considering price/performance, graphics capabilities, PS/2 server capabilities, and other factors, the RS/6000 family is selected.

Figure 7.2 shows an RS/6000-based local area network solution suitable for Johnson & Thornbush. The 16 MB Token-Ring Network was selected as the LAN for its high bandwidth and network management features.

Three workstations will be provided in the art department, one RS/6000 work-

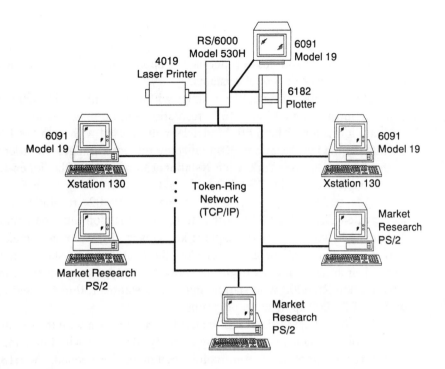

BASE SYSTEM

RS/6000 Model 530H
   * 32 MB Memory
   * 400 MB Disk
   * 1 Diskette Drive
   * 2 Async ports
   * 1 Parallel port
   * SCSI Adapter Card

OPTIONS

Token-Ring Network Adapter
150 MB Internal Tape Drive
32 MB Memory Card
857 MB disk select option
Internal CD-ROM Drive
POWERGt3 Graphics Adpter
Mouse/Keyboard

PERIPHERALS

Existing PS/2s w/ Token adapter
4019 Personal Page Printer
6182 Auto-Feed Color Plotter
6091 Color Display Model 23
Mouse
(2) Xstation 130
  - Token Ring Adapter
  - Video Memory Upgrade
  - Mouse

SOFTWARE

AIX
AIXwindows Environment/6000
Desk-top Publishing application
Graphics application program
CD-ROM Information Base Library
AIX Network Management/6000
Personal Computer Simulator/6000

(PS/2 Software)
AIX Access for DOS users
TCP/IP for the PS/2

* Denotes standard equipment

Figure 7.2. Xstation 130s and the RS/6000 Model 530H server in a LAN at Johnson & Thornbush.

station and two Xstation 130 workstations. The two Xstation 130s included in Johnson & Thornbush's network will give two more artists simultaneous access to the RS/6000 graphics and desktop publishing application programs at a lower cost than providing two more RS/6000 systems.

The POWER Gt3 graphics adapter will be used in the RS/6000 workstation to generate images with 1280 × 1024 resolution and up to 256 colors from a pallet of 16.7 million colors. The 6091 Model 19 will be used with both the RS/6000 workstation and the two Xstation 130s to display full color images. In order to participate in the Token-Ring Network, each Xstation 130 must have the Token-Ring Network 16/4 Adapter/A and the RS/6000 will need the Token-Ring High-Performance Network Adapter. Further, to support the same 1280 × 1024 resolution with 256 colors as provided on the RS/6000 workstation, each Xstation must be equipped with the Xstation 130 Video Memory Upgrade kit. This configuration will make the Xstation 130 workstations behave and "feel like" the RS/6000 workstation, reducing confusion when an artist moves from one workstation type to another. A mouse will be added to the RS/6000 workstation and each Xstation 130 to be used for interacting with the RS/6000 application programs.

The 4019 Laser Printer will be used in conjunction with the desktop publishing application program to generate high-quality black-and-white documents including both text and graphics. If multicolor documents are needed, the 6182 Auto-Feed Color Plotter will be used. This plotter can create eight-color drawings and text on A- or B-sized paper or transparencies. The automatic sheet feed will allow the plotter to print multiple drawings unattended.

In addition to supporting the three art department workstations, the RS/6000 will be used as a file and print server by all PS/2 users on the network. As a file server, the RS/6000 will be the central repository for demographic information needed by many PS/2 users performing market research. In effect, a portion of the RS/6000 disk becomes a giant PS/2 disk shared by all PS/2s. As a print server, it will allow all PS/2 users to print documents on either the 4019 Laser Printer or the 6182 Plotter just as if these devices were attached to their PS/2. Although many printers are already attached to the PS/2s, the 4019 will be the first laser printer and the 6182 will be the first plotter made available.

The file and print server functions will be provided by the "DOS Server" function in the AIX operating system on the RS/6000 along with the "AIX Access for DOS Users" licensed program that runs on the PS/2s. AIX Access for DOS Users will allow the PS/2s to access the printer, plotter, and demographic information stored on a shared volume on the RS/6000 disk. The demographic data will be stored in the DOS format on the RS/6000 disk rather than in AIX format so that the PS/2 users can use the data with the DOS application programs they currently use. Each PS/2 will also require a Token-Ring Network Adapter and the "Transmission Control

Protocol for the PS/2" licensed program in order to participate in the TCP/IP-based Token-Ring Network.

Based on the needs of the three art department workstations and the PS/2 server workload, the RS/6000 Model 530H is selected. This will provide adequate performance while providing sufficient expansion capability for Johnson & Thornbush in terms of disk and memory size, and processor speed. The 400 to 857 MB SCSI Disk Select feature will be chosen to instruct the factory to install an 857 MB SCSI disk in place of the 400 MB disk used in the standard configuration.

The 2.3 GB 8mm Internal Tape Drive will be used to back up the information on the RS/6000 disk daily. The internal CD-ROM Drive will give all users in the network quick access to the RS/6000 Information Base Library of manuals. While all users on the network will have access to these on-line manuals, they will be most useful to the RS/6000 workstation users in the art department.

In addition to the AIX operating system, AIXwindows Environment/6000 is needed, since it is a prerequisite for the graphics and desktop publishing application programs. Finally, the AIX Network Management/6000 program will help the network administrator keep things running smoothly.

Based on the vast experience with DOS application programs at Johnson & Thornbush, the study team also decides to install the "AIX Personal Computer Simulator/6000" on the RS/6000 system. This will allow the user of the RS/6000 workstation users to execute multiple, concurrent DOS application programs. Although of secondary importance to Johnson & Thornbush, the AIX Personal Computer Simulator/6000 will also allow any authorized PS/2 user to sign on to the RS/6000 as an ASCII terminal and run many character-based (i.e., nongraphics) DOS application programs. Of course the PS/2 users can also do everything they could before the local area network.

The electronic mail functions provided in the AIX operating system and the Transmission Control Protocol for the Personal System/2 will allow any user to electronically send documents or quick notes to any other user. This will streamline the internal communications within Johnson & Thornbush. While there are many word-processing application programs available for the RS/6000 system, the word-processing application currently being used on the PS/2s works well, so there is no need to make a change. However, the documents generated on the PS/2s will be sent around the network using the electronic mail functions of the AIX operating system.

Large-Business Environment—Atole Enterprises

Our hypothetical large business is Atole Enterprises. This multinational corporation is a manufacturer of aircraft and enjoys financial prowess worthy of its Fortune 500 membership. The many benefits afforded by computers are no news to Atole Enterprises. They have been using computers in their day-to-day operations for many years. Atole has at least one large S/390 computer at every major Atole facility. These large computers are linked together in a computer network, enabling the electronic transfer of information all over the world. Atole has developed many custom application programs for the S/390 computers. We will look more closely at the hypothetical Atole site on the outskirts of Pensacola, Florida.

Atole–Pensacola is a large manufacturing and advanced research facility. The company installed an Ethernet local area network several years ago and has a collection of workstations that run the UNIX operating system and participate in that network. These workstations support engineering, manufacturing, and research activities. There is also a large S/390 computer with custom application programs and many terminals and printers attached. This system provides inventory management, basic accounting, order entry, and other financial reporting functions.

A study team was tasked with finding ways to reduce the time it takes to design, manufacture, and test new aircraft designs while improving quality. The study team found that while the design engineers are using some computer-aided design tools on open system workstations, the tools are fairly old and do not offer comprehensive three-dimensional design capabilities. The designers feel that improved three-dimensional design and modeling tools would allow them to design aircraft components more quickly and with fewer errors. For example, the improved interference checking between components of an assembly afforded by true three-dimensional modeling would uncover any design problems early in the design cycle. Further, they feel that the improvement in productivity afforded by three-dimensional design would enable them to more efficiently investigate new design alternatives, which would result in higher design quality. After evaluating several alternatives, IBM's **CAEDS** computer-aided design/computer-aided manufacturing application program which runs on the RS/6000 family was selected as the new strategic design tool for Atole–Pensacola. CAEDS stands for *Computer-Aided Engineering Design System*. The strengths of this product in the area of stress analysis will prove essential to Atole.

Another problem area uncovered by the study was a lack of control on released (completed) engineering drawings. As a result, manufacturing would unknowingly build useless components based on pre-released or old engineering drawings not reflecting the latest engineering change. These drawings might come from informal meetings between design engineers and manufacturing engineers, private files of drawings, and so forth. This lack of control results in expensive scrap and schedule delays.

To address this situation, Atole will use the S/390 computer as a central repository for all released (completed) engineering drawings. When engineering makes a design change, the released drawing will replace the older drawing on the S/390. When manufacturing needs a drawing, it will only be made available on the S/390 computer. Eventually, all design documentation (drawings, routings, bills of material, numerical control programs, etc.) will be delivered to graphics terminals on the manufacturing floor, resulting in a paperless manufacturing environment. For now, the design drawings will be pulled down from the S/390 and viewed or plotted via an engineering workstation provided for manufacturing. When engineering is done with the drawing, they will throw it away.

The study also found that aircraft wind tunnel testing was a lengthy process, consuming much of the entire development cycle for new aircraft. The testing process itself wasn't the problem; rather, the design problems found during this testing would require component redesign, remanufacture of a prototype, and retesting. The time spent in redesigning and in making the prototypes used in wind tunnel testing far exceeded the testing time itself. Atole needed the capability to simulate the wind tunnel testing in a computer in order to uncover any design flaws long before the first prototype was ever built. The simulator would take the three-dimensional model of the airframe as input and simulate all testing done in the actual wind tunnel. The results of the simulation would be displayed using animated computer graphics for easy interpretation. Although several simulation packages were examined, it was decided that the research arm of Atole–Pensacola would develop a custom wind tunnel simulator, which would give Atole a competitive advantage. After considering several alternatives, the RS/6000 was selected for the wind tunnel simulator project because of its strong performance, expansion capability, compatibility with the RS/6000 systems in Engineering, and available *Computer-Aided Software Engineering* (CASE) tools.

To implement these projects, additional workstations will be added to the Ethernet local area network already installed throughout the Atole–Pensacola site as shown in Figure 7.3. In the first phase, five RS/6000 engineering workstations will be added to the network so that Atole design and manufacturing engineers can begin gaining experience with CAEDS. RS/6000 Model 320H systems were chosen for their price/performance and desktop design. Two of these five workstations will be connected to the S/390 host computer to allow the released designs to be transferred to the S/390, creating the central repository of drawings. While one RS/6000 could act as a communications server for all other engineering workstations in the network, two will be directly connected in case one breaks down. In the research department, three RS/6000 workstations will be added to the network and will be used to develop the custom wind tunnel simulator program. Since the wind tunnel simulator is expected to be a very demanding application from a performance standpoint, the RS/6000 Model 550s were chosen.

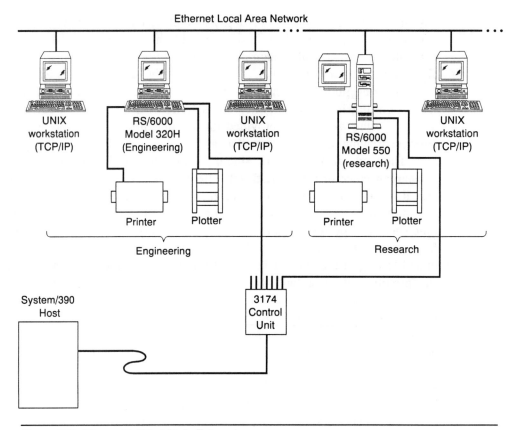

Figure 7.3. Ethernet LAN at Atole Enterprises.

Figure 7.4 shows the RS/6000 configuration that will be used as engineering workstations for Atole–Pensacola. The Model 320H processor will provide a computing base with sufficient performance to do the complex calculations associated with CAEDS' three-dimensional design and analysis capabilities. A 64 MB Memory Card will be installed in place of the 16 MB Memory Card in the standard configuration to improve system performance.

The second 400 MB SCSI Disk Drive will also be added providing 800 MB of total disk storage—enough for CAEDS and any models being developed. The POWER Gt4x (24-bit version) will provide the necessary graphics performance to support interactive design and analysis while generating lifelike images with up to 16.7 million colors. The Ethernet High-Performance LAN Adapter will allow the RS/6000 to participate in the Ethernet local area network. The 3270 Connection Adapter will allow the RS/6000 to be attached to the local S/390 computer via the same 3274 Control Unit used to attach standard terminals to S/390 computers. This

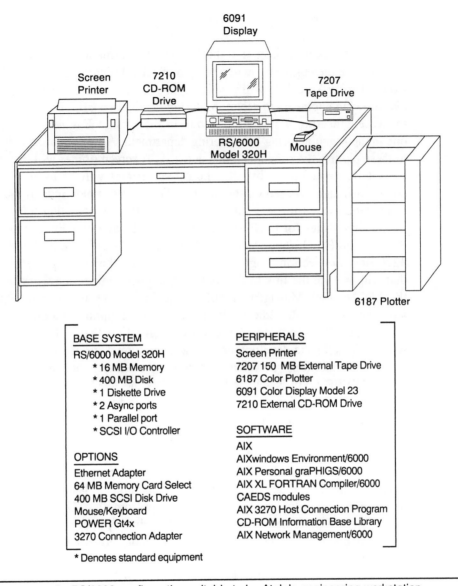

Figure 7.4. An RS/6000 configuration suitable to be Atole's engineering workstation.

link will facilitate sending released engineering drawings to the S/390 allowing for centralized control. Only two of the Model 320H systems will have this connection and they will share this communications link with all other workstations to send their released drawings to the S/390.

The 7207 150 MB External Tape Drive will be used to back up the workstation's disk in order to protect engineering designs in progress. The 7210 External CD-ROM Drive will only be installed on one engineering workstation but will provide all network users access to the CD-ROM Information Base Library. The mouse will provide the engineers with a way to efficiently interact with CAEDS. The 6091 Color Display Model 23 will provide enlarged views of the three-dimensional models, allowing engineers to see more design detail. Two 6187 Plotters will be attached to two engineering workstations — one in the Design Engineering department and one in the Manufacturing Engineering department. All workstations will have access to these plotters over the local area network. A screen printer will be attached to one workstation and shared by all. The screen printer will be used to generate hard copies of images as seen on the display. These color renderings of the three-dimensional models are for use in internal presentations and marketing activities.

Prerequisites for CAEDS include AIX, AIXwindows Environment/6000, AIX Personal graPHIGS/6000, and the AIX XL FORTRAN Compiler/6000. The AIX 3270 Host Connection Program will be needed by the two engineering workstations that will provide the link to the S/390. One other engineering workstation will have the AIX Network Management/6000 extension to AIX in order to help the network administrator keep the Ethernet local area network running smoothly.

Figure 7.5 shows the RS/6000 configuration that will be used as research workstations for the development of the wind tunnel simulator. The Model 550 will provide the additional power necessary for the wind tunnel simulation project. The 7235 POWER GTO is selected because it is the most powerful graphics circuitry available with the RS/6000 family in terms of performance and function. The added graphics performance of the 7235 will be necessary to support the heavily animated graphics required for the wind tunnel simulator. The two 32 MB memory cards in the standard Model 550 configuration will be exchanged for the two 64 MB Memory Cards, providing a total of 128 MB. This large memory will boost simulator performance by allowing much of the simulator program and data to stay resident in memory, minimizing virtual memory paging to and from disk. The standard 800 MB disk drive pair will be replaced with the 857 MB disk option, providing enough storage for development tools, the wind tunnel simulator software being written, and three-dimensional models used during development. The Ethernet High-Performance LAN Adapter will allow the RS/6000 to participate in the Ethernet local area network. The LAN will provide researchers access to the 3270 communications link and other resources available elsewhere in the network. One of the research workstations will be equipped with the 2.3 GB 8mm Internal Tape Drive to be shared by all research workstations via the Ethernet LAN. This tape drive will allow a single tape to back up all of the information on a workstations disk. The mouse will provide an effective input device for developing and interacting with the wind tunnel simulator program. The 6091 Color Display Model 23 will provide enlarged views of the wind

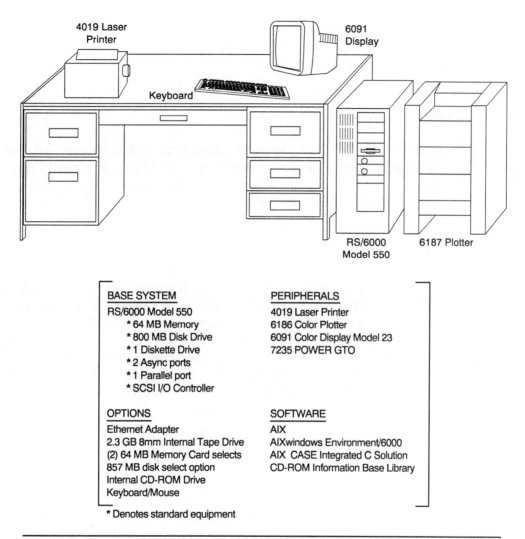

4019 Laser Printer

6091 Display

Keyboard

RS/6000 Model 550

6187 Plotter

BASE SYSTEM

RS/6000 Model 550
* 64 MB Memory
* 800 MB Disk Drive
* 1 Diskette Drive
* 2 Async ports
* 1 Parallel port
* SCSI I/O Controller

PERIPHERALS

4019 Laser Printer
6186 Color Plotter
6091 Color Display Model 23
7235 POWER GTO

OPTIONS

Ethernet Adapter
2.3 GB 8mm Internal Tape Drive
(2) 64 MB Memory Card selects
857 MB disk select option
Internal CD-ROM Drive
Keyboard/Mouse

SOFTWARE

AIX
AIXwindows Environment/6000
AIX CASE Integrated C Solution
CD-ROM Information Base Library

* Denotes standard equipment

Figure 7.5. RS/6000 configuration that will be used as a research workstation at Atole.

tunnel simulator graphics, allowing researchers to see more design detail. A 6187 Plotter will be attached to one research workstation and be shared by all. Finally, the Internal CD-ROM Drive will also be included on one of the research workstations to provide local access to the CD-ROM Information Base Library.

AIX and AIXwindows Environment/6000 will be included on the research workstations. The research personnel decide that the C programming language will be used in the wind tunnel simulator project. Further, they will use the computer-aided software engineering concepts basic to the CASE Integrated C Solution collection of programming tools to increase the productivity of the programmers and to help keep the project under control.

THE FINANCIAL DECISIONS

In addition to selecting the hardware and software to address identified needs, there are financial questions that must also be considered before you install your computer solution. Two important areas that must be addressed are cost justification and the "lease or buy" decision. Let's look at these issues.

Cost Justification

All businesses are the same in one respect: They exist to make profit. In the final analysis, the only reason for a business to buy a computer is to make the business more profitable. While academic, government, and nonprofit organizations don't have the profit motive, they still must decide how to invest their typically limited funds to best meet their objectives. In either case, therefore, the computer system must be **cost justified**. There are two halves to the cost-justification analysis: costs and benefits. The price you pay to the computer company is easily identified early in the project. What many people fail to consider are the other costs of owning a computer system. The costs of operating the computer installation after you buy it should also be considered over multiple years. Some costs that should be considered beyond the price tag include:

Hardware Maintenance: This is usually a monthly or annual fee you pay that basically is an extended warranty for the computer hardware. There are various alternatives, but the basic deal is that if your computer system breaks down, the service company will come out and effect repairs at no charge. You don't have to put your system on a maintenance contract, but if you don't you will have to pay an hourly fee and parts costs when your system breaks down. Since this parts/labor billing approach can be extremely expensive, most businesses choose to put their system on a maintenance contract.

Software Maintenance: In many cases, you will have to pay the software supplier an annual or monthly fee in order to get the corrections and updates to your programs.

Technical Support: Some companies charge fees for technical support, while others include some level of support in the price of their products. This support is a way for you to get answers to your questions and resolve any technical problems in either the hardware or software. This kind of support ranges from providing a telephone number to having permanently assigned personnel from the computer company on your premises. Sometimes this support is provided free of charge; other times it is on a fee basis.

Facilities: Many times it is necessary for you to modify your building to accommodate a computer system. These modifications might include running cable between workstations and the computer or modifying the electrical power services available. Fortunately, the cost of such building modifications is relatively low with RS/6000 systems as compared with larger computers, which may require water cooling and raised floors.

Education/Training: The people who will be using the computer system may need training. The computer operators will need to understand how to manage the day-to-day operations of the computer. The users of the computer system will have to understand the application programs. It may also be necessary to train your own programmer(s) to write custom application programs for your business. While RS/6000 systems are designed for ease of use, some training will still be necessary. There are many different types of training available, as discussed later in the chapter.

Communications Line Costs: If your computer system will be attached to remote workstations or other remote computers, you will incur communications line costs. There are many different communications services available today, and these costs should be considered in your justification.

On the brighter side, the computer solution is being purchased to solve identified problems or address known needs. That is, you will receive benefits after the computer system is installed. (Or else why install it?) While it is fairly easy to identify and quantify the costs associated with a computer system, it is often difficult to do the same for the benefits. This doesn't mean that benefits are any less real than costs; it simply means that they require some more work to uncover. Benefits are also more specific to your particular situation and so it would be impossible to list them all here. But some common benefits associated with the application of computer systems are discussed here.

Improved Business Cycle: The basic cycles of most businesses and other organizations have the same components. The business buys goods/equipment, takes customer orders for goods or services, delivers to the customer, and bills the customer. The most classic application of computer systems to these areas produces improvements in the basic business cycle, resulting in real dollar savings. These can be the result of many basic things such as collecting accounts receivable more quickly, or taking better advantage of accounts payable discount terms.

Inventory Reduction: There are many carrying costs associated with inventory. These include items like warehouse space, insurance, taxes, and interest expense. The proper application of computers can reduce the level of inventory that must be kept on hand, thus reducing carrying costs.

Improved Productivity: Given the proper tools, anyone in any part of an organization can do his or her job more efficiently. This allows an organization to get the same amount of work done in less time or with fewer people. Excess manpower can then be redirected to perform other tasks that help meet the organization's objectives. Further, as natural attrition reduces the workforce, it may be possible to not hire replacements, allowing for a reduction of the workforce over time.

Improved Quality: By providing more timely or better-organized information to personnel, organizations can often improve the quality of the services or products they provide. For example, in manufacturing environments, computers can be applied to everything from design simulations to statistical quality control.

Improved Customer Service: By allowing an organization to respond to customer orders, questions, and special requests, computer systems can improve customer service. These improvements can be things such as quickly responding to requests for price quotations and accurately quoting or meeting delivery dates.

Competitive Advantage: The items just discussed, which contribute to reducing costs, improving quality, and improving customer service, all work to improve the effectiveness of an organization. The flexibility provided by a computer system can also help improve your competitiveness by allowing you to respond more quickly to changing market demands. Change is inevitable, and it represents opportunity for the flexible and doom for the inflexible.

This list of general benefits is in no way comprehensive. Each organization will be able to add to this list based on its current situation and objectives. Once benefits have been identified, however, you are still not done. You should try to quantify the benefits in dollars and cents where possible to help focus on the areas with the largest payoff first. Quantified benefits also help when comparing computer investments with any other capital projects under consideration. However, quantifying benefits can be difficult and subject to judgment. Unlike the price of a computer, which can be looked up in a catalog, benefits must be calculated based on expected results. For example, if you feel that inventory can be reduced 10% by installing an inventory management application program, you would multiply 10% of your inventory value times the carrying costs to determine the annual benefit. This is not very difficult. Other areas are more difficult to quantify accurately. For example, if an engineer's productivity is increased by 15%, then you might multiply annual salary and benefit costs by 15%, yielding the annual savings. In this case, some would argue that since you still must pay the engineer full salary, there is no savings. However, consider that since the engineer can now spend 15% more time developing a product to enter a new market, for example, the actual benefit may be much higher than 15% of salary. You will have to decide what a benefit is worth to your organization. There are other benefits that typically are difficult to quantify and are thus often overlooked when tallying savings. Some benefits that fall into this category are increased sales (resulting from improved customer service) and lower employee turnover (resulting from improved working conditions and pride). The fact that these benefits (and others like them) are difficult to quantify doesn't make them any less valuable. It does, however, make them more often overlooked.

After the costs and benefits have been quantified, you can begin to evaluate the proposed computer project against other capital projects. Two often-used rulers with which to measure up a proposed computer system are:

1. The **payback period**, where the time to recover the investment from inflowing benefits is calculated.

2. **Net present value**, where the cash flows are calculated and then discounted based on the cost of money and risk associated with the project.

While this type of analysis can be valuable, don't overlook other aspects of the capital project such as its strategic value, its effect on customer-perceived quality and professionalism, and so on. Classic accounting techniques are easy to defend but don't always paint the entire picture.

Lease or Buy?

Just when you think you are through analyzing all the software and hardware alternatives, you are faced with a whole new set of questions concerning the acquisition method you will use. There are several methods commonly used to acquire a computer system. The most obvious alternative is to simply pay cash for the computer system, called an **outright purchase**. This is usually the least expensive way to acquire a computer system. However, it has a direct and usually substantial impact on the organization's cash flow and capital position. The next acquisition alternative is to finance the purchase price over a period of time, just as you would finance a new home. In this case, you simply make a down payment (of 10% for example) and take out a loan for the balance. The loan and interest are repaid through monthly payments, typically over a period of from two to five years. Since you must pay back the interest on the loan, this is a more expensive alternative than a cash purchase but it can reduce cash flow requirements. In either case, the title of the computer system passes to the business, as do any tax benefits such as depreciation. The purchaser of a computer also has the ability to sell the computer when it is replaced or no longer required, thus recovering the **residual value** of the computer system.

Another acquisition alternative is the **term lease**. In this alternative, the lessor (computer owner) grants use of a computer system to the lessee (the using company), who in turn agrees to make lease payments for some specified period of time (or **term**). Lease terms can be any length, but typically run from two to five years. If the lessee decides to terminate the lease before the end of the term, there is usually a termination fee. Some of the advantages offered by the term lease alternative include the conservation of capital and lines of credit. This allows the business to use this capital or credit to finance other investments. Two commonly found lease types include a **capital lease** and an **operating lease**. Capital leases are "rent-to-own": at the end of the term, you can purchase the computer system for a relatively small fee (e.g., 5 or 10% of the original cost). With a capital lease, the lessee is considered the owner and gets the tax benefits of ownership. Capital leases are much like a financed purchase, with the major difference being that a capital lease doesn't require the user to make a down payment as a financed purchase does. Operating leases are "real" leases, where there is no discounted purchase option at the end of the lease term. The lessor is considered to be the owner and thus retains the tax benefits of ownership. Because of this, the lessee typically makes a lower payment than with the capital lease alternative.

One final acquisition alternative is to rent the computer system month by month. This provides the most flexibility since this kind of arrangement typically only requires one month's notice to discontinue. Of course, you usually must pay higher rental payments to get this flexibility, and since the payment is usually not fixed, you are subject to increases.

The acquisition of computer software is a whole different story. Typically, you will not have the option to "buy" software. Most companies **license** software. A software license grants the licensee the right to use the software under the conditions specified in the document supplied by the software company, called the **licensing agreement**. Typically, these licenses allow the licensee to use the software on a specified computer system for a specified fee. Three common ways to pay for this license agreement are: **one-time charge**, **lease**, or **monthly charge**. With the one-time charge, the licensee pays a set price and retains the right to use the software indefinitely. This charge can be paid in cash or financed. The leasing alternative is really just another way to finance the one-time charge with no down payment. Finally, the monthly charge is like renting the software month to month indefinitely.

While I have introduced some basic lease/purchase alternatives in this section, the rules governing these various alternatives are complex and subject to change. The effects on a company's cash flow, income statements, balance sheets, taxes, and so forth, can also be strongly affected by these various acquisition alternatives. For this reason, you should consult the proper professionals to determine the best alternative for your situation.

USER EDUCATION

The discussions in the chapter so far should assist you in selecting the appropriate software and hardware to fit your needs. However, no matter what computer hardware and software you select, they will require people to operate them. In order to maximize efficiency and morale, these people (or **users**) must be provided with education in the use of the computer system itself as well as its software.

Proper education is critical to the success of any computer automation project. Inadequate education will prevent reaping the productivity benefits afforded by moving a task to the computer. The goal of this education is to make the users proficient at using the computer hardware and software and to make their interaction with the computer system enjoyable. If using the computer is enjoyable, the user will be more highly motivated. If using the computer represents a frustrating struggle due to inadequate education, the user will be less productive or perhaps avoid the computer altogether.

The education should cover both RS/6000 hardware and the software that will be used. RS/6000 hardware has been designed with close attention to making it as easy to use as possible. The videotape and the on-line education courses provided with every system provide a self-guided tour through RS/6000 basics. Chapter 3 discusses the types of courses that come with the RS/6000 and teaches the first-time user how to access this on-line education. These offerings should provide adequate education on RS/6000 hardware in most cases.

After the user is familiar with the computer system, he or she should be trained in the use of the AIX operating system and the application program(s). The amount of education needed on the AIX operating system will depend on the tasks being performed. Again, the videotape and the on-line education courses provided with RS/6000 systems are a good starting point for learning the AIX operating system. Traditional classroom education is available from IBM and others when more-detailed knowledge of the AIX operating system is needed. While the system's administrator will probably need such formal AIX operating system education, many times the operating system can be all but hidden from the users, minimizing their education needs in this area.

Education in the use of the application program is usually the most important thing for the users. The content of this education is dependent on the particular application program selected. Typically, manuals provided with the application program will contain step-by-step tutorials designed to train the user. Depending on the complexity of the application program, the experience of the user, and the quality of the tutorial, this education method achieves varying levels of success. There are other ways of getting application program education. Software companies offer classes tailored to teaching how to use their application programs. Many times businesses will send one person to a class of this type and then have the person teach other users upon returning. IBM, other software publishers, and consultants can provide information about various classes, books, videotapes, and so on.

IBMLINK

No matter what computer system a business chooses, the system and its users will require ongoing support. They will have questions that need answering, hardware problems that must be addressed, software updates that must be installed, and so forth. This support can be delivered in many different ways. Personnel from the computer manufacturer, the software company, the business's own staff, and so forth, are generally involved in supporting the computer system and its users.

In an effort to make this support more effective and convenient, IBM offers **IBMLink**. Just as electronic mail and on-line business information streamline a business's operation, IBMLink streamlines the support provided to the business.

Access to IBMLink is provided through the *IBM Information Network* (IIN). The kinds of things provided through IBMLink include the following:

InfoLink, which provides many of the same tools used by IBM personnel to support users. From InfoLink you can view IBM product announcement letters, hardware and software product catalogs, product prices, volume discount schedules, publication information, lists of local dealers, and so forth. You can also use hardware and software configuration planning tools to define and price workable computer systems with their various options.

OrderLink allows you to look at the equipment IBM currently has on order.

SupportLink provides a national database of technical questions and answers. This database can be searched by keywords to locate previously answered questions on a wide variety of technical topics. A user can also enter new questions, which will be answered by IBM support personnel and then added to the national question-and-answer database for others to view. Through SupportLink, you can also view Technical Bulletins and FLASHes posted by IBM. The "copy screen" function of SupportLink allows IBM personnel to interact with the user's computer system directly on his or her workstation while the users see the same screen image on their workstations. This helps resolve user questions and helps users learn the system, since they can watch the interaction on the workstation.

ServiceLink allows you to electronically communicate with IBM service personnel to report problems. Further, you (or IBM service personnel) can electronically search through IBM's software updates (e.g., *Program Temporary Fixes* [PTFs]), receive the software update electronically, and apply the fix. Problems detected by the RS/6000 system generate Alert messages that are automatically sent to IBM service without any user intervention.

User functions provide some simple electronic mail functions between IBM personnel and the users, thus reducing "telephone tag." You can also send comments back to IBMLink through these user functions.

With IBMLink, support is delivered electronically, improving access to technical and product information and streamlining communications between IBM and the users.

ERGONOMICS

No plan would be complete without addressing the human needs that directly affect the day-to-day productivity of computer users — **ergonomics**. Ergonomics is a science dedicated to investigating the designs for effective interaction between devices and human beings. Human beings have many physiological and psychological characteristics that should be considered when designing computers, software, desks, lighting, chairs, and so forth. Attention to ergonomics will increase effectiveness, work quality, health and safety, and job satisfaction.

RS/6000 terminals have been designed with careful attention to ergonomics. Everything from the power switch location to the length of the keyboard cable is scrutinized. Much effort is also expended fine-tuning the ergonomics of most application programs. In order to get the most out of your RS/6000 system, you must also provide an ergonomic environment for the users. Organizations such as the *Ameri*can *Optometric Association* (AOA) and the *New York Committee for Occupational Safety and Health* (NYCOSH) as well as IBM have probed deeply into the relationship between the computer and the user. Items such as desks, chairs, lighting, noise, and the like are important to productivity. Some of these steps are inexpensive and easily accomplished. Others may be expensive and accomplished gradually over time. Let's explore some specific steps you can take to help improve the ergonomics in your environment.

Comfort for the Eyes

The eyes, like any other part of the human body, can get tired as a result of intensive use. This fatigue, called "eyestrain," is nothing new to people who work long hours reading material. With the increase in computer use over recent years, however, we have seen an increase in eyestrain. Although eyestrain is only a temporary condition, it can cause a user to feel tired and irritated, especially if he or she continues to work due to the pressures of deadlines.

The eyes function most naturally at distances greater than or equal to arm's length. After all, throughout the majority of history, our vision needs were to pick fruits, not read contracts. When the eyes focus on anything closer than arm's reach, be it a computer terminal or a newspaper, the eyes are forced to look inward toward one's nose. This is extra work for the muscles that move your eye within your socket, resulting in fatigue. To reduce this fatiguing effect, the computer user should take breaks and go to an area where he or she can focus on more distant objects.

Another factor contributing to eye fatigue results from the work done by a muscle in the eye that re-forms the lens of your eye to maintain sharp focus. If you frequently shift your gaze between objects at different distances (such as a computer display and a paper on your desk), this makes the focusing muscles effectively do "push-ups." This also leads to tired eyes. To help prevent these eye "push-ups," it is desirable to put any paper that is frequently referenced during a computer session at the same distance and orientation as the computer screen. A clip-type holder used by secretaries to hold documents as they are typing works well for this.

Poor image quality can cause the eyes to constantly change focus in a futile attempt to correct the image. RS/6000 graphics displays and ASCII terminals provide high-quality images, helping to minimize eyestrain.

As if this isn't enough, there is still another contributor to eye fatigue commonly found in offices, namely, improper lighting. Your eye adjusts to all of the light in the field of vision. Unwanted light reflections called "glare" can appear in the user's field of vision, causing nonuniform light intensities. If the light intensity varies widely, the iris in your eye will continuously expand and contract to adjust for the light-level variance. To reduce the glare in the user's environment, RS/6000 displays and terminals have antiglare screens. Likewise, the workstation (desk, table, etc.) surface should have an antiglare or nonreflective surface. Windows are big culprits as far as causing glare, but almost everyone likes windows. You can reduce the amount of glare caused by windows by positioning your computer display screen at right angles to any window. You can also use curtains or horizontal blinds to direct the light away from the screen. Diffused office lighting will provide fewer "hot spots" and tend to provide the most uniform light and soften harsh shadows. For using computer displays, 30 to 50 footcandles of ambient light is optimum. The goal is to have the screen brightness be three or four times the ambient light. Since typical offices originally were designed to work with paper, not video displays, there is usually more light than this in an office. This may be difficult to change, depending on the type of lighting used in your office. You can try using fewer or lower-intensity bulbs or fluorescent tubes. Another possibility is to install dimmer switches.

Workstation Comfort

The workstation furniture shared by the computer and the user can also affect productivity. For this reason, attention should be given to the details of the user's workstation, that is, the chair and desk/table to be used.

A properly designed chair can help reduce back problems and make the user more comfortable and more productive. An improperly designed chair can lead to reduced alertness and shorter concentration spans. Users may not even realize they are uncomfortable as they unconsciously but constantly seek a more comfortable position.

What makes a chair a good chair? First, since a chair typically will be used by many sitters during its life with a company, it is important for it to be adjustable. The seat pan height should be adjustable from around 16 to 22 inches and should allow the feet to rest flat on the floor. Weight should be distributed through the buttocks, not the thighs. The front of the seat pan should roll off smoothly, as in the **waterfall** design, to provide for proper blood flow in the legs. A 20mm compression is about firm enough.

Backrests should adjust up and down over a two-inch range and backward and forward between 80 and 120 degrees for good support. Both the seat pans and backrests should be upholstered and covered in a material that absorbs perspiration.

If mobility is required, wheels or casters are recommended — unless the floor is slippery, which will make the chair unstable. Hard casters should be used for soft floors and vice versa. A five-legged chair will provide stability to prevent tipping. Seats should swivel if lateral movement is required.

Once the user is seated, his or her relationship with the computer display and keyboard will directly affect comfort, and thus productivity. The computer display should be positioned properly. The top of the computer display should be positioned 10 degrees below eye level, the center of the display at about 20 degrees below eye level and between 14 and 20 inches away. A tilt/swivel stand under the terminal or display allows the user to adjust the display screen angle as desired. Users should avoid using bifocal lenses since they must tip their heads back while reading the screens. This can lead to discomfort in the back and shoulders.

The keyboard should also be in a comfortable position. The RS/6000 systems and associated terminals all provide separate keyboards attached by a flexible cable, which allows the user to position the keyboard as desired. The keyboard height should allow the elbow to be bent at about 90 degrees during typing. Finally, provide sufficient desk space for documents used during the computer session.

What about Noise?

Noise is not conducive to efficiency. Irregular noise is more distracting than constant noise. Unfortunately, irregular noise is commonplace in almost any busy environment. It results from nearby conversations, telephones, printers, copy machines, and many other things. If possible, isolate noise sources such as impact printers and copy machines by placing them in isolated areas or separate rooms. Noise can also be reduced by installing doors, carpets, and other sound-insulating materials.

SECURITY

In many environments, computer systems are the very backbone of day-to-day operations. This makes the information stored on the computers an asset at least as valuable as cash. Like an organization's cash, computer information must be protected from loss or theft. Let's look at how this vital information can be protected.

Loss Prevention

An ever-present hazard when dealing with information (with or without computers) is the possibility that the information will be lost. This loss can occur in many different ways. A computer system's breakdown, such as a disk failure, can result in lost information. Further, operator error can cause data to be accidentally corrupted, resulting in lost information. Finally, a disaster (such as a fire or flood) can result in a loss of vital information. For this reason, **recovery** from the loss of vital information must be addressed.

One way to deal with the risk of losing vital information is to make backup copies of computer information at regular intervals (e.g., daily). Multiple backup copies should be made on a revolving basis and kept in a place safe from damage or loss. Three copies will allow at least one copy to be kept in safe storage at all times and provide for different levels of backup. In the event of an information loss, the computer system can be restored to the point at which the most recent backup copy was made. The AIX operating system and the various tape devices discussed in Chapter 2 are designed for these kinds of **save/restore** operations. Any changes to information after the point of the last backup will have to be re-created after the backup copy is used to restore the system. This may involve manually reentering the transactions since the last backup. The use of mirroring, discussed in Chapter 5, can also be used to decrease the likelihood of losing valuable information.

Theft Prevention

Theft prevention deals with protecting sensitive information from unauthorized disclosure. These security requirements vary widely from environment to environment. Consider your particular needs early in your planning.

RS/6000 systems provide various levels of security that help deter unauthorized access. Security is provided by the computer system itself along with the associated operating system. In fact, the RS/6000 systems and the AIX operating system have been designed to meet the stringent security requirements defined by the National Computer Security Center Trusted Computer System Evaluation Criteria Class C2. Depending on the needs of the environment, various levels of security can be activated, from no security to detailed access control. A security officer is usually assigned to manage the security of the system.

For sensitive environments, you may wish to consider restricting access to areas where RS/6000 systems or associated terminals are located. To help deter outright theft of the easily moved RS/6000 Model 320, a steel cable is available to secure the Model 320 System Unit to an immovable object. These site planning considerations should be considered early in a computer automation project.

SERVICE

While every effort has been made to make RS/6000 systems as reliable as possible, some computers will fail. If yours does, you must have a way of getting it fixed. All RS/6000 systems come with a one-year warranty that provides free on-site repairs from IBM's service division seven days a week, 24 hours per day. The various terminals and printers associated with RS/6000 systems each have their own warranty terms and periods ranging from three months to three years.

After the warranty period, you become responsible for maintenance of the system. IBM and others offer service agreements that, for a fee, provide postwarranty on-site service just like that provided during the warranty. There are various maintenance discounts available, depending on the level of system management procedures you are willing to implement in your organization.

If your system fails and you don't have any type of service contract, you will have to pay for parts and labor, which can quickly become extremely expensive. For this reason, most people choose to keep their systems on maintenance after warranty as a type of insurance policy.

APPENDIX A

Supported Peripherals

IBM conducted compatibility testing on selected equipment before announcing the RS/6000 family. This appendix shows a list of the devices found to be compatible at the time of the original testing. Peripherals not listed in this section are not necessarily incompatible with RS/6000 systems. Their absence simply means that they were not included in the original compatibility testing.

ASCII TERMINALS

Note: The IBM 3151, 3161, 3162, 3163, and 3164 are supported in 3161 mode (ANSI X3.64 Standard). National language support is provided through the use of Cartridge 8859/1.2 inserted into the terminal.

- IBM 3151
- IBM 3161
- IBM 3162
- IBM 3163
- IBM 3164
- DEC VT100
- DEC VT220
- DEC VT320
- DEC VT330
- WYSE 30
- WYSE 50
- WYSE 60
- WYSE 350

257

TERMINALS

- ❑ IBM Xstation 120
- ❑ VISUAL 640 XDS

GRAPHICS PROCESSORS

- ❑ IBM 5085, all models
- ❑ IBM 5086 Model 1

DIGITIZERS

- ❑ IBM 5084-M1
- ❑ IBM 5084-M2
- ❑ IBM 5084-M3

TABLETS

- ❑ IBM 5083 Model 021
- ❑ IBM 5083 Model 022

PLOTTERS

- ❑ IBM 6180 M1 Color
- ❑ IBM 6182 Color
- ❑ IBM 6184 Color
- ❑ IBM 6186 Color
- ❑ IBM 7372

MODEMS

- ❑ IBM 5822 DSU up to 56kbps
- ❑ IBM 5841 1200bps

- IBM 5853 2400bps
- IBM 5865 9600bps
- IBM 7861 up to 19.2kbps
- IBM 7868 up to 19.2 kbps
- Hayes Smartmodem 1200
- Hayes Smartmodem 2400
- Hayes V-Series 9600
- Racal-Vadic 1200PA
- Racal-Vadic 1200VP
- Racal-Vadic VI2422
- Racal-Vadic 2400PA
- Racal-Vadic 2400VP
- Racal-Vadic VI1222VP
- Telebit Trailblazer Plus

Note: Not all of the features supported by the listed modems are supported by the AIX Version 3 for RISC System/6000 software.

PRINTERS

- IBM 3812-002 Page Printer
- IBM 3816-01S Page Printer
- IBM 4019-001 LaserPrinter
- IBM 4201-002 IBM Proprinter II
- IBM 4201-003 Proprinter III
- IBM 4202-002 Proprinter II XL
- IBM 4202-003 Proprinter III XL
- IBM 4207-002 Proprinter X24E
- IBM 4208-002 Proprinter XL24E
- IBM 4216-031 Personal Page Printer
- IBM 4224-3E3 Serial Printer
- IBM 4224-3C2 Serial Printer
- IBM 4224-302 Serial Printer

- ❏ IBM 4224-301 Serial Printer
- ❏ IBM 4234-013 Dot Band Printer
- ❏ IBM 5204-001 Quickwriter
- ❏ DATAPRODUCTS LZR 2665
- ❏ DATAPRODUCTS BP2000
- ❏ HP LaserJet Series II
- ❏ PRINTRONIX P9012
- ❏ Texas Instruments Omnilaser

Performance Testing

Reprinted with permission from "IBM RISC System/6000 TPC Benchmark A and Benchmark B Performance," copyright International Business Machines Corporation 1991.

Disclaimer

The performance data presented are approximations which are believed to be sound. The degree of success, including actual system performance and throughput, which you may achieve in the use of IBM equipment and programs is dependent on a number of factors, many of which are not under IBM's control. Thus, IBM does not warrant or guarantee that you can or will achieve similar results and it is your responsibility to validate the estimates furnished and determine their relevance to your operation.

The pricing information contained in this presentation is believed to accurately reflect prices in effect on the indicated date. IBM does not warrant the pricing information in this document.

The graphs and data to be presented should not be used to size a proposed system for a specific workload. Better information about how a specific application might perform can usually be obtained by benchmarking the job on a specific system.

SPEC Benchmark Release 1 Summary

RESULTS: Benchmark No. & Name	SPEC Reference Time (seconds)	RISC System/6000 POWERstation 320 Time (seconds)	SPEC Ratio	IBM Corporation RISC System/6000 POWERstation 320	
001.gcc	1482.0	110.0	13.5	**Hardware**	
				Model Number:	POWERstation 320
008.espresso	2266.0	143.0	15.9	CPU:	20 MHz POWER 2032
				FPU:	Integrated
013.spice2g6	23951.0	1161.3	20.6	Number of CPUs:	1
				Cache Size Per CPU:	32K data/8K inst
015.doduc	1863.0	81.3	22.9	Memory:	32 MB
				Disk Subsystem:	2 - 320 SCSI
020.nasa7	20093.0	348.4	57.7	Network Interface:	NA
					Software
022.li	6206.0	391.7	15.8	O/S Type and Rev:	AIX v3.1.5
				Compiler Rev:	AIX XL C/6000 Ver. 1.1.5
023.eqntott	1101.0	58.7	18.8		(1) AIX XL FORTRAN Ver. 2.2
				Other Software:	None
030.matrix300	4525.0	14.0	323.2	File System Type:	AIX
				Firmware Level:	NA
042.fpppp	3038.0	72.7	41.8		**System**
				Tuning Parameters:	None
047.tomcatv	2649.0	43.5	60.9	Background Load:	None
				System State:	Multi-user(single-user logon)
Geometric Mean		SPECmark	32.8		
		SPECint	15.9	General Availability:	Hardware - Q1 1991
		SPECfp	53.1		Software - Q3 1991

Tested In: April, 1991	By: IBM - AWD	Of: Austin, TX	SPEC License # 011

Notes/Summary of Changes (*portability changes to the benchmarks)
001.gcc, 008.espresso, 022.li, and 023.eqntott were compiled with -O
013.spice2g6, 015.doduc, 042.fpppp, and 047.tomcatv were compiled with -O and pre-processor flags -P -Wp,-ea478
020.nasa7, and 030.matrix300 were compiled with -O and pre-processor flags (020.nasa7) -Pk -Wp,-ag=a, (030.matrix300) -Pk -Wp,-inlr,-inll=3
(1) AIX XL FORTRAN Alpha Version 2.2 used for testing !!

SPEC Benchmark Release 1 Summary

RESULTS: Benchmark No. & Name	SPEC Reference Time (seconds)	RISC System/6000 POWERstation 320H Time (seconds)	SPEC Ratio
001.gcc	1482.0	87.8	16.9
008.espresso	2266.0	113.7	19.9
013.spice2g6	23951.0	922.1	26.0
015.doduc	1863.0	64.7	28.8
020.nasa7	20093.0	276.6	72.6
022.li	6206.0	310.9	20.0
023.eqntott	1101.0	46.7	23.6
030.matrix300	4525.0	11.2	404.0
042.fpppp	3038.0	57.3	53.0
047.tomcatv	2649.0	34.6	76.6

IBM Corporation
RISC System/6000 POWERstation 320H

Hardware
Model Number: POWERstation 320H
CPU: 25 MHz POWER 2532
FPU: Integrated
Number of CPUs: 1
Cache Size Per CPU: 32K data/8K inst
Memory: 32 MB
Disk Subsystem: 2 - 320 SCSI
Network Interface: NA
Software
O/S Type and Rev: AIX v3.1.5
Compiler Rev: AIX XL C/6000 Ver. 1.1.5
(1) AIX XL FORTRAN Ver. 2.2
Other Software: None
File System Type: AIX
Firmware Level: NA
System
Tuning Parameters: None
Background Load: None
System State: Multi-user(single-user logon)

Geometric Mean	SPECmark	41.2
	SPECint	20.0
	SPECfp	66.8

General Availability: Hardware - Q1 1991
Software - Q3 1991

Tested In: April, 1991   By: IBM - AWD   Of: Austin, TX   SPEC License # 011

SPECmark = 41.2 (geo.mean)

Notes/Summary of Changes (*portability changes to the benchmarks)
001.gcc, 008.espresso, 022.li, and 023.eqntott were compiled with -O
013.spice2g6, 015.doduc, 042.fpppp, and 047.tomcatv were compiled with -O and pre-processor flags -P -Wp,-ea478
020.nasa7, and 030.matrix300 were compiled with -O and pre-processor flags (020.nasa7) -Pk -Wp,-ag=a, (030.matrix300) -Pk -Wp,-inlr,-inll=3
(1) AIX XL FORTRAN Alpha Version 2.2 used for testing !!

SPEC and SPECmark are trademarks of the Standard Performance Evaluation Corporation

SPEC Benchmark Release 1 Summary

RESULTS: Benchmark No. & Name	SPEC Reference Time (seconds)	RISC System/6000 POWERstation 520 Time (seconds)	SPEC Ratio	IBM Corporation RISC System/6000 POWERstation 520	
001.gcc	1482.0	111.3	13.3		Hardware
008.espresso	2266.0	143.1	15.8	Model Number:	POWERstation 520
				CPU:	20 MHz POWER 2032
013.spice2g6	23951.0	1169.5	20.5	FPU:	Integrated
				Number of CPUs:	1
015.doduc	1863.0	81.5	22.9	Cache Size Per CPU:	32K data/8K inst
				Memory:	32 MB
020.nasa7	20093.0	349.6	57.5	Disk Subsystem:	1 - 355 SCSI
				Network Interface:	NA
022.li	6206.0	392.3	15.8		Software
				O/S Type and Rev:	AIX v3.1.5
023.eqntott	1101.0	58.8	18.7	Compiler Rev:	AIX XL C/6000 Ver. 1.1.5
					(1) AIX XL FORTRAN Ver. 2.2
030.matrix300	4525.0	14.1	320.9	Other Software:	None
				File System Type:	AIX
042.fpppp	3038.0	72.8	41.7	Firmware Level:	NA
					System
047.tomcatv	2649.0	43.6	60.8	Tuning Parameters:	None
				Background Load:	None
				System State:	Multi-user(single-user logon)
Geometric Mean		SPECmark SPECint SPECfp	32.6 15.8 52.9	General Availability:	Hardware - Q1 1991 Software - Q3 1991

Tested in: April, 1991	By: IBM - AWD	Of: Austin, TX	SPEC License # 011

SPECmark
= 32.6
(geo.mean)

Notes/Summary of Changes (*portability changes to the benchmarks)
001.gcc, 008.espresso, 022.li, and 023.eqntott were compiled with -O
013.spice2g6, 015.doduc, 042.fpppp, and 047.tomcatv were compiled with -O and pre-processor flags -P -Wp,-ea478
020.nasa7, and 030.matrix300 were compiled with -O and pre-processor flags (020.nasa7) -Pk -Wp,-ag=a, (030.matrix300) -Pk -Wp,-inlr,-inll=3
(1) AIX XL FORTRAN Alpha Version 2.2 used for testing !!

SPEC and SPECmark are trademarks of the Standard Performance Evaluation Corporation

SPEC Benchmark Release 1 Summary

RESULTS: Benchmark No. & Name	SPEC Reference Time (seconds)	RISC System/6000 POWERstation 530 Time (seconds)	SPEC Ratio	IBM Corporation RISC System/6000 POWERstation 530
001.gcc	1482.0	89.9	16.5	**Hardware**
008.espresso	2266.0	112.0	20.2	Model Number: POWERstation 530 CPU: 25 MHz POWER 2564
013.spice2g6	23951.0	832.6	28.8	FPU: Integrated Number of CPUs: 1
015.doduc	1863.0	62.9	29.6	Cache Size Per CPU: 64K data/8K inst Memory: 32 MB
020.nasa7	20093.0	228.2	88.1	Disk Subsystem: 1 - 355 SCSI Network Interface: NA
022.li	6206.0	307.2	20.2	**Software** O/S Type and Rev: AIX v3.1.5
023.eqntott	1101.0	45.9	24.0	Compiler Rev: AIX XL C/6000 Ver. 1.1.5 (1) AIX XL FORTRAN Ver. 2.2
030.matrix300	4525.0	10.4	435.1	Other Software: None File System Type: AIX
042.fpppp	3038.0	57.0	53.3	Firmware Level: NA **System**
047.tomcatv	2649.0	31.8	83.3	Tuning Parameters: None Background Load: None System State: Multi-user(single-user logon)
Geometric Mean		SPECmark SPECint SPECfp	43.4 20.1 72.5	General Availability: Hardware - Q1 1991 Software - Q3 1991

Tested In: April, 1991	By: IBM - AWD	Of: Austin, TX	SPEC License # 011

Notes/Summary of Changes (*portability changes to the benchmarks)
001.gcc, 008.espresso, 022.li, and 023.eqntott were compiled with -O
013.spice2g6, 015.doduc, 042.fpppp, and 047.tomcatv were compiled with -O and pre-processor flags -P -Wp,-ea478
020.nasa7, and 030.matrix300 were compiled with -O and pre-processor flags (020.nasa7) -Pk -Wp,-ag=a, (030.matrix300) -Pk -Wp,-inlr,-inll=3
(1) AIX XL FORTRAN Alpha Version 2.2 used for testing !!

SPEC and SPECmark are trademarks of the Standard Performance Evaluation Corporation

SPEC Benchmark Release 1 Summary

RESULTS: Benchmark No. & Name	SPEC Reference Time (seconds)	RISC System/6000 POWERstation 530H Time (seconds)	SPEC Ratio	IBM Corporation RISC System/6000 POWERstation 530H	
001.gcc	1482.0	67.2	22.1	**Hardware**	
008.espresso	2266.0	84.2	26.9	Model Number:	POWERstation 530H
				CPU:	33 MHz POWER 3364
013.spice2g6	23951.0	639.5	37.5	FPU:	Integrated
				Number of CPUs:	1
015.doduc	1863.0	47.8	39.0	Cache Size Per CPU:	64K data/8K inst
				Memory:	32 MB
020.nasa7	20093.0	158.5	126.8	Disk Subsystem:	1 - 400 SCSI
				Network Interface:	NA
022.li	6206.0	230.9	26.9	**Software**	
				O/S Type and Rev:	AIX v3.1.5
023.eqntott	1101.0	35.1	31.4	Compiler Rev:	AIX XL C/6000 Ver. 1.1.5
					AIX XL FORTRAN Ver. 2.2
030.matrix300	4525.0	7.9	575.2	Other Software:	None
				File System Type:	AIX
042.fpppp	3038.0	45.6	66.6	Firmware Level:	NA
				System	
047.tomcatv	2649.0	24.1	109.7	Tuning Parameters:	None
				Background Load:	None
				System State:	Multi-user(single-user logon)
Geometric Mean		SPECmark	57.4		
		SPECint	26.6	General Availability:	Hardware - Q1 1991
		SPECfp	95.9		Software - Q3 1991

Tested In: Sept. 1991	By: IBM - AWD	Of: Austin, TX	SPEC License # 011

SPECmark = 57.4 (geo.mean)

Notes/Summary of Changes (*portability changes to the benchmarks)
SPECint Benchmarks were compiled with -O (001.gcc1.35 also used -lm)
SPECfp Benchmarks were compiled with -O -P -Wp,-ea478 and -lblas
020.nasa7 was compiled with -O -P -Wp,-ea478,-Rvpetst:vpenta and -lblas
030.matrix300 was compiled with -O -P -Wp,-ea478,-lsgemm:sgemv:saxpy and -lblas

SPEC and SPECmark are trademarks of the Standard Performance Evaluation Corporation

SPEC Benchmark Release 1 Summary

RESULTS: Benchmark No. & Name	SPEC Reference Time (seconds)	RISC System/6000 POWERstation 540 Time (seconds)	SPEC Ratio	IBM Corporation RISC System/6000 POWERstation 540	
001.gcc	1482.0	70.8	20.9	Hardware	
008.espresso	2266.0	93.5	24.2	Model Number:	POWERstation 540
				CPU:	30 MHz POWER 3064
013.spice2g6	23951.0	691.8	34.6	FPU:	Integrated
				Number of CPUs:	1
015.doduc	1863.0	52.4	35.6	Cache Size Per CPU:	64K data/8K inst
				Memory:	64 MB
020.nasa7	20093.0	188.2	106.8	Disk Subsystem:	2 - 320 SCSI
				Network Interface:	NA
022.li	6206.0	256.3	24.2	Software	
				O/S Type and Rev:	AIX v3.1.5
023.eqntott	1101.0	38.4	28.7	Compiler Rev:	AIX XL C/6000 Ver. 1.1.5
					(1) AIX XL FORTRAN Ver. 2.2
030.matrix300	4525.0	8.6	526.2	Other Software:	None
				File System Type:	AIX
042.fpppp	3038.0	47.3	64.2	Firmware Level:	NA
				System	
047.tomcatv	2649.0	26.5	100.0	Tuning Parameters:	None
				Background Load:	None
				System State:	Multi-user(single-user logon)
Geometric Mean		SPECmark SPECint SPECfp	52.4 24.4 87.3	General Availability:	Hardware - Q1 1991 Software - Q3 1991

Tested In: Feb., 1991	By: IBM - AWD	Of: Austin, TX	SPEC License # 011

Notes/Summary of Changes (*portability changes to the benchmarks)
001.gcc, 008.espresso, 022.li, and 023.eqntott were compiled with -O
013.spice2g6, 015.doduc, 042.fpppp, and 047.tomcatv were compiled with -O and pre-processor flags -P -Wp,-ea478
020.nasa7, and 030.matrix300 were compiled with -O and pre-processor flags (020.nasa7) -Pk -Wp,-ag=a, (030.matrix300) -Pk -Wp,-inlr,-inll=3
(1) AIX XL FORTRAN Alpha Version 2.2 used for testing !!

SPEC and SPECmark are trademarks of the Standard Performance Evaluation Corporation

SPEC Benchmark Release 1 Summary

RESULTS: Benchmark No. & Name	SPEC Reference Time (seconds)	RISC System/6000 POWERstation 550		IBM Corporation RISC System/6000 POWERstation 550	
		Time (seconds)	SPEC Ratio		
001.gcc	1482.0	51.5	28.9	**Hardware**	
008.espresso	2266.0	67.0	33.8	Model Number:	POWERstation 550
				CPU:	41.67 MHz POWER 4164
013.spice2g6	23951.0	507.3	47.2	FPU:	Integrated
				Number of CPUs:	1
015.doduc	1863.0	37.7	49.4	Cache Size Per CPU:	64K data/8K inst
020.nasa7	20093.0	139.2	144.4	Memory:	64 MB
				Disk Subsystem:	2 - 400 SCSI
022.li	6206.0	183.6	33.8	Network Interface:	NA
				Software	
023.eqntott	1101.0	27.6	39.9	O/S Type and Rev:	AIX v3.1.5
				Compiler Rev:	AIX XL C/6000 Ver. 1.1.5
030.matrix300	4525.0	6.2	729.8		(1) AIX XL FORTRAN Ver. 2.2
				Other Software:	None
042.fpppp	3038.0	35.0	86.8	File System Type:	AIX
047.tomcatv	2649.0	19.2	138.0	Firmware Level:	NA
				System	
				Tuning Parameters:	None
				Background Load:	None
				System State:	Multi-user(single-user logon)
Geometric Mean		SPECmark SPECint SPECfp	72.2 33.9 119.7	General Availability:	Hardware - Q1 1991 Software - Q3 1991

Tested in: Feb., 1991	By: IBM - AWD	Of: Austin, TX	SPEC License # 011

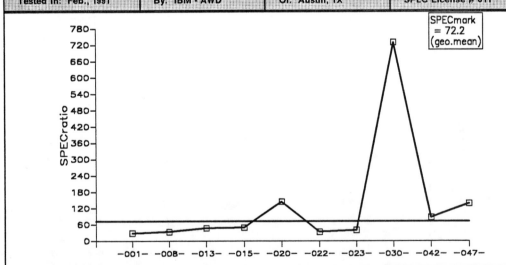

Notes/Summary of Changes (*portability changes to the benchmarks)
001.gcc, 008.espresso, 022.li, and 023.eqntott were compiled with -O
013.spice2g6, 015.doduc, 042.fpppp, and 047.tomcatv were compiled with -O and pre-processor flags -P -Wp,-ea478
020.nasa7, and 030.matrix300 were compiled with -O and pre-processor flags (020.nasa7) -Pk -Wp,-ag=a, (030.matrix300) -Pk -Wp,-inlr,-inll=3
(1) AIX XL FORTRAN Alpha Version 2.2 used for testing !!

SPEC and SPECmark are trademarks of the Standard Performance Evaluation Corporation

SPEC Benchmark Release 1 Summary

RESULTS: Benchmark No. & Name	SPEC Reference Time (seconds)	RISC System/6000 POWERstation 930 Time (seconds)	SPEC Ratio	IBM Corporation RISC System/6000 POWERstation 930		
001.gcc	1482.0	87.3	17.0		**Hardware**	
008.espresso	2266.0	112.0	20.2	Model Number:	POWERstation 930	
				CPU:	25 MHz POWER 2564	
				FPU:	Integrated	
013.spice2g6	23951.0	832.9	28.8	Number of CPUs:	1	
				Cache Size Per CPU:	64K data/8K inst	
015.doduc	1863.0	62.9	29.6	Memory:	32 MB	
				Disk Subsystem:	1 - 670 SCSI	
020.nasa7	20093.0	228.1	88.1	Network Interface:	NA	
					Software	
022.li	6206.0	307.1	20.2	O/S Type and Rev:	AIX v3.1.5	
				Compiler Rev:	AIX XL C/6000 Ver. 1.1.5	
023.eqntott	1101.0	47.1	23.4		(1) AIX XL FORTRAN Ver. 2.2	
				Other Software:	None	
030.matrix300	4525.0	10.4	435.1	File System Type:	AIX	
				Firmware Level:	NA	
042.fpppp	3038.0	57.0	53.3		**System**	
				Tuning Parameters:	None	
047.tomcatv	2649.0	31.9	83.0	Background Load:	None	
				System State:	Multi-user(single-user logon)	
Geometric Mean		SPECmark	43.4			
		SPECint	20.1	General Availability:	Hardware - Q1 1991	
		SPECfp	72.4		Software - Q3 1991	

Tested In: April, 1991	By: IBM - AWD	Of: Austin, TX	SPEC License # 011

SPECmark = 43.4 (geo.mean)

Notes/Summary of Changes (*portability changes to the benchmarks)
001.gcc, 008.espresso, 022.li, and 023.eqntott were compiled with -O
013.spice2g6, 015.doduc, 042.fpppp, and 047.tomcatv were compiled with -O and pre-processor flags -P -Wp,-ea478
020.nasa7, and 030.matrix300 were compiled with -O and pre-processor flags (020.nasa7) -Pk -Wp,-ag=a, (030.matrix300) -Pk -Wp,-inlr,-inll=3
(1) AIX XL FORTRAN Alpha Version 2.2 used for testing !!

SPEC and SPECmark are trademarks of the Standard Performance Evaluation Corporation

SPEC Benchmark Release 1 Summary

RESULTS: Benchmark No. & Name	SPEC Reference Time (seconds)	RISC System/6000 POWERstation 950		IBM Corporation RISC System/6000 POWERstation 950	
		Time (seconds)	SPEC Ratio		
001.gcc	1482.0	51.9	28.6	**Hardware**	
				Model Number:	POWERstation 950
008.espresso	2266.0	66.9	33.9	CPU:	41.67 MHz POWER 4164
				FPU:	Integrated
013.spice2g6	23951.0	507.4	47.2	Number of CPUs:	1
				Cache Size Per CPU:	64K data/8K inst
015.doduc	1863.0	37.6	49.6	Memory:	64 MB
				Disk Subsystem:	1 - 857 SCSI
020.nasa7	20093.0	139.2	144.4	Network Interface:	NA
				Software	
022.li	6206.0	183.4	33.8	O/S Type and Rev:	AIX v3.1.5
				Compiler Rev:	AIX XL C/6000 Ver. 1.1.5
023.eqntott	1101.0	27.5	40.0		(1) AIX XL FORTRAN Ver. 2.2
				Other Software:	None
030.matrix300	4525.0	6.2	729.8	File System Type:	AIX
				Firmware Level:	NA
042.fpppp	3038.0	35.1	86.6	**System**	
				Tuning Parameters:	None
047.tomcatv	2649.0	19.2	138.0	Background Load:	None
				System State:	Multi-user(single-user logon)
Geometric Mean		SPECmark SPECint SPECfp	72.2 33.8 119.7	General Availability:	Hardware - Q1 1991 Software - Q3 1991

Tested In: Feb., 1991	By: IBM - AWD	Of: Austin, TX	SPEC License # 011

SPECmark = 72.2 (geo.mean)

Notes/Summary of Changes (*portability changes to the benchmarks)
001.gcc, 008.espresso, 022.li, and 023.eqntott were compiled with -O
013.spice2g6, 015.doduc, 042.fpppp, and 047.tomcatv were compiled with -O and pre-processor flags -P -Wp,-ea478
020.nasa7, and 030.matrix300 were compiled with -O and pre-processor flags (020.nasa7) -Pk -Wp,-ag=a, (030.matrix300) -Pk -Wp,-inlr,-inll=3
(1) AIX XL FORTRAN Alpha Version 2.2 used for testing !!

SPEC and SPECmark are trademarks of the Standard Performance Evaluation Corporation

TPC Overview

♦ **Transaction Processing Performance Council (TPC)**

- TPC formed in 1988 to develop benchmarks for Transaction Processing application environments

- 40 vendors have joined the council, including IBM

- TPC Benchmark A: Standard workload definition completed 11/89 which reduces DebitCredit implementation inconsistencies

- TPC Benchmark B: Standard workload definition completed 9/90 which replaces TP1 benchmark

- Several vendors are now releasing TPC Benchmark A and B results

- More workloads are under consideration which attempt to go beyond the simple application represented by TPC Benchmark A and TPC Benchmark B

TPC Benchmark A Transaction Profile

♦ Read 100 bytes from terminal, including ACCOUNT, TELLER, BRANCH ids along with dollar amount.

- Begin Transaction
  - → Update Account Record:
    - — Read Account balance from Account record
    - — Set Account balance = Account balance + transaction dollar amount
    - — Write Account balance to Account record
  - → Write to History File
    - — Account id, Teller id, Branch id, dollar amount, time stamp
  - → Update Teller Record with new Teller balance
  - → Update Branch Record with new Branch balance

- Commit Transaction

♦ Write 200 bytes to terminal, including ACCOUNT, TELLER, BRANCH, dollar transaction and account balance.

TPC Benchmark A Scaling Rules

◆ For every TPS measured:

- 100,000 ACCOUNT records

- 10 TELLER records

- 10 terminals

- 1 BRANCH record

- 2,592,000 HISTORY records: Due to requirement for enough disk space to hold 90 eight hour days worth of history records at reported tps (must be stored on disk)

◆ Enough system log space to hold 8 hours of system recovery log data (must be stored on disk)

TPC Benchmark A and B Test Environments

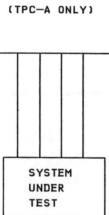

◆ TPC Benchmark A and B

- Simple transaction processing application defined by detailed specifications

- TPS at point where 90% of transaction response time is less than 2 seconds

- ACID functionality test for transaction processing system required

- Rules for reporting TPS and $/TPS defined

- Full Disclosure Report must be filed with TPC administrator

- Audit of measurements is recommended

- TPC Benchmark A requires Remote Terminal Emulator (RTE) to simulate users

- TPC Benchmark B is similar to TPC Benchmark A but no simulation of terminals is required (simplifies testing)

- **TPC Benchmark A results ARE NOT comparable to TPC Benchmark B results**

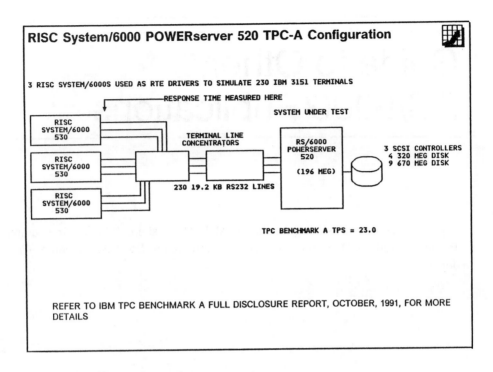

RISC System/6000 POWERserver 520 TPC-A Configuration

3 RISC SYSTEM/6000S USED AS RTE DRIVERS TO SIMULATE 230 IBM 3151 TERMINALS

RESPONSE TIME MEASURED HERE

SYSTEM UNDER TEST

RISC SYSTEM/6000 530

RISC SYSTEM/6000 530

RISC SYSTEM/6000 530

TERMINAL LINE CONCENTRATORS

RS/6000 POWERSERVER 520

(196 MEG)

3 SCSI CONTROLLERS
4 320 MEG DISK
9 670 MEG DISK

230 19.2 KB RS232 LINES

TPC BENCHMARK A TPS = 23.0

REFER TO IBM TPC BENCHMARK A FULL DISCLOSURE REPORT, OCTOBER, 1991, FOR MORE DETAILS

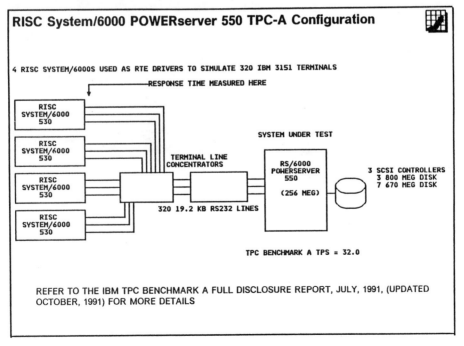

RISC System/6000 POWERserver 550 TPC-A Configuration

4 RISC SYSTEM/6000S USED AS RTE DRIVERS TO SIMULATE 320 IBM 3151 TERMINALS

RESPONSE TIME MEASURED HERE

RISC SYSTEM/6000 530

RISC SYSTEM/6000 530

RISC SYSTEM/6000 530

RISC SYSTEM/6000 530

SYSTEM UNDER TEST

TERMINAL LINE CONCENTRATORS

RS/6000 POWERSERVER 550

(256 MEG)

3 SCSI CONTROLLERS
3 800 MEG DISK
7 670 MEG DISK

320 19.2 KB RS232 LINES

TPC BENCHMARK A TPS = 32.0

REFER TO THE IBM TPC BENCHMARK A FULL DISCLOSURE REPORT, JULY, 1991, (UPDATED OCTOBER, 1991) FOR MORE DETAILS

APPENDIX C

Guide to Other RS/6000 Publications

Online Documentation and Books

IBM provides many documentation offerings in a variety of media for RISC System/6000 products. Much of the user and technical reference documentation is available in both hardcopy book form and in a form designed for online use with the InfoExplorer hypertext retrieval system.

The following sections describe the user and technical reference documentation that is available. All publications described in these sections are soft-bound 8 1/2 x 11-inch documents that are 5-hole punched to fit in standard binders (unless otherwise indicated).

In the publication descriptions, a ● indicates that the publication is included in the CD-ROM Hypertext Information Base Library. A ■ indicates that one copy of the publication is included with each system unit.

Online Documentation

IBM provides online documentation with most RISC System/6000 software products at no additional charge, and offers an optional CD-ROM Disc containing most of the available RISC System/6000 documentation. All online documentation is designed for use with the InfoExplorer hypertext retrieval system (part of the AIX licensed program). IBM has developed online documentation that describes the following RISC System/6000 products:

- The RISC System/6000 system units
- The following devices that attach to RISC System/6000 system units:
  - Xstations
  - 7203 External Portable Disk Drive Model 1
  - 7204 External Disk Drive Model 320
  - 7207 150MB External 1/4-Inch Cartridge Tape Drive Model 1
  - 7208 2.3GB External 8 mm Tape Drive Model 1
  - 7210 External CD-ROM Drive Model 1.

- The following licensed programs that are used with the RISC System/6000 system:
  - IBM AIX Version 3 for RISC System/6000
  - IBM AIXwindows Environment/6000
  - IBM AIX XL FORTRAN Compiler/6000
  - IBM AIX XL Pascal Compiler/6000
  - IBM AIX Network Management/6000
  - IBM AIX System Network Architecture Services/6000
  - IBM AIX 3278/79 Emulation/6000
  - IBM AIX 3270 Host Connection Program/6000
  - IBM AIX Personal Computer Simulator/6000.

Online Documentation that comes with RISC System/6000 Software Purchases

The online user documentation that comes with the aforementioned licensed programs consists of the following information that applies to the purchased programs:

- Conceptual and procedural information about general user tasks, system management tasks, and communications tasks
- User information about user interfaces
- Reference information about commands
- Procedural and reference information about editors
- Reference information about programming languages to support programming tasks
- Reference information about special functions of the licensed programs included in the purchase
- Task-oriented and reference-oriented information that provides navigational paths through the online documentation
- Glossary information.

The Comprehensive Online Documentation Offering

IBM RISC System/6000 CD-ROM Hypertext Information Base Library, SC23–2163, is an optionally available CD-ROM disc that provides users with most of the RISC System/6000 documentation. CD-ROM Hypertext Information Base Library contains all of the documentation (both text and graphics) that IBM has prepared for use with the InfoExplorer hypertext retrieval system. CD-ROM Hypertext Information Base Library requires a CD-ROM drive.

General Documentation

IBM provides several books that contain general information about the RISC System/6000 hardware and software offerings. The following paragraphs describe these books.

IBM RISC System/6000 General Information and Planning Information Kit, GK2T–0237, describes the RISC System/6000 system units and devices and the IBM hardware and software that support them. This kit contains information that may be needed while making purchasing decisions and while planning for the installation of RISC System/6000 products. *General Information and Planning Information Kit* contains the following items packaged in a folder:

* *IBM RISC System/6000 Hardware Offerings Overview,* GC23–2188, a booklet that describes RISC System/6000 system units and associated devices, adapters, and cables.

* *IBM RISC System/6000 Software Offerings Overview,* GC23–2189, a booklet that describes IBM licensed programs that are designed to run on the RISC System/6000 system unit.

* *IBM RISC System/6000 Communications Connectivity Overview,* GC23–2190, a booklet that describes some methods of connecting the RISC System/6000 system unit to other systems.

* *IBM RISC System/6000 Documentation and Training Offerings Overview,* GC23–2192. ●

* *IBM RISC System/6000 Planning for Your System Installation,* GC23–2191, a booklet that presents an overview of planning for the RISC System/6000, and provides the site planner with information and tools for effective planning.

Getting Started with IBM RISC System/6000, GBOF–1535, two books that describe how to use the basic features of the RISC System/6000. One copy of both books is provided with the operating system.The set includes:

* *Getting Started: Using IBM RISC System/6000,* GC23–2377, describes basic user tasks relating to both RISC System/6000 hardware and software.

* *Getting Started: Managing IBM RISC System/6000,* GC23–2378, describes basic system management tasks for the RISC System/6000 system.

IBM RISC System/6000 Problem Solving Guide, SC23–2204, serves as the primary reference should a user encounter a problem with the system hardware or software that cannot be corrected by the normal message actions. This book provides the user with steps that may either return the system to a normal operating condition or give the user sufficient information to place a service call. Additional copies of this publication are provided free of charge, and can be ordered from your IBM representative. ● ■

IBM RISC System/6000 Quick Start Guide, SC23–2195, a quick reference that provides a new RISC System/6000 system user with information about how to perform common tasks, such as logging in and logging off and accessing online documentation. Topics include AIX Version 3 for RISC System/6000, InfoExplorer, System Management Interface Tool (SMIT), and InfoTrainer. ■

Task Index and Glossary for IBM RISC System/6000, GC23–2201, contains three important elements of the RISC System/6000 system: 1) lists of RISC System/6000 tasks and where they are documented in the library; 2) an error message index; and 3) a glossary of technical terms and abbreviations used in the RISC System/6000 library. Copies of this book are provided free of charge, and can be ordered from your IBM representative. ●

IBM RISC System/6000 Technology, SA23–2619, contains a collection of articles written by engineers and programmers. These articles describe some technological advances in hardware and software design that have been incorporated in the RISC System/6000 products. This book is an 11 x 8 1/2 inch document that contains no hole punches for binder storage.

RISC System/6000 Hardware Books

Books are available that describe the installation, usage, and technical aspects of all IBM devices that can attach to the RISC System/6000 system unit. The following sections describe the books pertaining to the RISC System/6000 system units.

Installation and Service Guides ■

IBM provides an *Installation and Service Guide* with each RISC System/6000 system unit. The *Installation and Service Guide* describes how to install the system unit or drawer and how to perform some routine maintenance and service procedures (such as analysis of power problems and replacement of some parts). The guides for the various 7015 drawers, two of which cover only service considerations, are included with each system unit if the particular drawer is ordered. The following installation and service guides are available for RISC System/6000 system units:

- *IBM RISC System/6000 7012 POWERstation and POWERserver Installation and Service Guide, SA23–2624*

- *IBM RISC System/6000 7013 POWERstation and POWERserver Installation and Service Guide, SA23–2622*

- *IBM RISC System/6000 7015 POWERserver Installation and Service Guide, SA23–2628*

- *IBM RISC System/6000 7015 POWERserver CPU Drawer Service Guide, SA23-2649*

- *IBM RISC System/6000 7015 POWERserver SCSI Drawers Installation and Service Guide, SY23-0160*

- *IBM RISC System/6000 7015 POWERserver Async Expansion Drawer Service Guide, SA23-2651*

- *IBM RISC System/6000 7016 POWERstation Installation and Service Guide, SA23–2626.*

Operator Guides ■

IBM provides an *Operator Guide* with each RISC System/6000 system unit. The *Operator Guide* describes the system unit and its operator controls and gives information about operating the system unit and safety considerations for relocating the system unit. The following *Operator Guides* are available for RISC System/6000 system units:

- *IBM RISC System/6000 7012 POWERstation and POWERserver Operator Guide, SA23–2623*

- *IBM RISC System/6000 7013 POWERstation and POWERserver Operator Guide, SA23–2621*

- *IBM RISC System/6000 7015 POWERserver Operator Guide, SA23–2627*

- *IBM RISC System/6000 7016 POWERstation Operator Guide, SA23–2625.*

Xstation Guides

IBM provides a *Setup and Operator Guide* with each Xstation. The setup and operator guide describes Xstation setup and operation, as well as problem determination information.

The *Service Guide* describes how to perform some routine maintenance and service procedures (such as analysis of power problems and replacement of some parts).

- *Xstation 120 Setup and Operator Guide, SA23–2656* ■

- *Xstation 130 Setup and Operator Guide, SA23–2635* ■

- *Xstation 120 Service Guide, SA23-2657*

- *Xstation 130 Service Guide, SA23-2636*

IBM RISC System/6000 Xstation 120 Technical Reference, SA23-2661, provides a programming interface for a user to program the Xstation. This publication does not include hardware specifications for the Xstation 120, except concerning connection points.

IBM RISC System/6000 Xstation 130 Technical Reference, SA23-2648, provides a programming interface for a user to program the Xstation. This publication does not include hardware specifications for the Xstation 130, except concerning connection points.

Diagnostic Books ■

IBM RISC System/6000 POWERstation and POWERserver Diagnostic Programs Operator Guide, SA23–2631, guides both users and trained service personnel through diagnostic procedures that check for correct operation of the system unit and some attached devices. This book describes diagnostic procedures for all models and types of the RISC System/6000 system units.

IBM RISC System/6000 POWERstation and POWERserver Diagnostic Programs Service Guide, SA23–2632, guides trained service personnel through procedures in analyzing a service request number and provides service personnel with reference information to support service tasks. This book covers all models and types of RISC System/6000 system units.

Technical Reference Manuals

IBM RISC System/6000 POWERstation and POWERserver Hardware Technical Reference–General Information, SA23–2643, provides technical descriptions of the RISC System/6000 features and options such as processors, system and virtual memory interfaces, system input and output interfaces, data formats, keyboards, the mouse, and tablets. This book is written for programmers and engineers who plan to build adapters or devices. ●

IBM offers technical reference manuals that describe the specific RISC System/6000 system units in detail. These books include diagrams and descriptions of the system units and their features, such as processor boards, input/output boards, operator panels, and connectors. The following technical reference manuals are available:

- *IBM RISC System/6000 Hardware Technical Reference – 7012 POWERstation and POWERserver,* SA23–2660 ●

- *IBM RISC System/6000 Hardware Technical Reference – 7013 and 7016 POWERstation and POWERserver,* SA23–2644 ●

- *IBM RISC System/6000 Hardware Technical Reference – 7015 POWERserver,* SA23–2645 ●

- *IBM RISC System/6000 7015 POWERserver SCSI Drawers Technical Reference,* SA33-3207.

IBM RISC System/6000 POWERstation and POWERserver Hardware Technical Reference – Options and Devices, SA23–2646, provides technical descriptions of options, adapters, and attached devices that can be used with the RISC System/6000 system unit. A supplement to this publication, SA33-2630, is also available. ●

IBM RISC System/6000 POWERstation and POWERserver Hardware Technical Reference – Micro Channel Architecture, SA23–2647, describes the Micro Channel architecture used in the RISC System/6000 system unit.

Other Hardware Books

IBM RISC System/6000 POWERstation and POWERserver Translated Safety Information, SA23–2652, contains safety warnings written in various languages concerning the RISC System/6000 system unit and associated devices. A copy of this publication is also included with each IBM Xstation. ■

IBM External Device Safety Information Manual, SA23-2671, discusses safety considerations for the various external devices. A copy of this publication is provided with each external device.

RISC System/6000 Software Books

Some IBM books for RISC System/6000 software products describe functions that are available in a variety of licensed programs. For users who need to find information, but who do not know where the function is packaged (in AIX for RISC System/6000 licensed program or in another licensed program), this organization simplifies the search for information.

Other IBM books for RISC System/6000 software products describe functions that are available in a specific licensed program. These books usually focus on a topic that is covered by a single licensed program. For example, *XL C Language Reference for IBM AIX Version 3 for RISC System/6000* contains language reference information that applies to the functions available through the IBM AIX Version 3 for RISC System/6000 licensed program only.

AIX Installation Guide ●

AIX Version 3 for RISC System/6000 Installation Guide, SC23–2341, discusses various methods of installing and maintaining the operating system. It also covers how to start up a pre-installed system for the first time. When installing other licensed programs, you can use this guide in conjunction with the installation information provided with the other licensed programs. Additional copies of this publication are provided free of charge, and can be ordered from your IBM representative.

Books that Describe Functions of Multiple Licensed Programs

The documents described in this section provide information about functions available through the following licensed programs:

- IBM AIX Version 3 for RISC System/6000

- IBM AIXwindows Environment/6000

- IBM AIX Network Management/6000

- IBM AIX System Network Architecture Services/6000

- IBM AIX 3278/79 Emulation/6000

- IBM AIX 3270 Host Connection Program/6000

- IBM AIX Personal Computer Simulator/6000.

Each book listed in this section focuses on specific types of facilities (for example, commands or files) or on particular functional topics (for example, graphics programming concepts). The content of each book crosses the boundaries of licensed programs in order to more completely cover its subject. For example, *AIX Commands Reference for IBM RISC System/6000* contains information about the commands that are packaged with each of the previously listed licensed programs.

AIX General Concepts and Procedures for IBM RISC System/6000, GC23–2202, serves as the main resource for end users and system managers once they progress beyond the basic information contained in *Getting Started with RISC System/6000*. This book contains conceptual and procedural information about AIX for RISC System/6000 and is applicable to a variety of user interfaces. Copies of this book are provided free of charge, and can be ordered from your IBM representative. ●

AIX Editing Concepts and Procedures for IBM RISC System/6000, GC23–2212, describes some of the editors that are available for use with the RISC System/6000 system unit and includes suggestions of some effective uses of these editors (for example, to develop programs or to create and edit general text files). This book also contains procedural information for using particular functions provided with editors. Copies of this book are provided free of charge, and can be ordered from your IBM representative. ●

AIX Communication Concepts and Procedures for IBM RISC System/6000, GC23–2203, serves as the system manager and end user's main source book for procedures associated with using, managing, and customizing communications networks. This book contains information about many types of RISC System/6000 communications networks.Copies of this book are provided free of charge, and can be ordered from your IBM representative. ●

AIX Commands Reference for IBM RISC System/6000, GBOF–1531, provides reference information about commands and is written for end users, system managers, and programmers. This set of books contains examples and descriptions of the commands and their available flags. The command entries are arranged in alphabetical order. If you need additional copies of a particular volume, each volume can be ordered separately:

- *AIX Commands Reference for IBM RISC System/6000 Voume 1*, GC23–2376
- *AIX Commands Reference for IBM RISC System/6000 Volume 2*, GC23–2366
- *AIX Commands Reference for IBM RISC System.6000 Volume 3*, GC23–2367

  Copies of these books are provided free of charge, and can be ordered from your IBM representative. ●

AIX Calls and Subroutines Reference for IBM RISC System/6000, SC23–2198, provides reference information about system calls, kernel extension calls, and subroutines. This set of books is written for programmers. ●

AIX Files Reference for IBM RISC System/6000, GC23–2200, provides reference information about file formats, special files, and information associated with files (including keyboard and character tables). This book is written for system managers and programmers. Copies of this book are provided free of charge, and can be ordered from your IBM representative. ●

AIX General Programming Concepts for IBM RISC System/6000, SC23–2205, serves as the programmer's main source book for learning about the operating system from a programming perspective. ●

AIX User Interface Programming Concepts for IBM RISC System/6000, SC23–2209, serves as the programmer's main source book for learning about the user interfaces from a programming perspective. ●

AIX Communications Programming Concepts for IBM RISC System/6000, SC23–2206, serves as the main source book for information about the communications facilities from a programming perspective. ●

AIX Graphics Programming Concepts for IBM RISC System/6000, SC23–2208, serves as the programmer's main source book for learning about graphics capabilities from a programming perspective. ●

AIX Kernel Extensions and Device Support Programming Concepts for IBM RISC System/6000, SC23–2207, serves as the programmer's main source book for learning about the kernel extensions that enable programmers to address devices. ●

Books that Describe Functions of a Specific Licensed Program

The documents described in this section provide information about functions that are available in a single licensed program.

XL C User's Guide for IBM AIX Version 3 for RISC System/6000, SC09–1259, explains how to develop and compile C language programs on a RISC System/6000 system unit that has the IBM AIX Version 3 for RISC System/6000 licensed program installed. ●

XL C Language Reference for IBM AIX Version 3 for RISC System/6000, SC09–1260, describes the syntax and semantics of the C programming language that is implemented by the IBM AIX Version 3 for RISC System/6000 licensed program. This book is written for users who have some knowledge of C language programming concepts and some experience in writing C programs. ●

Assembler Language Reference for IBM AIX Version 3 for RISC System/6000, SC23–2197, describes the syntax and semantics of the assembler language that is implemented by the AIX for RISC System/6000 licensed program. This book is written for users who have some knowledge of assembler language programming concepts and some experience in writing assembler programs. ●

User's Guide for IBM AIX XL Pascal Compiler/6000, SC09–1326, explains how to develop and compile Pascal language programs on a RISC System/6000 system unit that has the IBM AIX XL Pascal Compiler/6000 licensed program installed. ●

Language Reference for IBM AIX XL Pascal Compiler/6000, SC09–1327, describes the syntax and semantics of the Pascal programming language that is implemented by the IBM AIX XL Pascal Compiler/6000 licensed program. This book is written for users who have some knowledge of Pascal language programming concepts and some experience in writing Pascal programs. ●

User's Guide for IBM AIX XL FORTRAN Compiler/6000 Version 2, SC09–1354, explains how to develop and compile FORTRAN language programs on a RISC System/6000 system unit that has the IBM AIX XL FORTRAN Compiler/6000 Version 2 licensed program installed. ●

Language Reference for IBM AIX XL FORTRAN Compiler/6000 Version 2, SC09–1353, describes the syntax and semantics of the FORTRAN programming language that is implemented by the IBM AIX XL FORTRAN Compiler/6000 Version 2 licensed program. This book is written for users who have some knowledge of FORTRAN language programming concepts and some experience in writing FORTRAN programs. ●

User's Guide for IBM AIX Ada/6000, SC09–1321, explains how to develop and compile Ada language programs on a RISC System/6000 system unit that has the IBM AIX Ada/6000 licensed program installed. One copy of the *Ada User's Guide* is provided with the AIX Ada/6000 licensed program.●

Language Reference for IBM AIX Ada/6000, SC09–1141, describes the syntax and semantics of the Ada programming language that is implemented by the IBM AIX Ada/6000 licensed program. This book is written for users who have some knowledge of Ada language programming concepts and some experience in writing Ada programs. One copy of the *Language Reference for IBM AIX Ada/6000* is provided with the AIX Ada/6000 licensed program. ●

Support Package Reference for IBM AIX Ada/6000, SC09–1395, describes how to use various support packages with Version 1 Release 2 of AIX Ada/6000. Support packages discussed include Ada support for a math library, AIXwindows, NLS functions, the GL library, and the XGSL library. This book is written for users who have an understanding of both Ada language and the AIX operating system. ●

User's Guide for IBM AIX VS COBOL Compiler/6000, SC23–2178, explains how to develop and execute COBOL programs on a RISC System/6000 system unit that has the IBM AIX VS COBOL Compiler/6000 licensed program installed. This book is written for users who have a good understanding of the COBOL programming language. One copy of the *VS COBOL User's Guide* is provided with the AIX VS COBOL Compiler/6000 licensed program.

Language Reference for IBM AIX VS COBOL Compiler/6000, SC23–2177, describes the IBM AIX VS COBOL Compiler/6000 licensed program implementation of the VS COBOL programming language. This book contains syntax and semantics descriptions representing COBOL at the ANSI 85 High Level and ANSI 74 High Level. This book is written for users who have some knowledge of COBOL programming concepts and some experience in writing COBOL programs. One copy of the *VS COBOL Language Reference* is provided with the AIX VS COBOL Compiler/6000 licensed program.

Programming Concepts and Reference for IBM AIX Computer Graphics Interface Toolkit/6000, SC23–2278, describes the functions available through the IBM AIX Computer Graphics Interface Toolkit/6000 licensed program for writing device-independent graphic software. This book is written for software application developers familiar with C, FORTRAN, and Pascal programming languages. One copy of the *Programming Concepts and Reference for Computer Graphics Interface Toolkit* is provided with the AIX Computer Graphics Interface Toolkit/6000 licensed program.

System Management Guide for IBM AIX Xstation Manager/6000, SC23–2264, describes how to install the IBM AIX Xstation Manager/6000 licensed program, how to add an Xstation interface protocol (IP) addresses and configuration parameters to the network and how to use the print capability provided with AIX Xstation Manager/6000. One copy of the *System Management Guide for IBM AIX Xstation Manager/6000* is provided with the AIX Xstation Manager/6000 licensed program. ●

IBM AIX Open Systems Interconnection Messaging and Filing/6000 User's and System Administrator's Guide, SC32–0012, describes how to use and manage AIX Open Systems Interconnection Messaging and Filing/6000.

IBM AIX AS/400 Connection Program User's Guide, SB35–4069, describes how to use the features of the AIX AS/400 Connection Program.

Index

B

C